Reading, Writing, and Computers

Planning for Integration

Sherry Hill Howie

California State University, San Bernardino

Allyn and Bacon
Boston   London   Sydney   Toronto

Copyright © 1989 by Allyn and Bacon
A Division of Simon & Schuster
160 Gould Street
Needham Heights, Massachusetts 02194

Photographs by Robyn C. Ocepek
California State University, San Bernardino
Audio Visual Services

Library of Congress Cataloging-in-Publication Data

Howie, Sherry Hill
    Reading, writing, and computers : planning for integration /
Sherry Hill Howie.
        p.   cm.
    Includes bibliographies and index.
    ISBN 0-205-11965-4
    1. Computer-assisted instruction. 2. Reading. 3. English
language—Composition and exercises—Study and teaching. I. Title.
LB1028.5.H675 1989
371.3′9445—dc19   88-27281
                                                                         CIP

Printed in the United States of America
10 9 8 7 6 5 4 3 2 1   93 92 91 90 89

CONTENTS

PREFACE

Reading, Writing, and Computers: Planning for Integration is intended for classroom teachers across the disciplines. All content-area teachers have a stake in the teaching of reading and writing as a means for their students to learn subject matter. We live in a multiliterate society in which people learn and gain information through a variety of technologies. The technologies of books, paper and pen, and computers can be compatible and reinforce each other as means to become literate. This book presents teachers with many different ideas on how to use the computer to help their students learn to think and to become literate in their disciplines.

This book was written to fill a need for synthesis and practicality. Current research has yielded many scattered ideas regarding writing, reading, and computer use in education, but there is a gap in understanding the integration of the three. The intent of this book is to bring the three areas together so that they interrelate and reinforce each other for more effective learning and communication. The ideas presented for integrating the three areas are based on the most current research, but they are made eminently practical so as to facilitate use by teachers and administrators. Such practical ideas promote integration for a well-planned curriculum.

The fields of computer science, artificial intelligence, linguistics, cognitive psychology, and education have contributed to the concepts presented in the chapters that follow. From research studies and from current literature in those fields, ideas have been translated into methodologies and strategies for more effective teaching. There is a necessary theoretical base for the ideas presented in Chapters 1 and 2, but the book as a whole is designed to be of immediate practical use to teachers. Chapter 6 contains recommendations for evaluation of software and lessons using software applications. Teachers at the upper elementary, secondary, and college levels will find lesson plans (fifty of them in Chapter 5), suggestions for using software, and recommendations for solving logistical concerns about the placement of equipment and machines. The book's practicality will also appeal to teacher trainers and administrators concerned about teacher development. The training of faculty in the use of computers is one important topic covered in this book. It certainly affects the integration of computers into a school, in terms of how widespread and how interdisciplinary the dispersion will be.

One problem in the writing of this book has been the speed with which ideas become obsolete in the field of computers. Writing down these ideas was akin to trying to hold back a huge boulder that keeps rolling down a hill. The act of putting the ideas into words is an attempt to stop the boulder for an instant at a certain place in the evolution of the technology.

However, the ideas will surely help teachers who are not already caught up in the evolution to become part of it. In fact, *Reading, Writing, and Computers* should help all teachers, both novice and advanced computer users, to gain knowledge, understanding, and wisdom in the use of technology. Teachers need to be the planners and directors in the evolution of technology in education, and this book can help them become leaders in the field.

Each chapter begins with a clear statement of purpose that will help the reader focus on the intent. Background for the major points is provided, and then practical applications are presented. The major focus of the book is on the integration of the computer into ongoing learning in a well-planned curriculum. The suggestions given may be adapted by teachers for their own purposes and needs. Chapter 4 provides ideas for the integration of computers in the school district, involving teachers in the planning stages at every level. Teachers know how best to teach, and they should be involved at every step in the process. The trends in technology presented in Chapter 3 will help teachers look ahead in implementing changes in the curriculum.

Many people contributed to the writing of this book. Most of the ideas stem from my years of teaching at the secondary and college levels, and my students and colleagues in Michigan, Wisconsin, and California have all contributed practical suggestions. I wish to thank them for their contributions and for their patience in undergoing experiments as I field-tested my hypotheses. My students' enthusiasm and encouragement have been a great source of inspiration in this project. I am deeply grateful to Hiram Howard for first believing in this book and encouraging me to develop it. Special acknowledgment is due Marianne Johnson of the Roseville, Minnesota, public schools for laboring over and greatly improving the original prospectus; her insight and suggestions helped steer my thinking more clearly. In the Writing Center at Cal State University, Carol Haviland was kind enough to read over some of the manuscript and make important suggestions for revision. I also thank Don Simpson, Principal at Shandin Hills Middle School, for permitting me to photograph the school's computer lab and the students who were using it. Special thanks to photographer Robyn C. Ocepek. I wish to express my gratitude to the Dean of my school, Dr. Ernest Garcia, and to my Department Chair, Dr. Adria Klein, both of whom supported this writing endeavor and allowed me time off from teaching duties to concentrate on the book. Most special thanks go to William Howie for his never-ending faith in me and continuous encouragement during the more than thirty years I've known him. Lastly, the book is dedicated to another writer who has served as my inspiration over the years — a dear, lifelong friend, the first person to believe in my abilities and to encourage me to develop them. I especially thank Jack V. Fogarty and dedicate *Reading, Writing, and Computers* to him.

Sherry Hill Howie

SECTION ONE
Preparation

Students preparing to read and write

CHAPTER ONE

Processes of
Reading and Writing

Learning by computer can transfer to learning from books

The purposes of this chapter are to define the reading and writing processes, interrelate them, and incorporate computer use in teaching them.
With this necessary background, teachers may then begin to plan to integrate technology into curricula for teaching reading and writing.

The Relationship of Writing to Reading

Reading and writing have been regarded as subjects that students must
be taught in school. After all, they are the *basics* of every person's education. The way these subjects have been taught has undergone some changes
over the past twenty-five years. In the 1950s and early 1960s, reading and
writing were taught together, usually in the English class. Most of the faculty
in other disciplines depended upon the English teacher to "teach those kids
to read and write"; they generally absolved themselves of responsibility to
reinforce in their classrooms what the English teacher was teaching about
language use. Most content-area teachers believed that reading and writing
were *subjects* that could not be fit into an already busy schedule of teaching
content.

In the late 1960s and early 1970s, English instruction began to separate
reading classes from writing classes. The idea was that reading and writing
were subjects that were best taught in isolation from each other. Courses
such as critical reading, literature, and expository writing divorced reading
from writing. The belief was that the separation would allow isolation of
skills in language use, so that they could be better identified and taught.

Today we know that such isolation of language skills is not an effective
way to teach students to read and write. Our understanding of language
processing has evolved through research in education, psychology, computer science, and linguistics. Particularly, the field of artificial intelligence
has given us ideas on how humans think and process information. It has
never been possible to cut open a human brain and watch an idea being
processed. In education, we have always proceeded on unfounded theories
about how our students think and then developed curricula to fit the theories
as best we were able. For the first time in the history of education, we are
now able to see theories proposed and tested out through simulations of
how humans process ideas.

Artificial intelligence investigators propose a theory called a *cognitive model*
and devise a computer program that uses the model. Then they test it out
on the computer and eventually on humans to see if it is valid. Through
such testing, we educators have gained much valuable knowledge about
what we should teach and how we should teach it. It is the purpose of this
book to translate some of these recent research findings into educational
practice.

When a computer processes language, it operates similarly to a human who reads and writes. Both reading and writing involve the processing of information in a cognitively active way. Writing is often thought of as an expressive process and reading a receptive, passive one. However, this view of reading denies the reader's active work in thinking and relating the material to background knowledge. Both reading and writing are active, thinking processes; when we teach them to students, we are virtually teaching them to think. Both reading and writing teach thinking, so what students learn can only be more solidly reinforced if the two processes are taught together, not separately. Teaching reading and writing together integrates the processes, interrelates them, and enhances the amount and strength of what is being learned.

A process is a means to an end. When reading and writing are thought of as processes rather than as school subjects, both are made more usable and teachable by all teachers, no matter what their subject. In writing, the process leads to composition, the product created by means of the writing process. In reading, the process leads to comprehension, the product created by means of the reading process. Both processes use information, and teaching, in a sense, is dispensing information. By using the process approach, every teacher (not just the English teacher) can help students use information more effectively. Teachers then become "information brokers" who teach students the means to the end, with a balance of emphasis on the process (the means) and product (the end). Every teacher in a faculty thus becomes responsible for giving students survival skills in a complex society, in which information currently doubles every twenty months. Considering reading and writing as processes that can be taught to students also allows all teachers to use them, not as burdensome extra subjects beyond their content fields, but as vehicles for having students learn their content areas.

Writing is a *composing system:* Elements of language—letters, words, sentences, and paragraphs, for example—are brought together into a whole product. In fact, the prefix "com" is derived from Latin and means "with or together"—drawing elements together into a composite. We see the same prefix in the word "comprehension," with regard to reading. Reading can also be considered a composing system. In reading, the reader recognizes symbols or words that suggest meanings already present in his or her memory store. The reader brings to the symbols the background knowledge and experience that has been stored there over a lifetime. The variety and the richness of the memories will determine how the reader interprets the symbols—that is, the nature of the composing that will occur. The reader composes meaning by relating what is known to him or her to what is new in a text, thus developing an interpretation that may differ from others' interpretations. The implications for teaching are that the teacher builds on and helps create the background knowledge of the students *before they begin to read,* so that composing from reading will be richer.

Holistic Text Approach

Since the language processing of reading and writing are composing systems, they should be taught from a holistic (whole) text approach. The larger the view of the text that students can get from the start, the better. This is easy in writing, because students have to start with a main idea, then outline, brainstorm, or map out their main points to develop that idea. The "main idea" approach should be used in the composing process of reading, as well. The SQ3R method provides a holistic text approach. In it, students Survey (skim) a text, ask Questions about it, Read it, Recite it (as in notetaking), then Review to remember it. It gives students the opportunity to get an overview of the main idea before they begin segmenting elements of the text into details that support that idea. Using mapping techniques is another excellent holistic text method: Before they even begin reading, students provide all the associations in their experience that relate to the ideas in the text. With the holistic text approach, students can then begin drawing on their background knowledge and experience related to the main ideas in the text. They may begin composing immediately as they get into the details of the main point; they may build bridges from what they know to what they don't know right from the very beginning. Such bridge-building allows more effective composing, which will result in better reading comprehension. It reinforces the approach used in writing.

Writing to Teach Reading

When both reading and writing are understood as composing systems tying elements of language together to construct meaning, their relationship becomes clearer. The justification for teaching them simultaneously becomes stronger. Many teachers agree that reading helps students in their writing. When students read someone else's writing, they are able to mimic it because they have a model to understand language use. Through reading, students gain a sense of language—its style, structure, fluency, and rhythm. Because of this experience in reading, students become better writers; having understood one process of language, they are able to use another, related process. Because the processes of reading and writing are so closely related, the reverse is also effective: Having students write teaches them to read better. To compose is to comprehend. Teaching students the process of writing, wherein they engage in language manipulation and kinesthetic experiences with language, also teaches them the process of reading, because they have had "hands-on" experience with written language. Through writing, students gain background knowledge and experience that allow them to build bridges from what they know to what they don't know in reading. It gives them the sense of "having been there" and reduces the threat of having to deal with the unknown.

Because composing in writing results in better comprehending in reading, students should be given the opportunity to write in each of their classes. The math teacher would probably encounter less student anxiety about math story problems if the students wrote their own problems and had to think through the logical structuring of mathematical language. The science teacher would experience more success with student understanding of lab experiments if students wrote their own, using the inductive logic of experimental procedure that is scientific language. The processes of reading and writing are so intertwined that not to teach them together, across the curriculum, is to shortchange students. Teaching the two processes together allows students to learn better how to acquire and use information.

The Process Model

Reading and writing are systems for processing information. Reading processes information in a cognitively active way that leads to meaning. Symbols are recognized and related to the memory store; they are interpreted according to the background knowledge and experience of the reader. Information is processed and meaning gained through reading. The reading process may be taught to students as an act of information processing that involves several stages: preparation, implementation, and application. The teacher can take these stages into account in constructing lesson plans and thus model the process that students are to learn. Also in writing, information is processed by the writer in the stages of preparation, implementation, and application. The teacher can teach information processing to students in a process model, thus concretely reinforcing the abstract concepts of how to read and write. This book is designed on this process model in order to reinforce understanding of it.

Reading and writing can be taught as one process consisting of several stages — concrete steps a student can use to gain the ends of comprehension and composition. Teaching processes should involve every teacher, because processing is the means to attaining and using information in every content area. Reading and writing are not subjects isolated from content; rather, they are the *access* to content. Using the two processes together strengthens and reinforces both of them and results in more effective language use by the students. Also, use of the processes across the curriculum, in every content area, by every subject teacher, integrates student development in the use of language. Teachers must begin to work together on problems of literacy. In this information age, teaching our young people to process information prepares them to survive as citizens.

The Steps of the Process

Reading and writing are such interrelated language processes that they may be taught together as one process, using the same steps to accomplish respective goals. The computer, because it simulates human language processing, may be used effectively to teach processing. The purpose of this chapter is to explain the processes and to provide suggestions for how to teach them using the computer. Thus teachers may use the process model in the classroom and design their lesson plans according to the model.

Figure 1-1   Steps in the processes of reading and writing

Step 1: Preparation
  Problem solving
    Establishing purpose
    Tying in background knowledge and experience
    Data gathering
  Brainstorming
    Social exchange
    Motivating
    Language generation
  Mapping
    Building bridges from known to unknown
    Giving learner confidence
    Dealing with fear of unknown
  Readiness
    Previewing
    Prewriting
    Initial drafting
    Understanding pattern of communication
    Recognizing audience

Step 2: Implementation
  Interacting actively with print (i.e., composing new ideas and from old ideas)
  Processing language (i.e., reading and writing)
  Thinking through language

Step 3: Application
  Applying new concepts learned
  Revising for an outside audience
  Editing
  Transferring of learning away from the computer

The process model of teaching reading and writing has three basic steps, as outlined in Figure 1-1. The steps are designed to combine reading and writing into one process so that they may be taught together, strengthening and enhancing each other. The important concept to remember is that the reading/writing process must be taught to students by the teacher in an ongoing curriculum. The computer will *not* teach students to write; the *teacher* teaches students to write using the steps of the process, and the computer is used as a convenient tool for the actual writing. Good teaching will never be replaced by a computer.

Teaching students these steps of language processing is actually teaching them to think, because as they progress through the process they use increasingly higher levels of cognitive understanding. Consider the application of Bloom's taxonomy of cognitive development to language processing (see Figure 1-2).

Figure 1-2   Bloom's taxonomy applied to language processing

Processes of Reading/Writing	Bloom's Taxonomy of Cognitive Stages
Preparation	Recall of knowledge
Probing background knowledge	From memory store
Gathering data	From resources
Setting purpose and audience	
Implementation	Comprehension
Reading ⎫	Application
⎬ Composing	
Writing ⎭	
Application	Analysis
Revision	Synthesis
Sociocentric extension	Evaluation
Transfer of ideas	
Integration with experience	

Step 1: Preparation

The first step of the process is *preparation.* Probably as much as 80 percent of the time spent on reading and writing activities in the classroom should be on *preparing* students to do so. This step is a difficult one because it requires careful planning and creative approaches that engage student interest and cooperation. It is a crucial step, because it lays the foundation for the other steps and may determine the success of the entire lesson.

Among the approaches the teacher may use to prepare students to read and write are problem solving, brainstorming, mapping, and readiness activities. All of these approaches use the holistic (whole) text approach, which begins with the main ideas before there has been any segmentation into parts. Students become comfortable with an overview of the ideas and then find details for them by reading and writing. The problem-solving approach considers reading and writing as means to solve problems. Readers answer their questions by reading, and writers discover what they know about a subject by writing about it. To activate such questions and such discovery, the teacher helps students to establish a purpose for reading and writing. In reading, the purpose will be the main points that the writer makes. Purpose pertains to what the reader is to gain from the reading. The teacher carefully considers what major ideas or understandings students are to gain from the reading, then leads the students to explore what they already know about the topic by tying in their background knowledge and experience. In writing, the approach is similar in that students are led to identify clearly their purpose for writing, which will affect the major points they need to get across to the reader. The purpose in writing pertains to what the reader or audience is to gain from reading the piece.

In the problem-solving approach, students ask questions about main ideas which can be answered only by reading and writing. Students are faced with a dilemma. They are curious and have questions, but they may resist reading, perhaps out of habit or previous unsuccessful experiences. They are stimulated because they recognize their purpose for reading and writing; they become curious and feel unfulfilled until their curiosity is satisfied. A teacher can effectively bring students to this point so that their only recourse is to do the reading and writing in order to solve the problem. Students with such curiosity become highly motivated, with intense desire to get answers to their questions. The teacher's role is to present the ideas to be learned as problems to be solved through reading about them or writing to think through the solutions. Gathering information about the main ideas is part of solving problems, which interrelates reading with writing a composition or taking notes.

Using the problem-solving approach may help students to realize the benefits of reading and writing, not just in the classroom but in many life circumstances beyond the school walls. For example, the driver's manual must be read and carefully studied before one can pass the driver's test — to solve the problem of getting a license. Also, we write job applications in order to be hired for work — to solve the problem of making a living. If possible, students should be taught the practical relevance of whatever it is they are doing. Seeing ways to solve actual problems prepares them for using reading and writing as survival tools.

The computer can be used in several ways to help students understand the problem-solving approach and to prepare them to read and write. First, it may be used to teach the problem-solving skills to be used in writing. Some excellent software programs present problems such as traveling mazes and discerning recurring patterns; other programs involve building graphic designs that help students with problem-solving skills. These programs can be used to pique students' interest for writing about the problems and the solutions they discover for them. Second, the computer can reinforce the concept of using reading and writing to solve problems. In using databases, both to enter data and to retrieve data about main ideas they are to read and write, students interrelate reading and writing and solve the problems of getting background knowledge and experience related to the ideas. They can gather and share ideas for their reading and writing. Third, the computer can be used to generate ideas for writing. Encyclopedia Britannica publishes outstanding literature programs that engage students in reading.

These programs may serve as catalysts for writing and further reading in the book.

Keep in mind that reading is slower on the computer, where the text is segmented into frames. Therefore, reading literature on the computer should be for introductory purposes only, to stimulate reading in the book or to serve as a catalyst for writing. For example, the beginning of a story may be displayed to the entire class on a large monitor or to small groups; then they can be asked to predict either verbally or in writing what the rest of the story will be about. There are also "story starters," which present story plots and subplots that can branch in different directions so that students must create their own subplots and solve the problem of how a story develops. Finally, the computer can be used to simulate experiences that students may use in their writing, providing solutions to such problems as survival on a westward trek, electing a president, or selling a product. There are many creative uses of the computer in the great variety of software available. Many of the software programs may be used to help students understand reading and writing as problem-solving methods that they can use throughout their lives.

Another approach the teacher may use to prepare students to read and write is brainstorming main ideas. In contrast to the usual view of reading and writing as solitary pursuits, brainstorming offers an opportunity for social exchange and should be planned to encourage such interaction. Brainstorming can involve the entire class in planning for reading and writing through an exchange of ideas about the topic. The great advantage of brainstorming is that it results in a rich reservoir of language generated by the students, which each individual may use later to write or read. It helps to generate vocabulary, concepts, and remembered experiences associated with the topic.

To use the brainstorming approach, the teacher asks the class *how* they want to write on a topic as well as *what* they want to write about it. For example, if the topic involves writing an autobiography, the students may contribute their ideas on what is to be included in it: where born, where lived, family and friends known, goals in life, and so on. Students will then be able to incorporate these key points into their own writing and to look for them in biographies they read. The important point is that the students themselves generate the ideas; the teacher does not impose them. With such student participation, there will be much more motivation to cooperate in the process.

In the autobiography assignment, students may be led to brainstorm about what they want to write by recalling content related to their own life experience. Each student can provide an anecdote or incident from his or her life which will, in turn, trigger the thoughts and memories of others. Such sharing should be a lot of fun for the students, but the main advantage is that they feel in command of the learning because they are generating the ideas. They are actively participating in their own preparation for reading and writing, which no longer seem threatening or intimidating. Students may experience security in such collaboration, realizing that they are "all in this together" and all have something to contribute.

The computer may be used to great advantage in brainstorming. Having generated ideas for how and what they are to read and write, students may enter the ideas on a planning disk made on a word processor. When a student (or better yet, a group of students working together) wants the information, it can be retrieved from the planning disk and printed out as a guide and resource for ideas. Students may be assigned to small groups to work on different topics, brainstorm within their own groups, and create planning disks for the next group that will be assigned their topic, on a rotating basis. The group may work together at each stage of the process, giving the students control over their learning and their product (the composition or the comprehension). Also, creating a planner teaches students to discern main ideas from subordinate details, to organize and plan information, and to be aware of structure and style in writing—their own as well as an author's. The teacher, of course, intervenes in and monitors each step of the process, verbally informing students of what they are experiencing.

When students feel that they are controlling their own learning, they are likely to show increased self-confidence and a more positive attitude toward the assignment. Students will cooperate more, be more motivated, and produce better results. Best of all, they learn the process that will help them outside of the classroom, transfer to other situations, and enhance their learning throughout life. The teacher must make sure that students are aware of what they are learning and how they are learning it. The teacher should carefully explain each step along the way, identifying the skills necessary and what is to be gained from doing each exercise, so as to establish purpose for reading and writing.

Another approach to preparing students to read and write is the use of mapping or webbing techniques. Mapping is based on a theory that all information about a subject is organized in our brains in memory clusters called *schemata*. All of a person's knowledge about *dog*, for example, comes from his or her experience with the concept. All of that experience and knowledge is grouped in a person's memory store into a *schema* (singular of *schemata*). When new information or experience relevant to the concept is introduced, the person relates it to what is already known about it and adds it to his or her existing schema of *dog*. The importance of this theory to teachers is that it can be used in preparing students to take in new information through their reading and writing. People's knowledge of concepts is not random, but organized. When a new concept is introduced to students, they will guess at its meaning in a systematic rather than a random way. Students will generally associate a new concept with ones they know according to three kinds of relationships: an example of it, a property of it, and the class of things it belongs to. The concept *dog,* for example, would be associated by students with collie (an example), with bark (its property), and with animal (its class). Teachers may use semantic mapping in several ways to build on student knowledge for new learning and to prepare them for reading and writing. Schema theory provides a basis for our holistic text approach to reading and writing, therefore, in that it illustrates why we need to build from the whole schema to the parts in student experiences.

One way teachers may use mapping is to write a topic on the blackboard and ask students to give their associations with the idea. (See Figure 1-3.) When students have responded fully, the teacher may designate the associations as either examples, classifications, or properties, then require that these three elements be addressed in the writing on the topic. Another possibility is to assign each of three small groups one of the elements to explore in greater depth, to become the "experts" in that element. For example, one group is the expert on explaining the properties of the topic. Each "expert" group then writes out a group essay on that element, which they later share with the whole class. Finally, all three elements are narrowed and organized into a whole composition on the main topic.

The whole composition may then be written by the class on the computer, using a large overhead monitor. One student sits at the keyboard, typing in the composition, as the class provides transition words to link ideas each group has generated on the topic. The class observes the composition taking place, while the teacher has a perfect opportunity to teach unity and cohesion of ideas as they are linked together. Unity may be taught to students as singleness of idea, the relating of all the ideas to the main topic. Students can determine whether unity is being achieved and can suggest improvements as they observe the composition being formed on the computer monitor. Cohesion, which relates to interrelationship of ideas, can also be guided by students during the composition, mainly through the use of effective transition words. Such a class composition should be on a simple topic at first, so that the emphasis will be on how to write rather than what to write. Use of the computer in this way links writing and reading and provides a social experience for all the students to share as they learn composing — for comprehension as well as for composition. Revision and editing may also be taught using the computer in this way.

A final approach to preparing students to read and write is the use of readiness strategies. Keeping in mind our holistic text approach, with main ideas introduced first, we engage the students in previewing and prewriting activities. In reading, the students should be asked to survey the text to determine its pattern of organization into units, chapters, and paragraphs and to note how new vocabulary words are introduced through italics, boldface, or highlighting. As the students survey, they are to ask questions about the topic and begin to wonder what it is about, what it includes, and

Figure 1-3   Semantic mapping (diagram adapted from Unit 2 of *Exploring Regions of the United States*. Follett Education Corp., 1969)

Step 1:   Read the title of the chapter students are to read. Illustrate that subject with a relevant drawing.

Step 2:   Try to predict what major concepts the author will present. Then check the chapter subtopics. Write these and connect them to the topic. Add a question mark at the end.

Step 3:   Read the material under the first heading. Stop to recall what was just read for self-testing. Add details to the topic questions on the map.

Step 4:   Review the map periodically to refresh the memory.

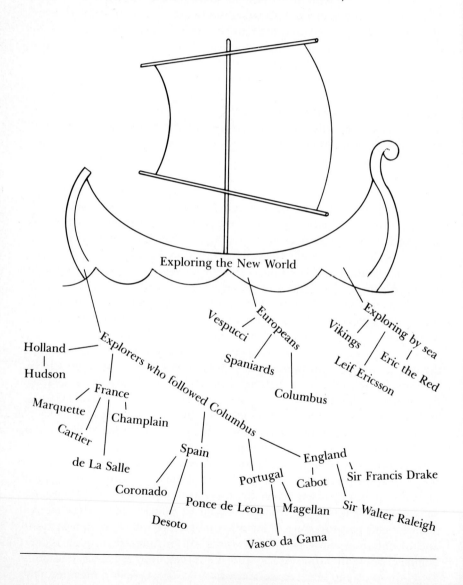

Exploring the New World

Vespucci
Europeans
Vikings
Exploring by sea

Holland
Explorers who followed Columbus
Spaniards
Eric the Red

Hudson
Leif Ericsson

France
Columbus

Marquette
Champlain

Cartier

de La Salle
Spain
England

Coronado
Portugal
Cabot
Sir Francis Drake

Desoto
Ponce de Leon
Magellan
Sir Walter Raleigh

Vasco da Gama

how it can be useful to them. Through such a survey, the students can gain text experience and familiarity, which prepares them, intellectually and emotionally, to read it. Surveying helps them to proceed from the whole to the parts, from overview to closeup, from synthesis to analysis. This preview approach in reading reinforces the prewriting step in composition. In prewriting, students choose a topic, narrow it, and select supporting details in preparation for writing the initial draft. Both prereading and prewriting build on students' existing background knowledge and experience, while adding what is necessary for teacher and students to achieve a common understanding of the assignment. In the preparation stage, students are thus led to tie in their associations and experiences, but they are also engaged in the teacher's expectations for performance and fulfillment of the reading and writing assignment. Therefore, the preparation step must also involve establishing clear purposes that reflect the teacher's expectations, so that students may rise to those expectations.

In connection with the readiness approach, word processors may be used to help students compose initial drafts. The word processors help put all the readiness ingredients to use. Sitting at the word processors, students may write their free associations about a topic, scroll back up through them, organize them, narrow them, and shape them into sentences suitable for a rough draft. Because revision is so easy on the computer, the rough draft may be composed freely—with the emphasis on expressing ideas, not on correcting errors. Shaping associations and thoughts into sentences during the creation of the rough draft prepares the writers to discover what they know about a topic and what direction they want to take with it. During the initial drafting using the word processor, writers process language easily, interact with the text visually and manually, and read and reread as they write. Although it has been found that composing on the computer takes more time than with pencil and paper, the extra time is justified by the greater amount of interaction with the text. Composing with a word processor provides a more dynamic connection between writing and reading while scrolling up and down through the text. This allows more previewing and prewriting readiness.

Step 2: Implementation

The second step of the process is *implementation*, the stage of actual reading and writing once the students have been fully prepared. This step carries out the plans and purposes set in the first (preparation) stage. Students know what they need to do and know that it can be accomplished only through reading and writing. In processing language, they also process their ideas, thus growing in thinking ability as well as in language use and skills.

We give shape to our impressions, feelings, and ideas through language. Writing is a way of discovering our ideas; if we prepare sufficiently for our discovery, we will come to know what we really want to say. We will have tied in what we have in our memory stores with what we want to express, giving shape to our experience and building more experience. Whether students write to an audience of the self (as in a diary) or to another person, they must process language to shape the ideas into expressible forms based on experience gained in life and in the preparation for expression. When there has been adequate preparation, the students are ready to implement their ideas.

Reading and writing involve composing ideas that build upon other ideas and lead to generation of still others. In processing language, one starts with one idea, then begins to get other ideas that lie stored in the experience and were not known to exist there. The computer, with its many varieties of software, provides abundant opportunities for students to interact actively with print, so that their ideas build other ideas and lead to discovery of what they know. Chapter 3 of this book explores this great diversity of software and how it can promote more cognitive involvement of the student in implementing the language processes of reading and writing.

Recent research indicates that there is a 10 percent improvement in reading ability with the use of reading programs in the implementation stage. The best improvement (25 percent) is seen with the use of vocabulary programs. Generally, the computer does not teach reading but gives practice in parts of reading. Shanahan's (1984) studies have found that there is a 45 percent overlap in skills progress when both reading and writing are taught together. There is improvement in both if they are taught together, but *there is no improvement in the other if they are taught separately.* Since reading is slower on the computer, it should be used as a springboard to further reading of literature in a book. The computer should be used to motivate reading. As emphasized before, the computer cannot teach writing; the teacher teaches the writing process in a well-planned curriculum. As a tool for practicing writing, the computer is preferable to the static paper and pen or the non-interactive typewriter. There are limited research results at this time; much more research is needed and will no doubt be forthcoming as the impact of computers on education continues to increase. The main point is that the computer needs to be integrated into a well-designed, carefully planned curriculum. It should never serve as a substitute for a curriculum or a teacher.

Step 3: Application

Through the process model of writing and reading, students have prepared for it in Step 1 (preparation), actually engaged in it in Step 2 (implementation), and in Step 3 are ready to apply it. In reading, *application* involves using the information gained from what was read in some way: in other learning, with regard to life circumstances, or as an aid to producing a product. An example of applying reading to other learning would be to use the ideas of one author to understand another author, as in a comparison exercise. Students may compare the ideas in one short story or essay to related ones in other writing. Ideas from reading may also be used in one's own writing; one's ideas are expanded and enhanced through reading. Reading may also be applied to life circumstances. For example, ideas are used to understand and clarify one's own place in history, or to reach the realization that all humans experience problems, concerns, and circumstances in common. Reading for solutions to problems experienced by others helps students gain background knowledge and experience in dealing with life. Application of ideas in reading also includes practical use of the ideas presented in procedural writing — for example, following a "how-to" book's instructions for making some product. These are some instances of how Step 3 (application) is used in reading.

This step is also used in writing when writers apply their ideas to outside audiences. Instead of egocentrically writing for themselves, they focus on the sociocentric concerns of shaping language to an outside audience. This focus applies a suitable style, relevant vocabulary, and more careful mechanics in an effort to communicate to another person or persons. Application in writing entails taking the ideas that one has initially expressed to oneself and applying them to other needs, those of audience and purpose. In Step 3, the audience and the purpose for writing have to be carefully rethought, as they might have changed from the original plan formulated in the prewriting stage. In application of the ideas to another audience, the writer revises, reshapes, and rethinks the language used, so that it suits the reader's needs for communication.

Step 3 also involves applying knowledge gained from computer use to learning away from the computer. When computer software is used in the process model to teach language processing, teachers must consider how that learning is to be transferred to traditional technologies for reading and writing — to books, paper and pencil, or typewriter. Composing in reading and writing may be practiced on the computer, but people do not read and write mostly with the computer in real life. The skills and learning acquired on the computer must transfer to learning away from the computer. This transfer is carefully planned in an ongoing curriculum (see Chapter 5). For example, students must understand that revision, although easier with a word processor, must also be part of writing with paper and pencil. Another example is that the learning or problem solving in a software program must be analyzed for the skills it teaches, so that students will understand how to use those skills elsewhere in solving problems. The problem solving in turtle graphics, for instance, should be discussed with students to help them realize its implications for logical thinking, for spatial organization, and for recursion of procedures. Then students should apply these implications to subjects they study and other problems they have to solve. Where is there a need for procedures in logic? Where does one find a need for spatial organization? Why is the concept of recursion valuable, and where else may it be used?

Thus the teacher must make a deliberate attempt to tie learning and experiences on the computer to learning away from the computer. Computer learning, therefore, is not perceived as isolated or unrelated to anything else. Good curriculum design by the teacher can ensure that such a tie-in is working. The application stage provides an excellent opportunity to review what students have learned in the process model, then to transfer it and apply it to other ongoing learning. Students must be led to *know what they know* so that they may use conscious options for learning in other circumstances away from the computer, the teacher, and the school. If teachers make this emphasis on transfer a habit after every experience students have, then students may also develop this habit of recognizing the relevance and later use of their learning. Learning then becomes connected, valuable, and usable in students' perceptions. The problems of motivating students to learn would be far fewer if teachers practiced this concept of transfer and emphasized it as a part of every review of learning. In reading and writing, transfer of learning should be part of the process model, as the learning is applied in Step 3.

Some teachers have found it most effective to print out hard copy of students' writing and have them revise the printed copy. Once the students have done this, they return to the computer, enter their revisions, and use spelling and style checkers to finalize the proofreading. Errors are often difficult to spot on a screen, so this approach may be preferable. Perhaps using both word processors and paper and pen will reinforce in students' minds the concept of transfer and revising and editing skills.

Prewriting and Prereading

Prewriting

Teachers may break down the process model of teaching composition and comprehension into very practical plans. The plan for teaching composition can include five learning steps for students (see Figure 1-4). Each step identified in Figure 1-4 takes students through the composing process to produce a composition intended for an audience beyond the writer. There should be opportunities for students to write only for themselves, such as in a diary or a journal. In such cases, writers might use only the first two steps to work out their feelings, thoughts, and ideas. Such ego-centered composition can help students learn to shape language for communication outside themselves.

The five steps to composition provide a disciplined framework for

Figure 1-4   The writing process in five steps

Step 1: Prewriting (up to 80 percent of the time)
  Brainstorm for ideas
  Choose a topic
  Incubate
    Establish purpose: persuade, inform, entertain, etc.
    Select mode: narration, exposition, etc.
    Determine the audience
  Narrow the topic
  Use databases for facts and details
  Choose supporting details
  Outline in order: time sequence, topical, story form
  Form small groups to discuss and organize information

Step 2: Initial draft
  Use word processor in small groups
  Take turns typing in as group members assist

Step 3: Preparing to revise the draft
  Print out the initial draft for each member of the group
  Proofread and discuss changes

Step 4: Editing and revising the draft
  Using a word processor, make changes
  Use spelling checkers and style analyzers
  Reread and discuss changes

Step 5: Finalizing the composition
  Scroll through and proofread
  Print out
  Read aloud to each other in the group to "hear" language

---

students to behave as writers. To become adept at any function, students must realize that they need to learn the discipline necessary to act, think, and perform. Students can be taught that a skill is learned behavior; the skills of writing require learning the behavior of a writer. These five steps teach writer's discipline and will be useful throughout life.

Most of the composing time should be spent on the Step 1 (prewriting), in which the teacher leads the students to select and narrow the topic. It is very important that some time be allowed for incubation or thinking about the topic. During incubation, students should be given the time and opportunity to explore an idea by gathering data, reading about it, discussing it, and discovering associations with it elsewhere. For example, if the topic of *protest* were assigned to students in a social studies class, students could read about various forms of protest (such as strikes, lawsuits, and rebellions), discuss the topic with other students and adults, and find current examples of it in a newspaper. During this time of incubation, students would be experiencing the implications of the concept and preparing themselves to deal with it in their own writing.

Part of incubation time should be devoted to thinking about the purpose for writing. Generally, there will be one of four purposes for writing a school assignment: to express a viewpoint, to inform with facts, to persuade through appeals, or to create in imaginative writing (see Chapter 2). Students can be told their purpose, but sometimes they may also be given the latitude to decide their own purpose for writing. In teaching students to determine the purpose for their writing, teachers should also take the opportunity to point out the purposes of the authors of the students' reading material. Thus, the value of recognizing purpose can be carried over from students' compositions to students' comprehension.

During incubation, students decide on or are directed to select the mode of composition for their writing. They will probably use one of the four modes that occur most often in student writing and textbooks (see Figure 1-5). These modes or styles of writing suit most composition needs, with

Figure 1-5   Modes of composition (from Howie, *Guidebook for Teaching Writing in Content Areas*)

Narration/description: tells a story using description, characters, a plot; compares and contrasts using coordinating conjunctions such as *but, or, yet.*

Story Components	Structure
goal	prose
characters	poetry
time	metaphorical language
place	creative use of language
incidents	plot
resolution	a point to make near the end
theme	

Procedural: relates a process step by step using words of transition.

Components	Structure
sequence	prose
imperative sentences (commands)	elliptical sentences (subject *you* is
unstated steps	eliminated)
abbreviations and symbols	sequence to be followed
referents	elements listed first and directions follow
product or final outcome	assume some reader experience

Time-order exposition: presents events in a time sequence with characters often mentioned; there is a problem to be solved and the sequencing is often cause and effect.

Components	Structure
cause and effect	prose
causality/motivation	sequence to be followed
final events most important	transition "ties" connect events

Figure 1-5, continued

Topic exposition: states an argument or clear topic; has supporting details and logical connections.

Components	Structure
no event sequence	prose
main idea or topic	clear statement of main idea
supporting details or examples	clear summary of topic
relationships connected logically	transition "ties" connect details
specialized vocabulary	concepts defined
often abstract information	relationships built for the reader between known and new concepts

narration/description the most prevalent mode of composition in elementary school, time-order exposition the mode introduced and developed in the middle grades, and topic exposition stressed most frequently in high school and college writing. The procedural mode is seldom taught at all, but is assumed to be understood in many content areas such as science and math. Procedural writing occurs in math story problems, lab experiments, recipes, and industrial arts manuals. The modes of composition have certain components and structural elements that students can be taught to recognize in their own writing as well as in that of others. By learning to recognize the various components and structures of the composition modes, students may begin to examine their own writing analytically. They become more conscious of the "compose" in "composition" and are thus led to apply elements of structure and style to their own work. At the same time, this consciousness of the elements of composition can have a positive effect on the student's reading comprehension.

Students should be given many opportunities to direct their writing to other audiences besides the teacher. In so doing, they become aware that their choices of tone, language, and style should be guided by their knowledge of the audience they address. The teacher may give the assignment of addressing a particular audience. Students may also experiment with audience in a group composition, in which they choose the vocabulary, tone, and style appropriate to communicate to a peer, an employer, a young child, or a college professor. By exploring the range of audiences, identifying the characteristics of each, and attempting to write appropriately, students fine-tune their writing skills and develop greater control.

An important part of the prewriting step is the narrowing of the topic to suit the constraints of the composition: length, purpose, audience, knowledge about the subject, and so forth. One way to help students understand how to narrow a topic for writing is to use the *restricting statement technique:* The key or main word of the topic is identified and then developed as a topic sentence with a restricting or controlling completion. An example is the topic of protest used earlier. This single word may be restricted with a viewpoint: "Protest is a way to fight injustice." The writer has a main idea or key word restricted by the rest of the sentence, which provides a limitation or control that the writer can focus on.

	Idea	Subject to be written about
Topic sentence:		
	Restriction	What there is to say about the subject

This topic sentence is then developed in the composition with the support of details, examples, or reasons, such as the following:

	Idea	Protest
Topic sentence:		
	Restriction	is a way to fight injustice.
Support:	Examples, details, or reasons	

With this kind of formula approach to topic restriction and support development, students may begin to grasp how a paragraph is structured and how ideas are related and tied together in expository composition. They should also be given the opportunity to locate this structure in well-written paragraphs of their textbooks. This sharpens their comprehension of how an author supports a topic, and it also gives the students models of effective writing.

The supporting elements (details, examples, or reasons) may themselves be developed into paragraphs in an expanded composition. The introductory paragraph could present the outline for the rest of the composition; if so, students should become conscious of the use of that kind of logical structure in their writing and their reading. If the support follows a particular order—cause and effect, story form, or spatial order, for example—students should be taught to recognize that order.

When students have prepared for composing in the prewriting stage, they may gauge their readiness for writing on an inventory checklist such as the one presented in Figure 1-6. The purpose of this inventory is to promote students' awareness of the prewriting stage and all the behaviors it entails and demands. Students may begin to realize that they have many options for communication and that careful selection among these options will result in clearer, more organized writing.

A word processor can be very useful to students in their prewriting preparation. The teacher can prepare a planning data disk with all of the prewriting prerequisites given in Figure 1-6 (using prompted writing) and have students fill them in as they incubate their ideas. The advantages of using a planning disk rather than a paper worksheet are that the computer focuses attention more, is more motivating, is more easily corrected or

Figure 1-6 Student prewriting worksheet

Topic
  Subject in general:
  Narrow to a specific aspect of the subject:

Purpose
  What I want the reader to know:
  What effect I want this to have on my audience:

Audience
  Who my audience is:
  What their special characteristics are:

Attitude
  How I feel about my topics:
  How my attitude will affect the tone of my writing:

Experience
  What I know about the subject:

  What I need to know:

  Where I can get information:

Persona
  The role or approach I should take toward my audience:

  I am an equal, an authority, or a character:

Mode
  The form of writing that is best (essay, letter, story, procedures):

  I will use description, time-order, procedures, or topic exposition:

---

changed, and tends to *expand the attention span* of the composer. Composing by computer takes more time than paper and pencil, and research indicates that it *increases* attention span. (This is in contrast to television, which, with its frequent interruptions, decreases attention span.) As the display of working text is larger on a monitor than on a worksheet, it lends itself more to social composing by a group. The prewriting preparation can thus be a social experience of a group gathered around the monitor, talking and exchanging ideas about the topic. Each student or each group could have a planning disk prepared by the teacher with the criteria to be addressed. The teacher may intervene in each group's response on the data disk, monitoring the replies so that students grasp every concept well.

   The teacher may also prepare a database on a file system, for students to access in preparation for writing. A database is a system for storing information, such as the telephone directory. A file system organizes information so that students can readily find it and print it out for their immediate reference. The following are some examples of possible file systems in different content areas:

Music History			Sports Player Files		
NAME:			PLAYER NAME:		
GENRES COMPOSED:			CLASS:	AGE:	BIRTHDAY:
STYLE CHARACTERISTICS:			PARENT NAMES:		
DATES:			ADDRESS:		
NATIONALITY:			UNIFORM NO:		
			SHOE SIZE:		
			BATS:	THROWS:	POSITION:

Business Inventory		Home Economics
ITEM NAME:		RECIPE CATEGORY:
UNIT COST:	QUANTITY:	SERVES:
SUPPLIER NAME:		INGREDIENTS:
ADDRESS:		PROCEDURE:
TELEPHONE:		HOW SERVED:
COMMENTS:		

Once a file system is established (see also Chapter 3), students may not only use it themselves but may also add to it from their own research. Adding to the database can be a valuable experience for students in learning that data should be organized, categorized, and classified for ready access and use. This helps them organize and structure their investigations into the unfamiliar and provides a logical means to report it. This sharing and exchanging of data can be stimulating and motivating, evoking the curiosity of students.

Once students have gathered data and background for their writing and fulfilled the criteria of preparation, they may write their rough drafts on a word processor. Then they edit and revise the drafts, using style and spelling checkers. Finally, they rewrite the composition on a "reference" disk, which other students writing on the same topic may use as an example of how to compose. This reference disk can include several samples of student writing (preferably composed in groups) that illustrate different audiences addressed, different modes of composition used, or different purposes established. It can be used, for example, to illustrate how a topic may be varied and what the effect is when it is varied. Use of the reference disk by students can be a variety of peer teaching; certainly, it is an example of peer modeling. Creating a reference disk by students for other students can be highly motivating; they will try to perform their very best so that peer judgment will be favorable. If the writing is by group composition, individual pressure may be lessened, but the teacher will have to decide which compositions are to be included in the reference disk. The disk may be used in the same class or in later classes taking the same course. Also, the best of students' compositions through the years may be gathered onto one disk as reference for later students who complete the same assignments. In any event, the reference disk can be used very effectively in the prewriting stage and can serve to integrate reading with the writing.

Prereading

In preparing students to read, teachers may break the plan into five steps that students can follow to achieve the maximum comprehension (see Figure 1-7). The steps are a directed reading lesson that provides a lesson plan for teachers, but a more important function may be as a guide for students to learn and use themselves. Students should be made aware of each step as they progress through it, so that they realize the skills they are developing and can use them in other circumstances beyond that lesson and outside the classroom.

Figure 1-7   Directed reading lesson

___

Step 1: Developing Interest

These preliminary activities should be multisensory and greatly varied, to make the abstract ideas as concrete as possible. These activities should be designed to motivate students, and they should also be used to engage student background knowledge and experience with the topic. This step is used to promote schema development, for affective as well as cognitive reasons. Examples:

1. Design a bulletin board to initiate thought and discussion on the topic to be studied. Have students contribute pictures to the display. (Suggested by Richard Kuhman, teacher.)
2. Bring in citizens from the community to talk about their experiences in a topic (recent history, an art or craft, business, etc.).
3. Read a legend or story aloud to students who have their eyes closed for listening. Have students visualize the scenes. (Suggested by Elly Gotfredson, teacher.)
4. Have students write a one-word response to key words, especially emotionally loaded words from the reading.

Step 2: Previewing

This step is necessary in a whole-text approach, so as to provide students with an overview of the entire selection to be read. Examples:

1. Map out chapter topic with subtopics. Predict main ideas the topic will cover. Compare the map with actual chapter headings and revise map.
2. Use SQ3R procedure to survey the selection to be read.
3. Ask students to rephrase the chapter headings into questions. Discuss and predict answers to the questions.
4. Skim the selection and pick out five key terms that relate to the topic. Discuss and tentatively define.

Step 3: Vocabulary

New vocabulary should be introduced in context. Technical terms and common words used in uncommon ways should be presented in context and illustrated, if possible. Preteaching the vocabulary is necessary to provide the schema necessary for the topic. Examples:

(continued)

Figure 1-7, continued

1. In groups of two, one student will find the new word in the glossary while the partner will locate the word in context. When they agree on the definition that applies in that context, one of them will write the definition on the vocabulary assignment sheet. One sheet will be turned in with both names on it. (Suggested by Carolyn Wilson, teacher.)
2. Students scan the selection. For any unfamiliar word they find, they write down the entire sentence the word is in.
3. Use a cloze exercise in which the unfamiliar words from the selection are included. Have students compare their answers to the actual text, noting the contextual uses of the new words.
4. Assign a student a word to locate in the selection. Have him or her read the sentence containing the word, and have the class guess the meaning.

Step 4: Reading

The actual reading may be performed in numerous ways; using a variety of formats will help sustain student interest. The reading can be oral, choral, silent, or done as homework. If it is assigned as homework, students might be assigned sections to prepare for oral reading the next day. The teacher should read some parts aloud at times to model the language used in the text.

Step 5: Evaluation

What is to be evaluated is the students' application of the reading. Activities can be creative and varied. Application of the concepts encountered in reading can increase student interest and retention of them. Examples:

1. Have students write a news article concerning the topic. Students can combine their articles into a booklet about the topic. (Suggested by Amy Knutson, teacher.)
2. Students provide everyday examples of the concepts illustrated in the text. They can write about a similar character they know, a personal experience they have had, or actual objects that relate to the topic.
3. Rewrite the selection as a play, a personal letter, a diary or journal, or some other form of writing.
4. A group of students makes a tape recording of one aspect of the selection. Play it for the class.

In Step 1, the variations of ways to develop interest are practically limitless, depending upon the imagination of the teacher. Developing interest in reading, first of all, involves probing student background knowledge, experience, and interest in the topic. Probing can be achieved through interest inventories (either oral or written), discussions, mapping and associating key ideas, or reactions to media and speaker presentations. The most effective transition into student involvement is through their interests and what they believe is relevant and meaningful. In addition to probing student knowledge and interest, it is important to build background that prepares them to understand concepts in the reading. Building student background involves providing sensory experiences with the new learning.

The more varied the sensory experiences in hearing about concepts and seeing them, the more students will be prepared to deal with their abstract representations in writing.

Psychologists tell us that we learn by taking in information through our senses and relating it to what we have stored in our memory. If our cognitive store contains some material related to the new information, then we adapt it to what we know, create new symbols for what we learn, and store it in our set of long-term memories. (See also Chapter 2.) The preparation stage (Step 1) is designed to create the necessary background for students to tie in new learning with their previous experience.

Some excellent computer programs can aid in this stage of developing interest. For example, simulation programs and problem-solving programs give students experience in thinking about the topic to be explored in reading. One problem-solving program teaches students to look for patterns of growth and death in a population of space creatures. Students look for patterns, relate them, and begin to predict patterns that will occur. Such problem solving can be transferred to the reading of mystery stories, for instance, where the reader looks for patterns of behavior in characters, discovers clues, and begins to predict the outcome of the story based on the patterns detected. This kind of problem solving may be used in social studies and science classes; patterns in history and in nature may be detected and a prediction established for their consequences. Thus, student experience can be built from simulated materials, similar presentations of ideas, and related concepts.

Previewing (Step 2) engages the whole-text approach that is so important in helping students gain an overview of the topic, the main ideas, and the format of text. Previewing gives a sense of familiarity with topic and text that builds students' confidence and experience when they do the actual reading. Previewing provides exercise in deductive thinking, which promotes an understanding of the general premise before reading for the specifics. This is helpful to students because it allows an overview of the main ideas before analysis of supporting details—a parallel to the writing process. (See Figure 1-8.)

Some of the ways students may gain an overview or a preview of what they are to read are through skimming, turning headings into questions, and scanning exercises. Skimming is a skill that students should be given opportunities to develop, as it allows between 50 and 90 percent comprehension while reading at a rate of 800 to 1000 words per minute. Practice in skimming can increase attention span and improve comprehension, because the students' focus is so concentrated and intense. The purposes for skimming are to gain impressions, understand the gist of the composition, and recognize the format of the text. In paper text, skimming involves quickly leafing through pages while running the eyes somewhat diagonally across the lines of print of each page. The exercise forces the reader to concentrate

Figure 1-8   Deductive logic used in the reading/writing process (whole-text approach)

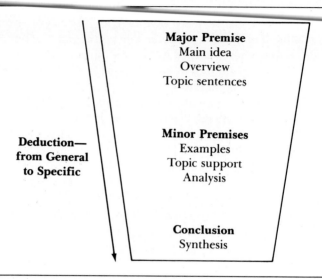

Deduction— from General to Specific

Major Premise
Main idea
Overview
Topic sentences

Minor Premises
Examples
Topic support
Analysis

Conclusion
Synthesis

on major impressions, ideas, and organization, synthesize them, and remember them. Students should be asked questions before they skim: "What is the main idea the author is going to talk about in this passage?" "How is this chapter organized so that you can read it more easily?" "What three major ideas is the author presenting on the main topic?"

Using skimming skills on the computer screen involves scrolling through the text in a word processor. Skimming text onscreen may actually be easier than doing so in a book, because it proceeds vertically. Text in a book proceeds vertically, then horizontally, then vertically, etc., requiring numerous eye-shifting patterns from page to page.

Students can achieve an overview of main ideas before they read by turning subheadings into questions. First, students should be guided through the chapter so that they recognize how the subtopics are presented—whether in boldface, capitals, or italics. When they recognize the subtopic, they use the title as the basis for a question that they will later read about to get the answer. For example, in a chapter on "Exploring the New World," one of the subtopics might be, "Europeans Rediscover the Western Lands." A question students might ask is, "Who were the European explorers of the western lands?" Actual reading would then answer the question.

Turning subtopics into questions is a problem-solving approach to reading, in that the students have generated questions that present them with a problem. The solution to the problem or questions is in the reading they must do to find the answers. Asking questions that need answers ensures active, cognitive involvement by students, because questions arouse curiosity and tension from not knowing. This technique for previewing also helps students develop critical reading and thinking skills by having them question whether or not the author fulfilled their expectations and fully answered their questions. Careful guidance can be given by the teacher to help students realize the value of questioning, then checking on the quality of the author's answers to the questions. This kind of critical reading can begin with very young students.

On the computer monitor, at the introduction of a software program, the main menu can be used to give students opportunities to turn headings into questions and to predict what the program will be about. The menu gives an overview—the macrostructure of the topic—which the students can use to gain familiarity with the topic, tie in their knowledge about it, and predict the treatment of it. They can then read the subtopics for analysis of the main topic and evaluate the author's treatment in terms of whether or not their predictions and anticipations were met and, if not, why not.

A third way students may experience a preview of the topic is through scanning exercises. Scanning is very quickly running the eyes through the text to locate a specific fact, name, date, or word. In a chapter on health and exercise, students may preview by quickly scanning for the word *aerobic,* for example, which may be a key word repeated numerous times throughout. The teacher may explain that the main topic concerns exercise and that repetition of the key subtopic, aerobics, helps provide cohesion of ideas. Cohesion of text involves relationships of ideas, achieved in part by repetition of key words. The skill of scanning helps students locate specific information rapidly and efficiently, a necessary skill in research or in everyday living. It can help students gain a sense of what is important to look for in their reading. Scanning skills can be developed through the use of a book or a computer screen. Students may flip through the pages of a book to locate specific data, scroll through the screens of a word processor, or run through an entire software disk, looking only for certain predetermined information. The effect of any of these exercises is to take students through the entire text as an overview, require them to concentrate and focus their attention, and provide emphasis on major concepts through key words.

The third step in the directed reading lesson is preteaching the vocabulary—having students experience the unfamiliar words before they encounter them in the reading. This step involves building students' backgrounds so that they possess the schema necessary for learning new ideas from the reading. Unusual vocabulary or technical words should be presented in context so as to have greater relevance for the students. One way to do this with a book is to ask a student to locate the word in the reading passage, read the entire sentence aloud to the class, and have them try to determine the meaning. The same technique may be used with text on a screen, especially a large overhead screen that the entire class can see while the student reads it aloud. The computer can also be used to generate vocabulary puzzles that the teacher or students create. The vocabulary words can be unfamiliar ones taken directly out of the reading. If students create the puzzle, they will have to take care in spelling. Some utility programs ask for clues to words in the puzzle, so students could use a dictionary to get clues for the new words they use in the puzzle. The word puzzle could then be given to the whole class to solve. Students could be assigned in groups to generate these word puzzles for the whole class prior to reading assignments. Each group can become an "expert" on the new words to be learned for a reading experience. This kind of activity can be tremendously motivating to students, not only to learn new vocabulary, but also to understand contextual uses of the words in the reading selection.

In previewing text in a book, students should be made aware of how the author presents new vocabulary—whether in italics, boldface, underlined, or in the margins. Textbooks use readers' aids to help introduce new vocabulary, and students should be taught to use those aids to advantage in gaining comprehension.

The fourth step in the directed reading lesson is the actual reading students engage in, whether in a book or on a computer monitor. They may read silently or orally to the teacher or class. If students read orally, they should be given the opportunity to prepare their performance. We no longer stick a book in front of students and just ask them to read aloud "cold." There may be testing times, such as in an IRI (Informal Reading Inventory), when students read from text without preparation (and the validity of this may be questionable), but this should never happen in usual classroom situations. When there are occasions for oral reading in content-area classes, students can preread the material, sound out the sentences and words, and lessen their anxieties by being prepared. Not all students are good oral readers, either. Poor ones should not be forced to perform, but rather given other ways to contribute.

Teachers should remember that silent reading in class is different from reading assigned as homework. Reading in class may be guided, monitored, and generally aided by the teacher so that it is on an instructional level of understanding for students. Homework reading taxes the reading ability of the students more, because it is done independently, without access to the teacher. Such reading necessitates much more preparation and preteaching by the teacher than reading done in the classroom. This preteaching is often neglected because teachers assume that both kinds of reading are the same. In homework reading, the first three steps of the directed reading lesson are crucial preparation stages if students are to be successful.

The use of the computer for reading in class has some advantages over the use of a book. The larger display of text on the screen allows opportunities for small groups of students to read together and discuss their reading as each screen appears. The computer offers greater possibilities for small groups to read together, discuss, and interact with the text in a social context. This is mainly because students see each portion of the text simultaneously; no reader lags a page or so behind another, as in book reading. The possibilities for peer help seem greater in this circumstance, and the poorer reader's fear of failure is lessened. Collaboratively responding to the text with answers or other input can result in greater feelings of success in reading. Furthermore, the teacher can monitor the reading and interactions more effectively, because all members of the reading group are at the same place in the text, discussing the responses, sharing ideas, and helping each other. The results in learning should be much improved over the usual method for silent reading in class, wherein everyone reads at different rates and is isolated from help by others.

The last step in the directed reading lesson, evaluation of the reading, should be approached creatively. The goal is not only to assess what the students have gained from their reading, but also to help them apply what they have learned and transfer the learning to other content areas. The teacher may evaluate what students gained in their reading by having them use it in other ways. For example, after reading a chapter about European explorers, the students could construct a map depicting the course of one or two of them, thus translating their knowledge into geography and cartography and graphically depicting what they have read. Another example would be to have the students read a story, then create a diorama of one of the key scenes, thus applying what they have learned in reading to an art project. In the art project, students would apply their learning to design, colors, and spatial arrangements of objects in order to depict their scene. They would have to read and reread for minor details and descriptions, then synthesize the information and symbolize it in a way other than words. A final example is to have students read a composition stored on a reference disk (from student writing or from supplemental material entered in by the teacher), then rewrite the information in another format. Students could rewrite a passage on ecosystems as a newspaper article and learn something about the journalistic style of the inverted pyramid. Students could rewrite a short story into a play, or a poem into a short story. There are numerous possibilities for applying reading and transferring what has been learned to other learning, limited only by the teacher's imagination. Both textbook and computer screen text can be used to help students gain information and to integrate it with other learning.

Prewriting and prereading may be seen as initial steps in the overall process of using information. The two are highly interrelated but may be broken down into teachable stages for students. Above all, students should be made aware of the steps in the process that the teacher uses, so that they know what and how they are knowing or learning. The steps can be identified for students, made meaningful to them as behaviors they need to engage in, and retained as conscious options for succeeding in situations away from the classroom.

This chapter has introduced the processes of reading and writing, pointing out their relationships and the ways in which each reinforces the other as language systems. The computer is ideal to teach these language systems because it is a language processor and simulates many of the ways people think and learn. Like any technology, the computer must be understood and carefully integrated into a well-designed curriculum. Such integration is necessary for effective teaching of reading and writing processes.

The focus of this chapter has been to introduce reading and writing as systems for processing language. In processing language, certain steps can be used for greater efficiency and effectiveness in language use. These steps may be taught to students so as to engage them in behaving like readers and writers. The computer is a technology with many unique advantages, which can enhance the learning of these behaviors. The chapters that follow will detail just how the computer can be valuable to the teacher and the students in reading and writing.

References

Anderson, J.R., and Bower, G.H. *Human Associative Memory.* New York: Wiley, 1973.

Geoffrion, Leo, and Geoffrion, Olga P. *Computers and Reading Instruction.* Reading, Mass.: Addison-Wesley, 1983.

Goetz, Ernest, and Armbruster, Bonnie. "Psychological Correlates of Text Structure." In *Theoretical Issues in Reading Comprehension* (Spiro, Ed. Hillsdale, N.J.: Erlbaum Associates, 1980.

Howie, Sherry Hill. *Guidebook to Teaching Writing in Content Areas.* Newton, Mass.: Allyn and Bacon, 1984.

Howie, Sherry Hill. "The Teaching of Reading in Technotronic Times: Values and Goals Clarification." In Twelfth NCAA Yearbook, *College and Adult Reading,* Vol. 12.

Moffatt, James, and Wagner, Betty Jane. *A Student-Centered Language Arts Curriculum.* Boston: Houghton Mifflin, 1968.

Pearson, David, and Johnson, Dale. *Teaching Reading Comprehension.* New York: Holt, Rinehart and Winston, 1972.

Rumelhart, David E., and Ortonly, A. "The Representation of Knowledge in Memory." In *Schooling and the Acquisition of Knowledge* (Anderson et al., Eds.). Hillsdale, N.J.: Erlbaum Associates, 1977.

Shanahan, Tim. "Nature of the Reading–Writing Relationship: An Explanatory Multivariate Analysis." *Journal of Educational Psychology,* 76, 466–477, 1984.

Spiro, Rand J. "Constructive Processes in Prose Comprehension and Recall." In *Theoretical Issues in Reading Comprehension* (Spiro, Ed.). Hillsdale, N.J.: Erlbaum Associates, 1980.

CHAPTER TWO

Uses of the Computer to Teach Processing

Students collaborating to learn

The purpose of this chapter is to detail ways the computer may be used to enhance the teaching of reading and writing. Computer programs may be used to build students background experience, establish purposes, and develop their thinking skills through different cognitive models. In particular, the computer offers problem-solving opportunities for students to develop skills they can use in processes that require clear, logical thinking.

Building Student Background Knowledge and Experience

Both writing and reading are composing systems for language, and the composing depends upon what the reader/writer knows. Therefore, a major factor in the process is ensuring that the language user has a sufficient knowledge and experience base. Each student reads or writes a text from a conceptual viewpoint that reflects his or her experience with the subject. The text consists of symbols that only suggest meanings that the language user already has stored in memory. Because of this, writers carefully select symbols that will evoke meaning according to the purpose and audience for which they are writing. Readers approach text as guides to help them construct meaning. Meaning is in the mind of the reader rather than in the text, so this factor has to be carefully considered in teaching comprehension as well as composition. The relationship between background knowledge and reading comprehension has long been acknowledged, but it has only recently been recognized as a possible major cause of reading failure. Research into causes of reading failure has often focused on problems in the text, such as sentence length, density of concepts, and difficult syntax. However, in our composing model of language use, we need to focus on the crucial factor of schemata—the knowledge structures that students possess and access to construct meaning. (See the beginning of Chapter 1.) Therefore, building background knowledge has to include student understanding of three areas: subject matter, vocabulary concepts, and kinds of text. This section will be concerned with these three areas in which teachers can help students become better at composing meaning.

Knowledge of Subject Matter

The teacher may use interest inventories, classroom probes, and other means to discover the backgrounds, experiences, and interests of students. Through such means, the students' existing memory stores may be understood and used as a base on which to build new knowledge. Teachers should make every effort to learn about their students for such purposes. There are also many time-tested methods teachers can use to build student background in prereading and prewriting stages, such as classroom presentations, field experiences, and use of media — including computers, which will be our focus.

A traditional method of building student background knowledge is through a presentation. James Flood (1986) outlines seven ingredients for an effective prereading presentation. These are appropriate for prewriting as well:

1. Relating new information to prior knowledge
2. Dealing with misconceptions and prejudgments
3. Establishing purposes for learning
4. Organizing new information into logical chunks
5. Providing transitions from one information chunk to the next
6. Summarizing the information of the text
7. Soliciting active responses and providing adequate feedback

In relating the new learning to prior knowledge, it is important to engage students' related life experiences, which they may draw on to associate with the new concepts. For example, if students are studying the theme of courage, it would be more useful to have them identify times in their lives when they have had to be courageous than to have them simply define the term without mention of associations and feelings they have experienced. In such sharing by students, the topic is made relevant. Students' biases toward the topic may also be discerned as they relate their associations with it. Understanding the students' biases and prejudgments, the teacher may guide their comprehension of the new subject matter.

Another way to help students learn new information is to establish very clear purposes for reading or writing. We have already identified purpose as what the reader is to gain from the reading. It is also important to identify the sequencing of the information to be presented — whether in a cause-effect sequence, time order, spatial sequence, or other — so that the students can recognize patterns of organization of the material. Because text should be approached from whole to part, students need to understand major chunks or divisions of information, such as can be organized into an *advanced organizer*. An advanced organizer on elements of design in art or music would include the major divisions of composition, balance, rhythm, and harmony. Understanding the major chunks, students will follow the process of filling in the details for each chunk as they learn. The overview is an organizer or synthesis for the analysis to follow in the learning.

Advanced Organizer

Elements of Design

Composition   Balance   Rhythm   Harmony

Then students need to have some understanding of how the parts fit together into a whole through transitions and how the ideas are related to each other. The summary of the most important information should help to provide this overview and relationship of ideas, not only by restating key terms, but also by providing a set of expectations for the reading and writing. The presentation allows for active student responses, so that the teacher can determine whether their thinking is on track for the new learning and can steer it in the right direction.

Another method for building student background experience is the use of field experiences, which take students right to the source and provide concrete contact with abstract ideas learned through books. Students have always benefited from trips to museums, outdoor science labs, and theatres to see plays, operas, and concerts. This method also includes bringing in speakers from the community to present ideas and share experiences that can give students a chance to interact with those "who have been there."

In addition, teachers have traditionally relied on media, particularly filmstrips, movies, television, and radio, to give their students background experience. With the versatility of the computer, however, use of media can be greatly extended to give students not just another media source, but a richer variety of experiences that are highly motivational. The following are suggestions for ways that the computer may be used to build background knowledge before reading and writing activities. Some of these suggestions involve taking common kinds of software such as word processors and using them in uncommon or creative ways. Many of these ideas have come from practicing teachers who have actually implemented them.

The first kind of programs may be thought of as *springboard* software, which serve to gain students' attention and help them focus on key points. Such software includes story starters and interactive story adventures, as well as word processors for brainstorming, mapping, and sharing information. The equipment needed is a computer with two disk drives and a large overhead monitor the whole class can see. The time required for the springboard software is about ten minutes, so the class is introduced to the program on the large monitor and has time to react to it with enough stimulus to begin reading or writing, independently or in small groups. Using a word processor in drive 1 and a data disk in drive 2, the teacher can begin to map out ideas with students on the topic they are to learn. As students give input, a student or the teacher types in the responses, which are projected on the large screen for the class to see. Perhaps the topic is the zoo, and students are asked to respond with whatever occurs to them regarding it. Responses will range from names of animals, to places they come from, to how they are cared for, to how a zoo is organized. After students' responses are typed in and displayed on the screen, they should be categorized by the class according to major subdivisions of information, which is easily done on the word processor with the editing functions of replace, delete, move, and change. (See Figure 2-1.) With this information graphically organized, students may begin to predict what the reading selection on zoos will cover. When they read, they may compare what they have *premapped* with the information the writer gives them. After they

Figure 2-1   Springboard activities

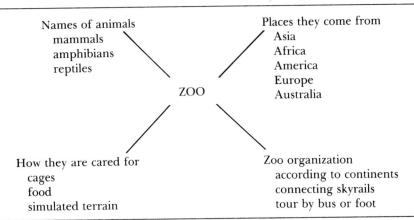

Names of animals
  mammals
  amphibians
  reptiles

Places they come from
  Asia
  Africa
  America
  Europe
  Australia

ZOO

How they are cared for
  cages
  food
  simulated terrain

Zoo organization
  according to continents
  connecting skyrails
  tour by bus or foot

read, students should construct another map, filling in with much greater detail what they have learned as a result of the reading. After the *postmap* is built, using the word processor and the large monitor, students may divide into groups, each of which is responsible for writing on one large chunk of the information in detail. When the groups have finished, they may collaborate as a class, building a class composition out of the major chunks of information, with a consistent point of view, appropriate transitions, and integration of ideas. The advantage of using the computer is that the maps may be printed out for each group and stored on a data disk for future use—for example, in comparison, precomposition, and postcomposition. The ease of rearranging the ideas and graphically displaying them is another advantage. Best of all is the social interchange that the overhead monitor allows. It focuses attention; students are together in their ideas, without some being left behind; and the teacher monitors the whole process, with immediate feedback and guidance.

Another springboard program is a story generator called "Story Tree," which allows students to make decisions about which branching subplot they wish to take. Again, the story starter can be displayed on a large monitor for students to view. At the point where they must make a decision on a story they have begun to create or one that exists on the disk, the students can be asked to work independently or in groups to complete the plot that was started. The different versions (actually, solutions to the story problem) may then be compared and critiqued for their logic, structure, and creativity.

Actually, nearly any program that students might use individually can also be used with the entire class to generate interest, focus attention, and build background knowledge for the reading or writing to follow. Such programs may be used as springboards for learning, or they may be used to give *experiential preparation,* as in simulations, which can be very effective as catalysts for language use. Most simulation programs can be used to cross content areas and integrate learning in what they teach. One example is "Geography Search" by McGraw-Hill, which integrates the content areas of geography, car-tography, history, literature, math, and science, while teaching skills of communication, research, recordkeeping, and critical thinking. Such a simulation can serve as a catalyst for writing and further reading in history and literature on the subjects of early navigation, exploration, and settling of new lands. This kind of an experience builds student background as well as interest, while providing a "realistic" situation in which communication with others is crucial and critical thinking is valuable. This kind of a pro-gram also encourages cooperative learning. For example, teams of students can be assigned to work together to solve the problems of sailing to the New World on ancient ships. Each team can be responsible for keeping its own records, writing its own reports, doing its own research, and informing the rest of the class of its progress. Such a project would truly integrate not only subject matter, but also the language processes of reading and writing.

Another kind of software that may be used to build student background in subject matter is an *information-organizing* program. A program called "Thinktank" (by Living VideoText, Inc.) may be used to help students outline major points they are to include in their writing as well as their reading. For writing, the teacher helps the class generate a skeletal outline of the main points of a topic, which the students may then expand (in-dividually or in groups) with subordinate details. With the use of a large monitor so that the class may see it, the program can serve as an electronic chalkboard that has many advantages over a regular chalkboard: printing out copies for students and revising, expanding, and collapsing the points. "Thinktank" may also be used to generate questions for students to fill in as they expand their topics. The program is appropriate for the first ten minutes of class, to review the ongoing writing and reading project and to provide focus for the learning for that period. The new ideas are added to the previous ideas, stored on the data disk to be used the next day, and printed out as a blueprint for student work for that day. The program is very effective for helping students to learn organization of information, to distinguish main points from subordinate details, and to develop ideas with elaboration. The outlines they generate may be expanded or collapsed with a push of a few keys, so that travel from the whole to part of a topic and back again is accomplished easily. Besides their usefulness for prewriting organization, the outlines may also serve to set up anticipations for reading: What do students *predict* the reading selection is going to be about? The predictions will be based on what they already know or guess about the subject and will serve to get them cognitively involved in it. Students may list the major points they think the author will cover. The list can be printed out, then filled in as a guide to be used as they read. When the details are filled in as a result of the reading, students may write their essay on the topic according to the expanded outline. "Thinktank" can be used for most content areas and in many creative ways—as an organizer, a data base, or a study guide. In these functions, it is useful for activities before, during, or even after reading and writing. A word processor can also be used for these functions, but it will not have the sophisticated functions of the "Thinktank" program.

Another program that has some similar functions is the "Quill" writing system, by D.C. Heath. It is an integrated system of three programs, centered around a word processor. The "Planner" program may be prepared by the teacher for students to use as they plan their writing. The "Quill Planner" contains a list of topics supplied by the teacher, one of which the student chooses. After the topic is chosen, the student is given a list of questions to answer about the topic, which are answered right on the disk. The answers to the questions serve as a database of information, from which students actually write out their essays. The planner can be teacher-made or created by the student. It can be displayed as a whole-class stimulus for writing or for reading, or it may be used by small groups or individuals. The lists may be printed out (up to ten copies at a time), so that students can use them for working at their desks rather than at the computer. Planner disks may be stockpiled for later use by other groups of students writing on the same topics. Thus, they serve as databases for different subjects and different kinds of writing, such as narrative, expository, and creative writing. They can give guidance not only in what to write, but also in how to write it.

Another information organizer that may help students to build background knowledge in subject matter is a database program, such as "PFS: File" by Scholastic, Inc. This program allows students to establish a format for storing information they can use in their writing and reading. When a topic is selected, the teacher can guide students in deciding what information is needed with regard to that topic; then the format can be set up. For example, if students are to study about United States presidents, they will need to know their names, when they served, their political affiliation, their major contributions, events during their time in office, and so on. All of these points serve as the format for later entry of the information that students will be able to go back and fill in for each president as they read.

```
Topic: U.S. Presidents
NAME:
DATES OF ADMINISTRATION:
POLITICAL PARTY:
MAJOR CONTRIBUTIONS:

IMPORTANT EVENTS:
```

The important thing students learn here is how to make decisions on what they need to know to become informed about the topic. The format can always be altered to include other information as students discover they need to change it. With this program, students gain a sense of responsibility for what they want to learn. Then they learn it and organize it according to the database they have preestablished. This gives a clear purpose for the reading they are to do, as they know just what they are to gain from it. Some of the points in the format are at the literal level, but the last two in the example above are decidedly at the inferential level (requiring higher thinking ability), which should be explained to the students. They should know that they will be required to draw conclusions and make decisions about what they believe are the major contributions and important events and that these points will be stated only indirectly in their reading. Using a database system such as this can be extremely valuable to students in organizing the information they gain in reading. This organization can later be used for their own writing. The database may be used to state a format, but questions could be asked just as easily, if that is easier for students: for example, "What are the major contributions?" Students could use these questions as a study guide for their reading or a quiz on what they have read. Applied creatively, information-organizing programs serve many purposes — not just as databases, but also as study guides, test generators, previews or reviews of learning. They can be created by the teacher or by the students; they may be used for whole classes, small groups, or individuals; and their applications are limited only by the imagination of the users.

The above are just a few of the many fine programs that can serve as springboards, experiential preparation, and information-organizing catalysts to help build student knowledge and background in subject matter. There is ample potential for teacher experimentation with such programs.

Building Knowledge of Vocabulary Concepts

Vocabulary should be pretaught so that students will have a working knowledge of important concepts as they read and write. If students are introduced to concepts ahead of time, they will experience a sense of familiarity that will give them confidence and success with the new learning. Introducing students to new vocabulary before reading and writing allows them to develop the schema references that are necessary to relate to new information. Preteaching vocabulary is therefore an important step in the reading/writing processing of language. Vocabulary concepts may be pretaught in many ways. For our purposes here, we will concentrate on three specific approaches to understand how the computer can best be of assistance in this preparatory step. Because software lends itself to numerous instructional techniques for learning, the student is not limited to mere drill and practice, although there are software programs specifically for that. Vocabulary instruction comes in many forms in different software: games, tutorials, and material generation programs, in which students can create word puzzles for themselves and for classmates. The most useful programs are the ones that focus on three approaches to teaching vocabulary in particular: the use of words in context, word associations, and experiential opportunities. This section will discuss some of the uses of these three approaches to teaching vocabulary concepts, with the intention of building students' background knowledge before reading and writing.

By learning new words in context, students learn to rely on clues of syntax or word order in sentence structures. For example, the unfamiliar word *pterodactyl* will appear in a sentence as a noun, probably preceded by an article: "The pterodactyl became extinct after the Cretaceous geologic era." Its position makes it the subject of the sentence, so the student has a clue that it is something with the property of having become extinct at some time period. Thus, the student will begin establishing some schema reference for the new word, based on its relationship to the other words. Learning words in the context of sentences has tremendous advantages over learning them in isolation — an approach that is not recommended. In choosing software to teach vocabulary, the teacher should be very careful to select approaches that use context over those that merely present lists of words or game formats with isolated words. New words need to be placed in some referential context for greater understanding as well as longer retention. This principle is consistent with our theory of language processing.

The following discussion deals with specific software packages that serve as examples of sound educational programs for teaching vocabulary; there is no intention of promoting any particular program or company. They are included here because of appropriateness of their principles, which can be helpful to the teacher in evaluating and selecting the best educational software available. Because technology becomes obsolete so rapidly and new software is introduced onto the market at the rate of about twenty-five pieces a day, our focus has to be on the *criteria* for selection rather than names of particular products.

Some software programs are "shells" that allow entry of new content, such as words that a teacher might want to include for relevance to ongoing lessons. The "Vocabulary Machine: Customized Spelling Lists" by SouthWest Educational Psychology Services is one such program. The teacher may insert both words and graphics to illustrate the words. Each word is presented in a sentence with a picture. The program also includes a recordkeeping system for a maximum of sixty students. Another program allowing custom entry of words is "Word Attack" by Davidson & Associates. In this package, words are presented with definitions and sentences illustrating usage in four activity programs. These are followed by a reinforcement exercise that uses arcade action in a game format. Another package that uses a cloze procedure as well as contextual clues is one by Sunburst, called "M__ss__ng L__nks." *Cloze* refers to the principle of closure: that the human mind logically seeks to fill in missing information in order to make sense out of the whole of it. This program capitalizes on this principle by deleting letters and words in selected passages of literature on nine levels of difficulty. The object is to give students practice in identifying and understanding grammar structures, word use, and effective writing. The teacher may also enter passages that tailor the program to the needs and interests of students in the ongoing curriculum. These are just some of the fine software programs available to help students learn vocabulary from context clues and to build background in what they are to learn. The fact that some of them can be customized is very important for making computer lessons transferable to classroom learning.

The word processor can be used effectively to create vocabulary lessons that are entirely customized. Cloze exercises may be constructed by deleting certain words from passages taken from literature or texts that students are going to read. The deleted words may be ones that are unfamiliar to students or ones that need to be emphasized as being very important to the meaning of the text. The deleted words are indicated by underlines, as in the example below. The passage can be displayed on a large monitor for the class to guess what the missing words might be. The missing words may be listed at the bottom of the passage so that students can choose where to place them. The following example is from Steinbeck's *The Pearl*.

Cloze Exercise

Kino deftly slipped his knife into the edge of the shell. Through the _____ he could feel the muscle tighten hard. He worked the _____ lever-wise and the closing muscle parted and the _____ fell apart. The lip-like flesh writhed up and then subsided. Kino lifted the _____, and there it lay, the great _____, perfect as the moon. It captured the light and refined it and gave it back in _____ incandescence. It was as large as a sea-gull's egg. It was the greatest _____ in the world.

pearl   knife   flesh   blade   shell   silver

An effective way to present this is to create the exercise on the word processor, then print out copies for students to work on independently before the whole-class exercise. Students thus have a chance to think quietly about what logically fits and then, in the whole-class exercise, get to share their ideas and compare their decisions with others. A program called "Mastertype's Writer" by Scarborough presents a split screen for word processing; this can also be used to display the text and the missing words at the same time. The original cloze test deleted every fifth word from a 250-word passage, resulting in 50 blank spaces for students to fill in. That procedure may be followed also, but it would be for a purpose different from ours, which is to teach specific vocabulary concepts in context.

Another approach to teaching vocabulary concepts to build student background knowledge is *word associations* of synonyms, antonyms, homonyms, analogies, and the like. This approach provides a reference point from which students may begin to build their schematic structures for a new word. In selecting software for this approach, it is important to look for a feature that allows students to get the right answer if they make a mistake. It will not be enough for students just to know that they have made a mistake; they should be provided a helpful, correct model to compare to their incorrect choice, so that their learning is reinforced with right answers. Many vocabulary games are faulty in that they do not correct wrong answers, so teachers should be alert to this problem with some programs. Another failing of some games is that they emphasize the points the "winner" accumulates — at the expense of the learning that should be taking place.

One fine educational computer program is "Word Pairs" by Microcomputer Workshops. The program is divided into two parts, the first of which uses definitions and examples to teach the students to discriminate between frequently confused pairs of words. Students can then practice using them in exercises that are provided. The second part is more complex; it asks students to find errors in usage of word pairs and to make corrections. The beauty of the program is that it contains a Help screen option, which the students may use at any time to view definitions. Continuous feedback is provided through helpful models. The teacher is also given an aid: At the end, the achievement of the student is detailed so that progress can be noted. This software presents the ingredients for a sound educational vocabulary package.

Hartley has a vocabulary program called "Analogies," which is keyed to different grade levels for middle school and secondary students. This program presents an organized method for understanding analogous word relationships, so that analogies are not presented in isolation but are grouped according to an overall classification, making them easier to understand and to remember. Furthermore, when students understand overall relationships such as cause-effect, synonyms and antonyms, and part-whole, they may begin to create their own analogies according to the classifications. The program presents the analogy and asks for an answer; if the answer is incorrect, it instructs the student to press RETURN for a hint that explains the relationship more clearly. Included in the program is a recordkeeping system that can help students and teacher keep abreast of progress. Analogies are important for students to experience because they contain subtle word relationships that may help students think more clearly and choose words to express themselves more carefully. This program is an example of sound educational software in its feedback to students, in its guidance of learning, and in its organized method of classifying information that students can structure and retain in their own minds.

The last approach to teaching vocabulary concepts for building student knowledge is rather comprehensive — it covers *experiential* opportunities. This approach ranges from games through material generation to virtually anything that personally involves students in creating or engaging in their own experiences with new words. Teachers can generate word puzzles and create vocabulary games, but it is important to let students be "teachers," too, so that they can take more of a responsibility for the learning and sharing of learning. One program for creating crossword puzzles and word finds is the MECC "Teacher Utility" software. Both students and teacher will find this very simple to use to generate vocabulary exercises out of the on-going reading and writing that take place in the classroom. After words are entered in, the puzzle is created — vertically and horizontally, diagonally, or all ways. A teacher's key is printed out along with the puzzle. Puzzles of this nature do not really teach vocabulary concepts, but they promote familiarity with the appearance of words and help students in spelling them. The meanings of the vocabulary would have to be taught either before or after the puzzle is completed. Another program that presents clues along with the new words is "Crossword Magic" by Mindscape. The teacher or student enters words and clues to their meanings, and the computer arranges the words into a crossword puzzle with the clues printed underneath. An answer key is also printed. The puzzles may be used for preteaching vocabulary or as reviews in postreading or postwriting, with words taken from students' own papers. Words students have misused or misunderstood in their own writing may serve as the basis for crossword puzzles, thus making the experience really relevant to their ongoing learning. These puzzles may serve as a focus for class attention if they are displayed on a large overhead monitor and completed with guidance from the teacher. They may also be played as games. Groups try to solve the puzzles within a specified time limit, competing against each other for fun.

There are plenty of software programs that use games and drill and practice formats for instructing students in vocabulary that is preselected and built in, but these may not be applicable to the ongoing learning in the class. These preselected formats must be chosen carefully by the teacher for relevance and transferability to the needs of the students. The words have to be at students' comprehension levels, and they should have appeal to their interests. A certain number of these programs could be kept on hand as supplements for remedial or enrichment purposes. However, shell programs into which words from the class curriculum may be inserted are the ones most integral to learning. Among many such good programs is "The Game Show" by Advanced Ideas. This is a quiz program, with animated color graphics, for an individual player or small groups. It can also be used for an entire class, using a large monitor. The program has prepackaged subjects (including vocabulary, biology, and cities), but it also allows more topics to be added to the disk, customizing it for students in any subject. This feature can be valuable in helping students build background in vocabulary concepts for prereading and prewriting purposes. The teacher should be aware of the advantages of this customizing feature when selecting software that teaches vocabulary; the choices are *not* limited to drill and practice or tutorial programs that preselect oftentimes irrelevant materials.

Again, the word processor may be used to create vocabulary exercises that the teacher can print out as worksheets or that students use on the computer and print out for the teacher. The treacher may ask questions about words, and students answer; the teacher may create a cloze exercise of a passage, into which students insert meaningful words; or the teacher may devise games that match words, require use of a dictionary, or necessitate logical multiple-choice selections. The word processor can be used creatively to promote student interest in words and in increasing their vocabularies in any subject area.

Building Knowledge of Text

Before reading and writing, students need to be instructed in the kind of text they are going to be using. It is not enough for them to be instructed in content only; they also need help in becoming text-wise. *Text* refers to two or more sentences that have structure, unity, and cohesion. Knowledge of these elements can help students' comprehension and composition considerably. As our approach to text is holistic, in that we consider the main ideas before we look at its parts, we can understand how students need an overview of the patterns and forms of text. For example, a short story differs in its structure and components from a math story problem, even though both can be considered complete compositions in themselves. Students should be taught that a short story is structured according to a story grammar (or recurring pattern), which they can recognize every time they read a story. That story grammar differs from the math story problem, which is also highly structured—with givens presented at the beginning and what to do with them at the end (somewhat like the format of a recipe). Also, an expository composition or a chapter in a textbook follows a predictable and recognizable pattern that students should learn to recognize in their reading and writing. An expository composition is structured logically, with an introduction, development of details, and a summarizing and restating conclusion. A well-written chapter in a textbook is also structured this way, so students can depend upon its predictability in their gaining meaning. With predictable text, students may validate their own guesses and find closure in the comfort of recognizable patterns. However, these patterns must be taught to students before they can use them.

Teaching patterns in text may be seen metaphorically as teaching rituals of communication. *Ritual* is a sociological term indicating a recurring, recognized, and accepted pattern that through its familiarity communicates something. A wedding ceremony is a ritual of communication that has expectations of participants, format, and outcome. A baseball game can also be considered a ritual in the same ways. Textbooks follow rituals of communication that we come to expect, if the book is to serve its purpose. Students may be introduced to the ritual of unit divisions, chapter subdivisions, sections and parts, prefaces and table of contents, and appendices. Education of the young may be considered to be introduction to the rituals of society, and rituals in literacy education are no different. One time-tested strategy for teaching rituals or patterns of texts is the SQ3R method, in which students are asked to Survey (skim) a text, ask Questions, then Read the text, Recite it as in notetaking, and Review it for memory retention. This strategy helps to make students text-wise, introducing them to the ritual used by the author to communicate meaning. An interesting software program by Sunburst teaches students to understand patterns in "The Pond." A frog, lost in a pond of lily pads, helps the user to recognize patterns and to make generalizations from the data offered through inductive thinking. This program teaches how to recognize structure, how to classify information, and how to draw logical conclusions based on that information. These are the reading and writing strategies we want students to develop as we teach them ritual.

Differences in kinds of ritual presented in content-area textbooks and in students' writing may be characterized as modes of composition. *Modes* are styles of writing that have certain identifiable structures and components that distinguish them one from the other. Four modes of composition (Howie, 1984) are found in middle and secondary school writing: narration/description mode, topic exposition mode, time-order mode, and procedural mode. The *narration/description* mode is the one taught almost exclusively to students in elementary school, where they learn to enjoy stories with characters, a plot, and lots of description. This is the mode students usually become most familiar and comfortable with throughout their schooling. The *time-order* mode is introduced in junior high school and is predominant in social studies and science text writing. It emphasizes cause and effect and historical sequencing of events. *Topic exposition* is taught mostly in high school and college; it emphasizes argument supported by details, examples, and reasons. In topic exposition, a student states a clear topic and develops it with support from research. The topic is often abstract and contains specialized vocabulary that has to be carefully defined.

The last mode of composition is the *procedural* mode, which is the least familiar to students because it is rarely if ever taught as a style of writing. This mode relates a process step by step; uses technical vocabulary, usually abbreviations and symbols other than words; and assumes the reader has enough prior experience to supply the unstated steps and inferencing required. This mode is used in such instances as math story problems, science experiments, home economics recipes, and industrial arts procedures. Because students are rarely taught this mode of writing, unfamiliarity with it may be a major cause of the "math anxiety" experienced by so many.

Resistance to this mode because of unfamiliarity with it helps to widen the dichotomies in our society between the liberal arts and the scientific, the humanistic and the technical, and the idealistic and the realistic. English teachers generally do not teach this mode; it should be taught by content-area teachers who are specialists in use of language in their fields.

These four modes of composition can be taught through the use of different software programs. The software can introduce students to the mode of composition in which they are to read and write and serve to induct them into its ritual.

Narration/Description Mode.   This first mode tells a story using description, often with characters and a plot, and sometimes uses comparison and contrast.

Story Structure	Story Components
Prose	Goal
Poetry	Time
Metaphors	Incidents
Plot	Resolution
A point to make at the end	Theme

An effective type of software in teaching this kind of text is the *story starter*. A program alluded to earlier, "Story Tree," by Scholastic, is one of the best of this type in that it lets students make decisions about how a plot is going to unfold by branching it in different directions. The built-in word processor permits students to write their own stories using this branching capability. With careful guidance from the teacher, students can use this type of program to become text-wise in the structure and components of the narrative/descriptive mode. Another kind of software to teach this mode is a tutorial that teaches components of composition. One by Micro Lab is "Myths, Magic and Monsters: Comprehensive Reading Skills," which presents stories introducing such concepts as main idea, speaker, and figurative language. The program could be used with individuals, small groups, or (on a large monitor) the entire class, to teach story grammar. "Quill Planner," mentioned earlier, can also help guide students with key words in developing each story component. For example, the teacher can enter the key terms of exposition, events in rising action, and climax and have the students write them out as they are guided. An outlining program such as "ThinkTank" can also be used for this purpose: Students expand with "paragraphs" each story component entered into the outline as a guide to story development. It would be more effective to have the entire class cooperate in story development initially, so that everyone understands and participates in the process. Narrative/descriptive writing created by students can be stored on data disks to serve as examples for other students to emulate. These disks can become libraries or databanks, effective in

motivating students because they were created by their peers. Storing student work in this way could also motivate them to write for different
audiences.

Time-Order Exposition.   This second mode presents events in a time
sequence, with characters often mentioned. There is a problem to be solved,
and the sequencing is often cause and effect.

Structure	Components
Prose	Cause and effect
Sequence	Causality/motivation
Transition ties connect events	Final events are most important

Expository writing *exposes* ideas. It is logically structured, with an introduction that states the topic, a body that supports and develops the topic, and
a conclusion that restates the main points and summarizes the ideas. The
essay may be sequenced in a time-order organization, indicated to the reader
by transition words such as the following:

Logical order

Time: then, after, one day, subsequently, first, second, meanwhile, immediately,
soon, when, yesterday, tomorrow

Value: initially, first, second, third, finally, next, last

Cause/effect: due to, thus, hence, because, since, therefore, consequently, accordingly, as a result

Such time-order exposition often occurs in social studies and history texts.
In reading these, students should be led to recognize important transition
words that provide the logical structuring. To recognize their importance
in reading may help students to realize their importance in writing. To
teach this mode of composition with the computer, a simulation such as
"President Elect" by Strategic Simulations, presented to the entire class,
would be effective in getting across the concept of cause and effect. This
program allows students to recreate an election, using historical figures from
the years 1960 to 1984. The students may run for office, speak out on issues,
and allocate campaign funds. The computer graphically portrays the status
of the candidates each "week" by analyzing the political climate constructed
from economic factors, the news media, and foreign circumstances. The
simulation creates "what if" situations based on many realistic factors. By
making decisions, students can see the effects caused by circumstances they
can control as well as those beyond their control. A record could be kept
of all the transition words they use orally to tie together their sequencing
of events during the simulation, then analyzed for their logical meanings
and helpfulness in communication. These words may then be used in
students' writing to indicate sequencing and time order.

Another program that is similar but has a different subject matter is "Starting a New Business" by Intellectual Software. This program has students set up a new business, making decisions that can lead to either wealth or bankruptcy. Their decisions on advertising, hiring, raising capital, incorporation, marketing, budgeting, etc. teach them causes and effects and generate a great many words that express that kind of sequencing. All along, during use of the simulation, students should be monitored and constantly made aware of their choices of language and specific words used to talk about the time ordering of the events. Students should be taught that the words they use are logical ones that they should also use in their writing to express time order and consequences to a reader. A student recorder could be appointed for the session, to write down the words the groups use during the simulation. Then the words on the list can be discussed by the class, identified in reading they do, and incorporated *consciously* into their own writing.

Topic Exposition.   The third mode states an argument or clear topic and has supporting details and logical connections.

Structure	Components
Clear statement of main idea	Main idea or topic
Clear summary of topic	Supporting details or examples
Transition "ties"	Specialized vocabulary
Concepts defined	Relationships connected logically
Relationships built between known and new concepts	Often abstract information

Because this is an expository essay, students should be taught that the overall structure consists of a clear introduction of the main ideas or topic, the body that supports and develops the main ideas, and the conclusion that sums up and restates the main points, so that the reader gets reinforcement and emphasis of the ideas. One way to teach this structure is to have students write the introduction and the conclusion first, before they write the body of the essay. The introduction and the conclusion are restatements and reinforcements of each other, providing the overview initially and finally of what the reader is to gain. This approach to teaching composition has validity; it is a holistic view — a synthesis — of what then the writer is to analyze within the body of the essay. Students should be led to understand this kind of logical structuring in their writing as well as their reading. Recognizing the logic of text composition will help them organize and think more clearly. Students should be informed of the logic of such structure and how it can help them develop their thinking ability as well as their communication skills. Any word processor may be used for composing the introduction and the conclusion and printing hard copy for comparison. One problem is that the full texts are not displayed together on the screen. A way to solve this problem is to use "Mastertype's Writer" by Scarborough, which displays two screens simultaneously. Using this "split screen," students may compose the introduction in the top screen and the conclusion in the bottom one so that both are displayed, for understanding, repetition of key words, and reinforcement of ideas. Revision of either is simple with the editing functions.

Some computer programs can help students learn to write topic exposition. Intellectual Software Company has an interactive program called "Persuasive Essay," which presents five topics for students to react to. On such a topic as "Mandatory Military Service," students are to formulate opinions. Then, through a step-by-step approach, they are led to write an opinion essay on the topic. The program teaches students the differences between fact and opinion, leads them to substantiate their viewpoints, and helps them be persuasive in their arguments. This software package could be used effectively as a springboard, providing a prewriting stimulus for the entire class, if projected on a large monitor so that all students can react and discuss their reactions. The whole class could then be divided into small groups of two to three students, to continue discussion and formulation and opinions. The small groups could take turns using the program for actually writing their essays, which they would later share with the entire class. Each group essay could be printed out and duplicated for sharing with the other groups. The essays could be compared and evaluated for their persuasive techniques and adherence to the criteria in the computer program. This peer evaluation of groups should not include assigning of grades to the essays, but only evaluation of what is effective and what needs improvement. Since all the students are being evaluated by their peers and by group (not individual) performance, there should be no fear of embarrassment. Rather, the production should be superior and the effort greater because they are writing for peer judgment. The teacher can make sure the groups are carefully balanced by selecting a better student to help the poorer ones in each group.

Another computer program to help prepare students for topic exposition is by Sunburst: "How Can I Find It If I Don't Know What I'm Looking For?" This program for the middle grades involves reference search. Questions are presented to lead students through a series of branching procedures that explore many different reference books. The beauty of this program, written by a classroom teacher, is that it can be customized to include the reference books available at the school library. Thus, the students will be learning about specific resources at their own school which they can use independently. They will be exposed not only to generic reference sources, but also to the resources of their own particular library, highly relevant to them. When students have identified or been assigned a topic for their expository essay, they can be taught how to research the topic in different reference books. Then, with the cooperation of the school librarian, the students can be assigned library study periods to gather their information before writing. They may use a program by Grolier called "Note Card Maker" to help them prepare bibliographies and note cards for the information they gather from the resource books. The program is a self-paced tutorial that demonstrates how to arrange note cards using a standard format. The program has a database management capability that allows users to sort and search for data, as well as a word processing facility to let them organize, select, edit, and print out note cards. Using these information management programs, students will be on their way to learning the research skills, collection of data, and organization of information that are necessary for prewriting. Very importantly, students will be involved in the ritual of communication that establishes accepted patterns for using information. They will be fusing the processes of reading and writing in order to engage in the ritual.

Procedural Mode.   This fourth mode relates a process step by step.

Structure	Components
Sequence to be followed	Sequence
Elements are listed first, and directions follow	Imperative sentences
	Unstated steps
Elliptical sentences (*you* sometimes deleted)	Abbreviations and symbols
	Final outcome
Technical vocabulary	Assumes reader experience

The procedural style of writing can be difficult to compose, because the audience to whom it is directed must be clearly identified. Usually the procedure that is explained is technical in nature, and specialized vocabulary has to be used. Reading this kind of composition requires visualization on the part of the reader. The point of it is an end product of some nature, such as the result of a scientific experiment, an assembled machine, or the solution to a problem. Because visualization is required, the language used has to be accurate and precise yet include enough description that the reader can follow the procedure to produce the end result mentally, then physically. The writer has to understand and aim for the sophistication level of the reader, whether a novice in the procedure or a veteran. However, procedural writing necessarily assumes that the reader has some experience with the symbols and abbreviations used, because that is the nature of this mode of composition.

Flowcharts. An effective way to teach procedural writing is to have students construct a flowchart of a procedure, then write out in specific detail all the steps involved in carrying out the procedure. Have students make a flowchart for a novice reader of the procedure for starting a car, for example. Use the accepted symbols of the flowchart: The elliptical circle indicates beginning and ending; the diamonds denote decisions to be made; and the rectangles specify directions to be followed in the procedure. (See Figure 2-2.)

Figure 2-2   Flowchart symbols

Terminal Symbol—starting or ending point of a flowchart

Direction Symbol—used to provide instruction for following a process

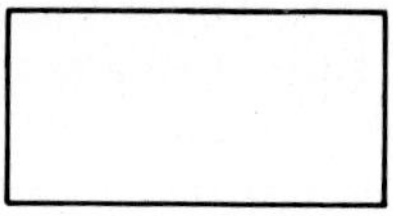

Decision Symbol—used at a decision point in a process

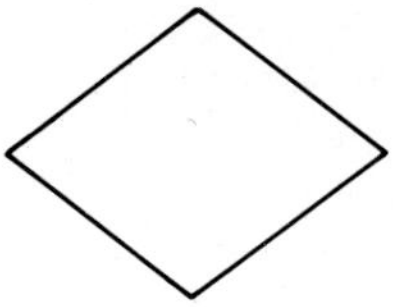

Output Symbol—used when printing an output

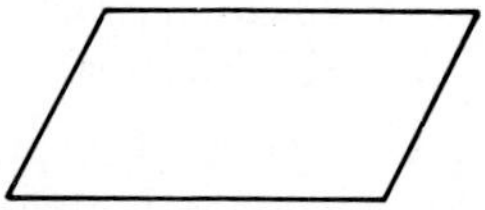

Procedural writing is valuable for students to experience because it makes the writer pay attention to important details that could simply be taken for granted. It teaches students to visualize every step in a process and to organize logically according to time order (first step to last). This kind of writing requires analysis of detail and great patience to cover every step that is necessary to reach the desired end product. Procedural writing is a prerequisite to computer programming, because computer languages are very precise and detailed. The greatest importance of procedural writing and reading lies in the thinking skills it develops in students: Linear, sequential logic must be applied to accomplish a purpose. The writer and the reader must practice this kind of logic to succeed with procedural writing. Most important, the writer must express the procedure clearly and concisely to an audience so that they can use it. This kind of writing uses both right-brain visualization and left-brain verbalization; it is a whole-brain exercise.

One very fine computer program that can give students practice in this kind of procedural thinking is "Operation: Frog" by Scholastic. This science program can be used to generate a lot of language use prior to reading and writing for any content area, not just science. Students learn the steps for dissecting a frog (without the mess), selecting the proper surgical instruments and proceeding step by step through the operation until "dissection." Then they are asked to reconstruct the frog using the reverse procedure. This program can be used to stimulate students' imagination, generate language use, and motivate them to write in detail what they have experienced in the simulation. It could be used with the whole class on a large monitor, or with a small group on a rotation basis. However, the teacher should act as guide at all times, intervening with questions that will develop students' thinking for their reading and writing of procedural text.

Another excellent computer program for experience in procedural thinking is "The Factory" by Sunburst, suitable for middle and secondary students. One of its major objectives is to illustrate the importance of sequence. Students are to create geometric "products" on a machine assembly line that they design. In this logical program, students inductively arrive at the solutions to the problems of design. They use spatial perception, visually discriminating between shapes and spaces. This is a math-based program, but it may also be used to motivate students for procedural writing. Ideally, it could be used as an across-the-curriculum assignment, integrating the sciences and the language arts. The program could be initiated in the math classroom and discussed there for its math values. Then it could be extended into the art class, where use of space, elements of design, and efficiency of graphic placement are emphasized. It could be further developed in science class, where the principles of physics regarding states and properties of matter are taught. Finally, it could culminate in English class, where students would write procedurally on the "factory" design they have built. This kind of a simulation program can serve as a catalyst for team teaching and integration of experiences in a relevant, meaningful school-wide curriculum.

Building student background knowledge and experience in the preparation stage of reading and writing is crucial. It requires a great deal of planning and thought on the part of the teacher. Since the preparation stage could amount to 80 percent of the time spent in the reading and writing process, teacher planning should be this proportion as well. Teacher planning should encompass building student background in the three areas of subject matter, vocabulary, and text forms, so that students can engage (cognitively and affectively) in using written language more meaningfully. Students will be more knowledgeable about the appropriate schemata and will feel more confident in applying what they know to what they do not know. The teacher's rewards will be the students' higher motivation and desire to cooperate in their own learning. Use of the computer can be very effectively employed in the preparation stage as a springboard stimulus to a whole class or a small group, as a concept builder for the new material, and as a catalyst for integration of the curriculum. Building student knowledge and background can be exciting for both teacher and students, if it is carefully planned and executed with variety.

Identifying Purposes for Reading and Writing

Purpose for writing involves what the audience is to gain from reading it. Thus, a writer considers the purpose for writing from the viewpoint of the audience. The reader is reading the author's work for a particular purpose, so in the precomposing stage the writer should be able clearly to identify the audience and the purpose for writing, so that communication will be effective. In assigning writing to students, the teacher should establish what the purpose is, preferably by having them identify it. If the understanding of purpose is student-generated rather than teacher-imposed, it will be more meaningful to students, and they will grow in their reading comprehension as well as their composition. Having students consider their writing in the way it impacts a reader can be a maturing experience in two ways. It asks them to move beyond egocentric concerns, "into the mind" of a reader — someone outside themselves — and it helps them connect writing with reading by understanding the role reversal of writer and reader.

The teacher can initiate this understanding in students by teaching them that there are generally four major purposes for writing anything for readers. The first is to express views or opinions on a topic. The readers' purpose in reading this kind of expressive writing is to learn of differing views on a topic of interest, to corroborate and substantiate their own views or to counter them. Students should understand that this expressive purpose allows them to write their opinions ("their side of the story") from a subjective stance, and that readers will have their own "side of the story." Therefore, in expressive writing, students should base their opinions on their personal experiences. Valuable preparation for expressive writing is to have students discuss their viewpoints on a topic with three different people before they write. In getting different reactions, students may strengthen or alter their beliefs, gain a clearer understanding of the position they want to take, and be able to understand how readers will react to their views.

A second purpose for writing is to present facts and data on a topic. The purpose for reading such factual writing is to get information, so readers look for accurate statements and sufficient detail in the presentation of facts. It is the writer's responsibility in factual writing to get accurate information from reliable sources before presenting the facts to the reader. Students need to be directed to sources of information so that they can gather factual detail. Once the facts are gathered, they must be organized and ordered logically, as in these suggested sequences:

Spatial order	Near to far, top to bottom or reverse, largest to smallest or reverse, etc.
Time order	Past to present, present to future, young to old
Cause and effect	If-then, because
Comparison	Likes and differences
Procedure	Directions, steps

In their writing, students should state the sequencing of their facts for the clarity of the information to the reader. In their reading, students should be able to identify the sequencing of factual information, if the text is well written. If there is not a discernable organization, students should be encouraged to criticize such poor presentation of facts.

A third purpose for writing is to persuade the reader to think or do something. The reader's purpose in reading this kind of persuasive writing is to be persuaded or refuse to be persuaded to think the same way the author does. The writer presents the reader with a choice: either to believe or to refute. The writer persuades through appeals and techniques designed to sway a reader's thinking. The classical appeals a writer may use are of three kinds:

Logos — appeals to reader's logic

Ethos — appeals to reader's ethics or morality

Pathos — appeals to reader's emotions

Readers may be persuaded through these appeals and through such techniques as advertisers and politicians use. Some effective, convincing techniques that students may use in their own persuasive writing include the following:

1. Name-calling, including mud-slinging
2. Glittering generality — that is, the use of favorable words such as "American made" or "Mom's apple pie" to color a viewpoint
3. Plain folks — "Think this way and you will fit in and just be one of us"
4. Testimonial — as when a movie star or other celebrity endorses a product although not an authority on its technical aspects
5. Bandwagon — "Everyone is doing it, so that makes it right"
6. The false dilemma, which presents an either-or situation: the wrong choice and the "right one" (the propagandist's)

From using these appeals and techniques in their writing, students should be guided to recognize them in their reading. Teachers should provide opportunities for students to read persuasive writing in advertisements, newspaper editorials, and political speeches, where they may identify persuasive techniques and appeals for better composition and comprehension.

A fourth purpose for writing is to use the imagination to create images in a reader's mind, as in a story. The reader's purpose in reading creative writing is to be entertained and to appreciate the imaginative use of language. Students need to understand the creative use of language, involving similes and metaphors, elaboration of descriptive detail, and such story structures as plots and subplots. Students should orally describe something that happened in their own experience—something that frightened them or inspired them, for example. Then the other students in the class, after hearing the description, can supply as many adjectives as they can think of to add to the account. After the adjectives are listed on the board, students may choose among them in the writing of their own related experiences.

The computer can be used to help students learn to write for a purpose. A word processor is especially helpful in storing compositions written for different purposes, which students may access as models for their own writing. The teacher can enter examples from literature or have students enter their own writing on blank data disks: one disk containing examples of factual writing, another for expressive writing, a third for creative writing, and so forth. Through reading such models for their writing, students are making the connection in the reading-writing relationship.

There are also computer writing programs that instruct students in writing for a purpose. One program teaches specific skills in format, tone, arguments, facts, supporting details, and mechanics for the purpose of writing letters, reports, and persuasive essays. Another program approaches writing as thinking and uses interactive dialogue to guide students as they develop purpose, strategies, and evaluation of their writing. Still another program teaches students the art of persuasion by providing five relevant topics on which students can formulate opinions and write. The skills of differentiating fact from opinion, reasoning clearly, and providing sufficient facts are emphasized so that students apply what they learn. There are also some excellent story starters, such as one program that begins a story and asks students to take different branches of the plot to develop a creative story. Another computer program helps students learn creative use of language by having them generate poetry based on a phrase formula given in the program. Other programs to be used in helping students learn to write for a purpose include databases that allow writers to store and retrieve information they need for factual writing. Using a file system, students can store their own facts, organize them, sort them, and retrieve them in order according to their writing needs. Another program teaches students to create note cards, although it is actually a database system. A tutorial demonstrates how to arrange note cards and presents a standard format for gathering information for a research paper. Students create the cards, and the word processing capabilities allow them to organize, select, edit, and print in any order.

These are just a few of the many possible software selections teachers may use to help students learn to write for a purpose. Approximately 80 percent of the educational software developed in the last six years is geared toward language skills, so there is a very wide selection of programs to choose from on all age and grade levels. Teaching language processes with a language processor need never be restricted to a dull routine.

Writers need to be aware of their purpose for writing, which relates to what the reader is to gain from the writing. Therefore, the writer must clearly identify audience and purpose for writing in the prewriting stage if communication is to be effective. When writers have the ability to understand audience and purpose in their own composition, they may be taught to recognize them in their reading, for better comprehension. Understanding these role reversals should facilitate the reading-writing connections. However, students must be taught to make the transfer and use the connection as they progress in their understanding of language processing.

Models of Thinking in Computer Programs

Researchers in the fields of psychology and artificial intelligence have proposed theories of how humans think. Such a theory can be developed into a computer program and tested as a simulation of human thinking. The computer is similar to a human brain only in limited ways; in many respects, it cannot duplicate the functions of the infinitely more complex brain. The terminology differentiates between *brain* and *mind*. The brain is the physiological organ and all its neural connections; the mind is defined as the functions of the brain. For educational purposes, we can note that the computer and the mind are alike in three essential ways: the capability of processing information with language; memory storage, both short-term (RAM) and long-term (ROM and data disks); and retrieval of information, from both random access memory and key-word associations. The mind can retrieve information randomly stored in the memory by recalling an event or piece of information, and it also remembers by associating events or pieces of information through mnemonic devices.

The computer is similar to the human mind in that it is an information processor. It uses language functions to process information, as does the mind. Because of this similarity, the computer can help teachers to teach the language processes of reading and writing. Teaching processing is teaching thinking. Certain models of thinking (cognitive models) underlie the better-designed instructional software. We need to understand these cognitive models so as to realize how the thinking skills of students are being developed and manipulated by software designers. We want to recognize the models so that we are able to alter them to develop varieties of thinking skills in our students and to meet their cognitive needs.

One theory proposes that there are generally two ways humans solve problems. One way is from the top down, in a highly structured, sequential procedure that has prescribed steps and results in only one right answer or solution. (See the left side of Figure 2-3.) This way of thinking is

Figure 2-3   Opportunistic problem-solving planning: two styles of control

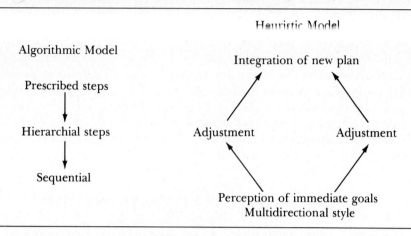

strongly convergent. We teach this kind of problem solving in flowcharts and algorithms that we use with students. Computer programs that use this theory of algorithmic problem solving tend to consist of drill and practice and tutorials that lead students through sequential and hierarchical steps to a prescribed solution. These programs appear to be at a more literal level, and more concrete on Bloom's taxonomic scale of cognitive ability. This model of problem solving has its place in educating students to think, but it tends not to be true to the way real life forces us to solve problems. We set goals in life to solve problems, but we do not often use a strictly linear approach in the way we solve them.

The other way humans solve problems, according to this cognitive theory, is from the bottom up, making choices and choosing alternatives that are not prescribed but are discovered along the way. (See the right side of Figure 2-3.) We set goals, but we do not achieve them linearly. Rather, we alter original plans, discover new directions, and change our minds about what to do to accomplish our goals. This kind of problem solving is scary, because a person must take a risk that he or she will make a mistake. However, this is much more true to life, and teaching this kind of divergent risk-taking is a crucial experience for students in preparing them to make important life decisions. The computer programs that use this model of problem solving are called "heuristic" programs and are found in some programming languages, some material generation programs, and some educational games. This kind of problem solving tends to be more abstract and inferential, involving higher levels on Bloom's taxonomy of cognitive development. Most current software is not based on this kind of model, but in the next ten years there should be much more such software available to foster higher-level cognitive skills in students.

Other models of cognition currently being researched for their application to computer programs to be used in human learning are based on theories of information processing. Learning is explained as the processing of information that is acquired through our senses of sight, sound, touch, taste, and smell. The information is acquired as symbols that represent the information and are matched to symbols already in our memory store. If the new information is relevant, or matches that which we have stored, it is translated into symbols and stored in our memory. (See Figure 2-4.) These new symbols become our knowledge and experience.

Figure 2-4   Learning as information processing

Cognitive System

Set of memories

Symbols

Manipulation process

Acquired through the senses as information, related to the memory store, and stored in the existing set

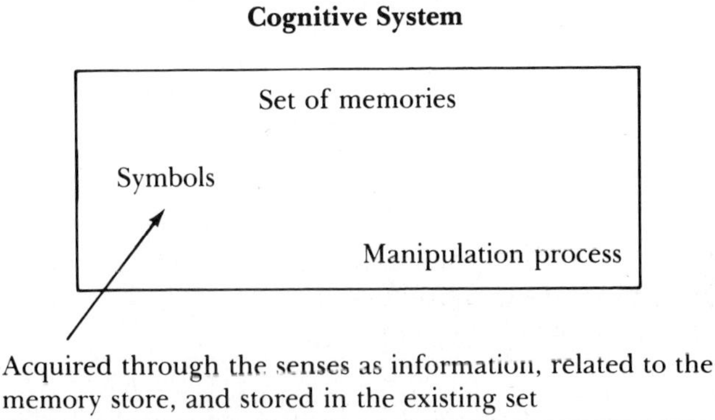

Current software promotes learning in three different ways: (1) memory skills in sequencing, regrouping, rote, whole-to-part, and mnemonic systems; (2) discrimination, attributes, and rules; and (3) problem solving in mazes, programming, and constructing designs. There are several leading software companies that employ theories of cognition derived from research on learning and thinking.

When teachers are aware of the models of thinking that underlie the computer programs they use with students, they will understand how to diversify the opportunities for students to learn. Teaching literacy should be highly varied to make sure that students get many opportunities to develop thinking and memory skills, for acquiring information is made more complex by the fact that we need to retain it and apply it. In our process model, we teach preparation for acquiring information, then implementation in actual reading and writing. The final step in our process is application of the information used. In reading, it is to use what we read for our interests; in writing, it is to shape the information for an outside audience. Using models of cognition as presented in different software can diversify our teaching of literacy, foster growth on different levels of thinking, and get at students' different learning styles.

Problem-Solving Opportunities

This book on planning for integration of language processes balances process with product. Technology should be thought of a means to an end —

important for the human activities for which we use it. Books, paper, and pencil are the traditional technologies we use to transmit information about ourselves and our culture. However, the importance of a book is not in its publication, but in the human activities of reading and writing it. Similarly, the importance of the computer as a technology lies in the human activities involved with its use. Literacy involves three components: a technology, systems of knowledge, and cognitive abilities (Norton, 1985). All three must be taught so that learners may share in socially recognized goals and make use of common technologies and knowledge systems.

The book has been the predominant transmitter of our literate culture since Gutenberg's invention of the printing press in 1437. A book offers problem-solving activities of a specific nature that students must master in order to become literate. The thinking required for a print-oriented culture can be characterized as follows:

1. Linear, sequential reasoning as the result of a steady accumulation of information. The thinking is systematic, summing up relevant facts with correct inferencing and organization throughout the reading.
2. Deductive reasoning, wherein the problem solver starts with statements taken as true, then tries to see what other statements can be logically derived from them. Deductive thinking implies analysis of the parts in order to identify relevant information that makes up the whole. The problem solver's or reader's task is essentially to rearrange information to suit his or her own perspective.
3. If-then reasoning, which encourages the reader to construct coherent, rational arguments in order to arrive at the "truth." The problem solver links information according to cause-and-effect relationships.
4. Reasoning in a closed system, in which problems are restricted to those posed within the context provided. The problem solver or reader deals only with the parameters set by the writer.

Interestingly, the computer may be seen as offering alternative ways of problem solving and developing other ways of thinking. Drill and practice and tutorial programs continue much in the linear mode of reasoning, offering sequential and cumulative information that leads to one right answer for the problem solver. However, other kinds of programs (specifically, the Logo language) may offer students problem-solving opportunities that are different from those afforded by print. The research is still skimpy on the effects of Logo on thinking skills and abilities, perhaps because the right questions are not being asked about the new technology. Students have been found to increase their originality, fluency, and divergent thinking with use of Logo. Also, they are more willing to take risks and experiment (reported in Norton, 1985). Because of its interactive nature, the computer can afford students the opportunity to act out ideas they imagine or fantasize. With the computer, students are able to experiment, test their hypotheses, create, and evaluate their intuitions. The word processor for writing allows the kind of testing and experimentation capabilities that may be more conducive to the writing process than static print activities. Priscilla Norton (1985) suggests that use of the computer may provide the following problem-solving opportunities as alternative ways of thinking:

1. Patterns and connections that result from relationships observed and tested. The problem solver is not restricted to seeing only those relationships proposed by an author, but is encouraged to form new patterns and discern new connections. The reader looks for an underlying structure in a problem in order to find the patterns, so that new ones may be made.
2. Inductive reasoning, in which the problem solver begins with a set of observations and makes a generalization based on them. The generalization can then be tested through simulation to see if it works.
3. "What-if" reasoning, which develops flexibility in thinking. The problem solver is encouraged to take chances and to experiment rather than just to see the consequences of a given event described in print. The problem solver realizes in testing and evaluating that there is no single right answer, but rather the possibility of several different solutions to a problem.
4. Reasoning in an open system that does not restrict the problem solver to the parameters proposed by a writer in print. The reader is encouraged to use personal experience and general knowledge in order to arrive at a solution to a problem. The ability to experiment and test out one's own hypothesis frees the problem solver from the solutions or "truths" proposed by a writer.

The point is not that print is bad or that the computer is good and will solve all problems in education. The preceding discussion is meant to suggest that use of different media such as print and the computer may offer different opportunities for teaching and learning in developing abilities to think and solve problems in our complex society. We have become a multimedia society, using technology of many different varieties to help us use the glut of information that affects us daily. As teachers, we should be aware of and concerned about the possible effects of the media upon us and our students, so that we may use it wisely. Ours is becoming an information-based society; we teachers are information brokers, the middlepersons between the data and the students. We must be open to providing many alternative ways of dealing with information and teaching students to become problem solvers so that they can make decisions about the information and its use.

As referred to above, Logo is a software program that is actually a programming language. It was developed by Seymour Papert of MIT and based on Piagetian concepts of cognitive development. Papert believes that computers can be used to bring concrete experiences of abstract ideas to children and provide opportunities for systematic thinking that will improve the quality of intellectual growth (Papert, 1980). Certainly, Logo provides a radical alternative to the drill and practice programs so predominant in educational software. Logo is much more than just a graphics program, but this capability is probably the most important from an educational standpoint.

The graphics are created by a "turtle" (or a "rabbit" on the Macintosh's "Experlogo"), actually a triangle that leaves a trail for drawing geometric shapes. After five to ten minutes of orientation, even a small child can begin to experiment and create shapes that teach spatial relationships, which are important for reading readiness. Logo presents a trial-and-error approach to learning that encourages risk-taking in making decisions. It fosters the skills of visualization and prediction, which are both important in reading development. Most importantly, it allows students control over an environment they have created, so that they feel success and self-confidence in manipulating tangible items for intangible abstractions.

The Logo graphics may be used for preparing students to read and write through many varieties of activities. As a class group, students may construct a design on paper or the blackboard, then test it out on the computer. The graphic may be printed out and incorporated in a creative story that is narrative/descriptive — the graphic described with adjectives and adverbs carefully chosen. The graphic procedure may be used in a procedural essay that details, step by step, how the graphic was designed. The graphic may also be used in expository writing, as the central focus of the topic. For example, a polyspiral may be designed, using the procedural mode in Logo, and students may write about the factor of recursion as it is used to create the graphic figure, providing details, examples, and reasons why the recursion capability is efficient and effective. Small groups of students may be assigned to create graphic designs, then write comparison-contrast essays describing differences between the designs or differences between the methods of creating them. For preparation for reading, Logo graphics may be used as a catalyst for understanding the decision-making of main characters or historical persons. Were those characters risk-takers, and with what result? What are the characteristics of a conservative, a liberal, a right or left-winger in politics? Logo affords opportunities to try out various options in a simulation, without undergoing the real-life consequences. With teacher guidance, can students make a connection between their concrete experiences and the abstract points in story plots at which characters make decisions? Finally, Logo may be used to cross content areas, integrating curricula from math, art, the sciences, and English, as well as the processes of reading and writing in each of those fields.

For language activities specifically, there are also Logo listing and word processing routines that allow students to enter words, phrases, and clauses to create poetry such as haiku. There are creative story starters, generated from random selections of the variables of nouns, adjectives, verbs, etc. that students enter. Students enter lists of words according to their parts of speech, then the computer sorts through them to select them randomly and arranges them in the logical order or sentence structure programmed for them. With Logo list processing, especially with "Apple Logo," students may manipulate language, learn the parts of speech, and create some interesting uses of language. What they generate can be used to stimulate creative writing. It takes the teacher a while to learn how to teach this program, but the effort will be worth it.

There are other computer programs that may be used as opportunities to teach problem solving and to develop thinking abilities preparatory to reading and writing. Besides programming languages such as Logo, other types of programs include simulations, databases, and word processors. The following software has educational characteristics desirable to teach problem solving in each of the types.

Simulations are terrific for giving students hands-on experience with no real risk. They provide lifelike, realistic situations that students can live through, learning about the risks and the choices that they must be prepared to deal with when the time in real life comes. One of the better simulations is by Learning Company (Addison-Wesley), and is entitled "Rocky's Boots." Actually, this is a complete package that includes lesson plans and student activity worksheets in the school edition, a great resource to the teacher. The program uses several senses of the learners, involving sound, sight, and touch. The object is to build a "logic machine" piece-by-piece, moving parts about to test each one individually and as part of the entire machine. While building this machine, students are making decisions, predicting outcomes, solving problems of the parts, and experimenting to see what works best. The student has complete control over the construction of the machine and experiences success when right decisions are made, which develops self-confidence and a feeling of accomplishment. If the teacher asks questions about how something was done and why it was or was not successful, students will be able to transfer learning of this experience to stories, biographies, historical events, science experiments, and artistic works that they encounter. Students should be asked to analyze the way they think and go about solving problems. Simulations can be used before reading and writing to give students a concrete experience that they can then transfer to abstract causes and effects they experience in print. For example, young students can be asked to explain *why* they moved a graphic part on the screen and *what* the outcome was. Then they can read a story and be asked why a character acted in a certain way and what the result of the character's action was, with their own experience behind them. Older students can be more introspective and analytical, probing *how* they arrived at solutions to problems in "Rocky's Boots" — whether by perceiving patterns of organization, by trial and error, or by mathematical calculations. Then, perhaps, they may analyze events in history as to how decisions were made, what alternatives there might have been, how they affected other events, and so forth. Through this all, students should be made consciously aware of which logical skills they are developing, what the point of the simulation exercise is, and how they can transfer their learning to other ongoing reading and writing. This affects the teacher's job as monitor of the learning process.

Another type of software, very valuable for its use in teaching students problem solving before reading and writing, is the database. With the use of databases, students will be engaging in simultaneous reading, writing, and computer use, integrating the processes in a very meaningful way. A file or database is an organized collection of information on a specific subject (such as a telephone directory or an almanac, to name a couple of databases we commonly use). A computerized data management system simplifies storing, updating, organizing, and retrieving information from data files. The educational purposes behind using databases are many, but one is that they help students arrange information in useful ways. Students can decide what information they need to learn about a topic such as countries of the world, design a format for the information they intend to collect on each country, enter it, then access it for later use. In retrieving the information, students can discover similarities of culture in the countries they study, analyze political relationships, and look for economic or other trends. The databases can serve as a very meaningful preparation for ongoing reading and writing, relevant especially because the students themselves have prepared and formatted the data. There are many good database software programs; one that is especially easy and useful for students is "PFS: File" by Scholastic, Inc. In files with a lot of text in them, this is a handy organizer that keeps the files on disk while they are being worked on.

Beverly Hunter (1985) suggests three stages for teaching the use of databases to students.

Stage 1: Using and exploring existing databases

Stage 2: Building files on existing forms

Stage 3: Designing an original database

In Stage 1, students examine data files that someone else has prepared to help them organize their reports or investigate new information. They learn the purpose of databases and how they are useful. They come to understand the ease of use of the files in the ways they are organized. In Stage 2, students are given a blank form that they may use to collect and organize data. The teacher provides the format or key points that guide students' research. The teacher may design the format with students' help, asking them what they need to know about a topic and what commonalities there are in what they will find about a topic. For example, in research on countries of the world, small groups of students may each study a particular country, finding information on economic conditions, political situation, population, and relations with the United States. These factors would constitute the format of the database and serve as a guide to students' research and organization of information. Students must be cautioned in this stage to check and doublecheck the accuracy of the information they enter into the database. This stage of learning about databases provides a great exercise in critical reading and writing, logical thinking and planning, and responsibility for accurate reporting of data. In Stage 3, students are ready to plan, design, build, and use their own databases. This stage requires analysis of the problem to be investigated and decision-making as to how the problem is to be approached. Students design a file, including the format, content, and screen layout. Then they gather the data and check its accuracy. Finally, they enter it and use it. Students may also decide how the information is to be used, whether in their writing or in oral presentations, but it should be used to further their communication with others in some way. In every stage of students' learning to use databases, the teacher should guide and monitor their experience, explaining what it is they are learning and why it is important for development of thinking and communication skills.

The last type of software that we will consider for problem-solving opportunities preparatory to reading and writing is the word processor. When students write, they have a problem to solve: that of shaping their language for an outside audience. Writers begin with a major topic, but during writing they explore how it can be expressed. Writing is discovery, and ideas are often not clearly known even by the writer until they are discovered in the process of writing. Problem solving in writing is thus the discovery of what one's ideas are and how they may be communicated most effectively to a reader. One method for getting students to focus entirely on discovering their own ideas about a topic while using a word processor is "invisible writing," a technique suggested by Dr. Stephen Marcus of the South Coast Writing Project. The teacher turns off the monitor, but not the computer, leaving the screen dark during students' composing. They should experience a free flow of ideas, undistracted by seeing errors or fearing errors. The result should be concentrated thinking about the topic — a focus on solving the problem of idea expression. After the ideas are formulated, the monitor may be turned back on for the purposes of reading, revising, and editing of mechanical errors. For most students it may be better to print hard copy for their reading and revising. Text may not actually exist for many students unless it is printed out. The size of the screen and the display on the word processor may be a problem as well. The larger the text display, the easier it is to read and revise. Students may read and revise their printed copies, then return to the computer to enter their revisions and editing. The student will want to use the writer's aids of style analyzers and spelling checkers to facilitate this part of the writing process (see Chapter 3). Most of writing is revising and reshaping, a kind of hypothesis testing that asks "what-if" questions, experiments with them, and selects from alternatives. Word processors, especially those that aid in composition planning and production, can facilitate problem solving in writing and reading because of their interactive nature and the ease of revision.

There are many fine word processors available (see Chapter 3). The easiest ones to use typically have the least amount of space and capability. The least expensive for students to use are not "disk intensive" — meaning that a single master disk may be booted into several computers — thus saving money, since a disk is not needed for each student. Such a word processor is "Bank Street Writer" by Scholastic, which comes with a fairly good tutorial for students to learn by. This is a fine, inexpensive word processor for student learning, but it is limited in its capabilities. Another inexpensive and very easy word processor for students is "MECC Writer," which has an extensive support system of other disks that are compatible with the "Writer." There is a keyboarding disk, a speller disk, a database, a creative story maker, and more. MECC has even established a scope and sequence chart, K-12, for the use of this entire word processing courseware. Word processors for student use differ in quality, capabilities, and cost from the personal word processors that one may choose; the choice is up to individual taste and need. Clearly, though, a useful word processor is a necessity for student use in reading and writing. It can be regarded as a tool for helping students develop problem-solving abilities, crucial for managing our complex information age. However, the computer is always to be considered a "transparent technology": it does not teach writing and is not the end in itself, but is a means to experiencing and practicing writing.

Chapter 2 has discussed the use of the computer to prepare students for reading and writing and suggested methods, software, and activities that may facilitate this important step in the literacy process. Perhaps as much as 80 percent of reading and writing time is spent in preparing to do so. Students need to have a clear purpose and an adequate background knowledge of the content, vocabulary, and text form in order to engage in the ritual of commonly accepted patterns of communication of our society. The computer is a means to this end of effective communication. It provides a tremendous diversity of techniques and a different way of having students think that is beneficial to developing problem-solving abilities. Teaching students the steps of the reading/writing process teaches them to think, and use of the computer as a language processor provides the means for human language processing.

References

Britton, James. "The Composing Processes and the Functions of Writing." In *Research on Composing* (Cooper and Odell, Eds.). National Council of Teachers of English, 1978.
Brown, Ann L. "Metacognitive Development and Reading." In *Theoretical Issues in Reading Comprehension* (Spiro, Ed.). Hillsdale, N.J.: Erlbaum Associates, 1980.

Cohen, Paul R., and Feigenbaum, Edward A. *The Handbook of Artificial Intelligence,* vol. III, Los Altos, Calif.: William Kaufman, 1982.

Flood, James. "The Text, the Student and the Teacher: Learning from Exposition in Middle Schools." *The Reading Teacher,* April, 1986.

Howie, Sherry Hill. *Guidebook to Teaching Writing in Content Areas.* Boston: Allyn and Bacon, 1984.

Hunter, Beverly. "Problem Solving with Data Bases." *The Computing Teacher,* May, 1985.

Johnson, David, et al. *Circles of Learning.* Alexandria, Va.: Association for Supervision and Curriculum Development, 1984.

Kinneavey, J.S. *A Theory of Discourse.* Englewood Cliffs, N.J.: Prentice-Hall, 1971.

Minsky, M. "A Framework for Representing Knowledge." In *The Psychology of Computer Vision* (Winson, Ed.). New York: McGraw-Hill, 1975.

Norton, Priscilla. "Problem-Solving Activities in a Computer Environment: A Different Angle of Vision." *Educational Technology,* October, 1985.

Papert, Seymour. *Mindstorms: Children, Computers and Powerful Ideas.* New York: Basic Books, 1980.

Pearson, David, and Johnson, Dale. *Teaching Reading Comprehension.* New York: Holt Rinehart and Winston, 1972.

SECTION TWO

Implementation

Using the computer in teaching

CHAPTER THREE

The Range of Computer Applications

Learning on the computer

The purpose of this chapter is to explore the range of educational computer programs so as to make teachers and curriculum planners aware of the options that are open to them in their planning. The computer not only offers new content to be learned and practiced; it also provides new ways to experience it. The computer is a "transparent technology," a *means* through which learning and experiences may take place. Educators need to understand applications of educational software and classify types of software in order to implement the processes of reading and writing, as well as to appreciate future trends of technology in education so as to plan ahead.

Understanding Applications of Educational Software

To grasp the complexity, applications, and purposes of the rapidly expanding field of educational software, we shall use the framework suggested by Robert Taylor (1980). Although such a framework may be helpful in categorizing the numerous computer programs, Taylor himself cautions against becoming so bound to the labels as not to realize possible uses for them beyond the framework. It is a guide to help teachers understand the possible applications for their educational purposes. Taylor classifies the applications of computing in education into three modes—*tutor, tool,* and *tutee.* He makes mention of a possible fourth mode, that of "toy," but he does not employ it because he believes it to be subsumed under the other three modes. However, this fourth mode may help explain some of the newer software that we will investigate. (See Figure 3-1.)

The first mode (computer as *tutor*) is also known as computer-assisted instruction, or CAI. The computer acts as a patient, knowledgeable teacher's aide. Information about a topic is prepared on a computer program by a person who is expert in programming and in that subject. The software

Figure 3-1   Four applications of educational software

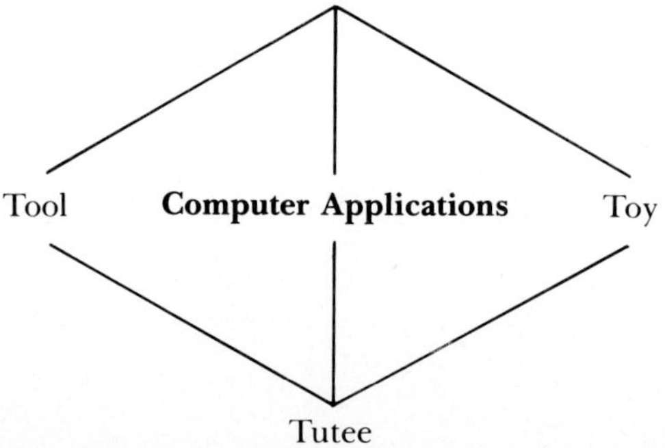

presents some subject matter, and the student responds. The computer evaluates the response and then determines what to present next. In the best programs, it provides positive feedback if the response is correct or gives the correct answer if the student response is wrong. For wrong responses, the program should branch to more practice in the concept until the student masters it. Many complete tutorial programs store and report students' scores, thus relieving teachers from the tedium of recordkeeping. The educational function of "tutor" is found in "drill and practice" programs and in tutorial programs. Its use can benefit students at all levels of ability. It helps developmental students practice and retain new ideas, provides remediation for weak students, and enriches the instruction of better students. This function can individualize instruction — not so much because the program can be tailored to each student, but because it can free the teacher to be with individual students who need extra help. The value of this function is in reinforcing what has been taught. This type of software must not be seen as a substitute for the teacher, but rather as an aid to what the teacher has taught. It is therefore crucial to evaluate this kind of software to be sure it fits the ongoing curriculum.

In Taylor's framework, the second mode of educational software is as a *tool*. To function as a tool, the program must have some useful built-in capability that may be used to implement an end such as calculation, graphic illustration, or word processing. This category of educational programs includes teacher utilities that provide for computer-managed instruction (CMI). Such utility programs help the teacher keep files and records, work out grading procedures and storage, create word puzzles and games, authoring systems for writing lessons, and much more. Such utilities save teachers time by performing mechanical and "administrivial" tasks. Also, the tool function is used for information management — for example, in data-based management in file systems and spreadsheets. These are tools that teachers can use and that students can be taught to use as resources for research and factual reporting. The tool mode is also seen in word processing programs that provide the capability of creating documents. Writer's aids such as spelling checkers, thesauruses, and style analyzers can also be classified as tools.

Although they did not exist when Taylor established his classification, such programs as planners and story starters, with their capabilities of inspiring and facilitating writing and reading, may be categorized in the tool mode. Fine graphics programs such as "Print Shop" may be labeled as tools that implement an end, both in CMI for teacher use and in illustrations of learning for student use. The tool mode is therefore educationally useful both in CMI and CAI, for the purposes of managing and assisting instruction. Students need to learn data, but it is crucial that they learn to organize and structure it so that it is manageable. Teaching the tool mode of computing also prepares students for occupations outside of education, in which the computer is primarily regarded as a tool in data processing and management of information. It is necessary to understand and to become competent in this mode, but it is not the primary use in educational computing.

The third major area of application for educational software is the *tutee* mode, which is potentially the most exciting for learning. In this mode, the student teaches the computer — or, more precisely, programs it to do what he or she wants in a language it understands. Seymour Papert (1972) gets most excited about this mode; he created the Logo language program for children to use in the tutee mode. In this mode, students can "discover" mathematical principles in geometric shapes they create with turtle graphics. Using Logo, students can see the relevance of knowing grammatical parts of speech as they create poems through list processing. Logo also allows students to experience hypothesis testing of alternative solutions to problems, using inductive reasoning. This mode has application in many content areas: math and science, music and art, and particularly in English. A school district in Minnesota is using it to cross content areas in students' learning. Other educational programming languages besides Logo may be used to teach students to teach the computer. The best way to learn is to teach, and students should have the experience of being teachers. The computer is the ideal tutee; it is patient and receptive, and its disks can always be reinitialized to start over. To use the computer as tutee, the student controls and manipulates abstractions on a concrete level, thus applying knowledge rather than just acquiring it. The tutee mode of computer use can be a very powerful educational medium. Students can experience learning inductively, discovering knowledge rather than just having it presented to them, and taking risks in communicating ideas.

Taylor suggested a fourth mode of application — *toy* — but did not actually use it. It is conceptually useful to us in categorizing one type of software that is just emerging and another that has existed a while. He proposed the toy mode to indicate user interaction with games, simulations, and other software that can be manipulated and "played with." In using the term, we do not intend it in its usual sense of a trifle of little value; rather, we use it to mean an implement that may be played with and enjoyed. The playing can be very creative and dynamic. Playing involves action and interaction with the components of the thing played with. A capacity to be played with, however, need not diminish the educational importance of a thing. After all, learning should be enjoyable, and this mode offers such an opportunity in ways that provide concrete experiences to learners.

Besides simulations and games, a new type of educational software that is described by this mode is *interactive fiction,* wherein students read narrative prose to learn story structure and characterization. The manipulative part of this software is that the student may become one of the characters, entering into the story so as to experience the action and become personally involved. Reading such a story is therefore an active, dynamic experience, an interaction with the components being played with. Another, similar type of software is called "text adventures." Students help to create the adventure, using resources and reference materials such as atlases, almanacs, and encyclopedias. This type of software also presents the opportunity to interact with the text in a dynamic, personal way that is meaningful and enjoyable.

The term "toy," therefore, helps us to designate such learning experience. Simulations can be thought of as toys in that the user plays out the roles introduced in the scenario in a dynamic and personal way. We will not consider games under this particular mode as separate from all the other modes, because games actually occur in the other modes—in tutor, and tutee, and tool (where they may be created).

With this framework, we can begin to classify the many software programs that are available to teach the processes of reading and writing. We can also subdivide the categories into eight types, which indicate the format as well as the function of a program. Through such classification, it is possible to choose the type that is most appropriate to a particular curriculum. The different types, used for different learning purposes, also allow varied opportunities for developing thinking skills and meeting individual learning needs. Awareness of this variety therefore permits the teacher to offer many opportunities to help students grow. Consider the variety of software according to the following classifications:

Tutor: Skill builders
Tool: Word processors, writing aids
         Planners, story starters, graphics
         Information management
         Teacher utilities
Tutee: Programming languages
Toy: Simulations
         Interactive fiction, text adventures

Each of the eight types of educational software will be examined in detail, according to its functions and applications in teaching reading and writing. Because technology changes so rapidly and new software is introduced at the rate of about 400 pieces a month, the descriptions of type, format, and educational value will be stressed rather than specific examples of each type. The most current, applicable examples of each type of software will be used by way of illustration, but it is not the intent of this book to promote a particular software product or company.

Types of Software for Teaching Reading and Writing Processes

TUTOR: Skill Builders

Approximately 95 percent of all educational software produced currently is of the "drill and practice" variety. This instructional design was the first to be computerized, because it simulated homework assignments and text-book exercises familiar to all students. However, if computerized drill and practice programs offered only the same benefits as paper exercises, their expense and programming effort would be unjustified.

In its function as tutor, the drill and practice application is considered a major component of CAI, which literally means "Instruction that is assisted or aided through use of the computer" (Harrod and Ruggles, 1983). Along with computer-managed instruction, CAI is included in the larger organizational concept of computer-based instruction, which encompasses all forms of computer use in education. CAI offers two dimensions in the teaching-learning process: computer as a medium of instruction through its *delivery* and computer as a learning tool through its *interaction* with the student. (See Figure 3-2.) These uses of the computer in instruction give it a tremendous advantage over paper and pencil. Because of their well-planned delivery and interaction capabilities, drill and practice programs may be well justified in their use.

Drill and practice software is intended to reinforce instruction that students have already been given by the teacher. It provides a practice medium for concepts taught in an ongoing curriculum. The programs may assist students in previewing as a part of initial instruction, reviewing forgotten concepts, and overlearning skills in mastery learning. Drill and practice does not require teaching new material; it simply presents repetitions of already designated content and checks student responses against preprogrammed answers.

Many educators believe that drill and practice software is the least interesting and most abused of all computer applications in education. Mark Grabe (1986) examined three important objections to this application. The first concerns the repetitive, sometimes dull work of drill and practice; many educators believe that it is not creative or stimulating to students' minds. However, the purpose of drill and practice is not to be creative. Its intent is to provide practice in a concept supposedly taught creatively *by the teacher* — to reinforce ideas. To teach new ideas is the role of the teacher. What the computer can do that paper worksheets cannot is to give the learner immediate feedback so that he or she is guided to correct practice in the right concepts. The program interacts with the learner, responding to correct answers, incorrect answers, and ways of thinking. The paper worksheet cannot perform this function, and students using it may persist in inaccurate repetition without realizing their inaccuracies.

Figure 3-2   Computer-based instruction

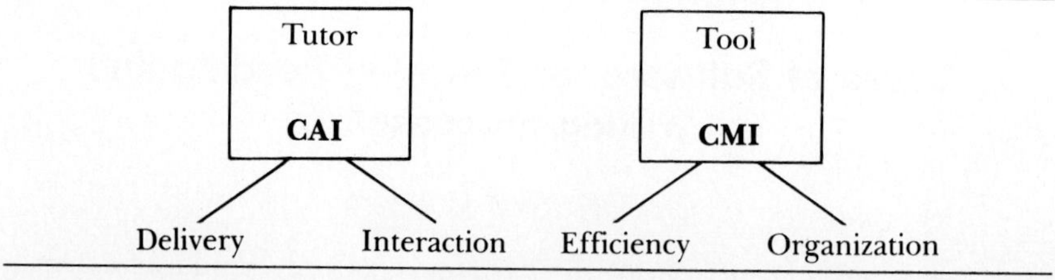

A second objection some educators express about these programs is that they are too costly. Yet, as Grabe points out, this objection may not take into account the economic value of teacher time spent in grading and scoring countless numbers of worksheet pages, a task that can be expeditiously performed by an efficient recordkeeping drill and practice program. Besides, these programs actually tend to be less expensive than other kinds of software, because they are not meant to be innovative or creative. Such programs can free a teacher to plan creative presentations of ideas and to spend more time with individuals who need a lot of human attention in their learning.

The third objection is that computerized worksheets are useless. If properly programmed, however, effective drill and practice software can counter the negative effects of paper worksheets. It can give a student immediate feedback and respond in such a way that students begin to reconstruct and evaluate the ways they think about a problem solution. In a typical case, paper worksheets are handed back a day or two later with a red-inked grade that students look at and throw away. There is no opportunity to rethink or remember how or why they answered as they did.

These objections are not to be taken lightly. Many times, they are justified — especially in the case of earlier drill and practice software. By and large, however, the capabilities of such software are making it more instructionally effective and valuable.

In order to select high-quality drill and practice software for effective student learning, teachers need to understand some of the principles of design (Dennis, 1979):

1. A distinction must be made between students' correct answers and their learning; a single correct answer has only a small probability of indicating student learning.
2. The probability that real learning has occurred increases if there are several correct responses on a topic over a period of time.
3. The use of related exercises on a topic increases the possibility of differentiating between memorization and learning. The more correct responses to varied exercises on a topic, the more indication there is that learning is taking place.
4. The more specific feedback students receive to their incorrect responses, the more they will be helped to learn.
5. When incorrect responses occur, subsequent exercises should present more variations on the items missed than on the ones that were successfully answered.

Using these principles of effective design, educators may be able to select better drill and practice programs for students. The kind of practice offered in the program should also be analyzed for its interaction with students — the way it presents exercises and expects a response. Dennis (1979) calls the exercise "the questioning episode" and looks for the following components in a well-designed program:

1. A question or directive statement
2. An opportunity for student response

3. Computer interpretation of student response that distinguishes between
   a. Correct replies
   b. Incorrect but conceptually correct replies
   c. Likely-to-occur incorrect replies
   d. Unidentifiable replies
4. Specific feedback to the type of student reply
5. A time element established for the practice

The value of the computerized drill and practice is that it can be programmed to interpret and classify student answers so that the feedback is specifically tailored to the individual — a capability no paper worksheet has. The learners may therefore be guided to analyze their own reasoning and to understand how they arrived at an answer. With such metacognitive awareness, learning involves how to arrive at a correct response in addition to what content is correct. The software can be programmed to make distinctions in students' incorrect replies. Some replies are incorrect, but in line with the main ideas. Other student responses may be incorrect because they are logically inaccurate. There are also unidentifiable replies that are totally unexpected and untraceable in their logic. A really effective drill and practice program can be made to distinguish between different replies so that students learn from their incorrect responses rather than continuing to repeat them.

If students are to learn from their mistakes, the program must be truly interactive and specific in its responses. Dennis outlines some necessary components in an effective feedback system. Messages to students should contain the following:

1. Confirmation of correct answers and reinforcement of why they are correct
2. Confirmation of correct thinking and help in constructing a correct answer
3. Information regarding predictable incorrect answers, with reasons that make it possible to find remedies
4. Information about unidentifiable incorrect answers, with suggestions for seeking help

Clearly, "yes or no" feedback to students, without further explanation, is not instructional. Students should be told why their responses are accurate or inaccurate, so that they become aware of strategies for problem solving. Good teaching would include guiding students in transferring this awareness beyond the computer into other learning situations.

An example of a drill and practice program that meets most of the criteria for an effective program is a literature package published by Pomfret House, Encyclopaedia Britannica Educational Corp., 1983. The package includes a student book that has the literary selection to be read, a teacher's manual with lesson plans and ideas for transfer "away from the computer," and a computer disk of student exercises. The program includes most of the desirable features of an effective drill and practice program for students.

1. It calls the student by name throughout the exercises, which personalizes the interaction.
2. Extremely interactive, it gives encouraging, polite, matter-of-fact feedback in a conversational style.
3. For an incorrect response, it gives a helpful explanation to guide students in correcting their thinking.
4. It assigns students to levels of remediation on the basis of their scores.
5. The teacher, using a hidden option, may modify the assignment of levels and display or delete student test scores.
6. It includes recordkeeping for the test scores of up to thirty students.
7. It gives all of the reasons behind the selection of questions. This promotes students' awareness of their reading habits, vocabulary, knowledge of grammar, and comprehension.
8. It lets the students further apply and reinforce the vocabulary concepts used in a story in a timed word game, which is included as follow-up to the exercises.

To use the program, the student reads the story in the booklet. A sound filmstrip of the story is also available, if needed. Then the student uses the computer disk, which is designed to be used independently. The exercise disk should first be prepared by the teacher so that it is tailored to the students' individual needs, on the level chosen by the teacher. There are three levels of difficulty, based on student performance on the pretest, but the teacher can preselect the levels to override the computer's decision by means of the teacher's options that are built into the program.

All of the exercises take about twenty minutes to complete. They include synonyms, context clues, word relationships of mood, classification and meaning, and comprehension of important details in a cloze exercise. All the vocabulary and comprehension questions are directly tied to concepts in the story and reinforce understanding. Feedback is immediate and politely given: "That is correct, Juanita." If a student response is incorrect, the correct answer is usually given so that the student does not persist in false thinking: "That is incorrect, Juan." At the conclusion of all the exercises, the student's score is displayed.

I. Program scoring

Activity	Level I			Level II			Level III		
	No. of ans.	Pts/ ea.	Value	No. of ans.	Pts/ ea.	Value	No. of. ans.	Pts/ ea.	Value
Vocabulary	5	4	20	5	4	20	5	4	20
Word meaning	4	5	20	4	5	20	4	5	20
Synonyms									
1st try	6	5	30	7	4	28	8	4	32
(2nd try)		(2	12)		(2	14)		(2	16)
Comprehension	3	10	30	4	8	32	7	4	28
			100			100			100

II. The number of accepted words in the timed word game.

III. Preprogram activities are not calculated into the scores but are noted in the program summary as a means of evaluating the student's effort.
   a. Responded (yes/no) to reading the story.
   b. Requested _____ definitions out of 20.
   c. Answered _____ correctly on the pretest.

Note: The student must take the entire test before the scores are available for viewing.

Based on the score, the teacher may decide to change the level for the student on the next reading selection. The students' scores will be stored on the disk, which the teacher can print out or just copy from the screen. In the manual, student records are provided so that students themselves can keep track of their progress.

Finally, students may play the timed word game so as to get further practice in the story's concepts. They may play individually or in a small group, and the program will display the name of the highest scorer in the friendly competition.

The teacher's manual suggests several transfer activities away from the computer, such as writing about the story, rewriting the ending, or preparing reports on related topics. It also recommends further practice in the new vocabulary learned: context usage in sentences, syllabication of the words, and finding synonyms, antonyms, or homonyms for the new words.

This is an elegant, sophisticated program, very easy for both student and teacher to use. It goes a long way toward meeting the criteria for effective drill and practice programs.

TUTOR: Tutorials

Tutorial programs usually include a drill and practice exercise section after a tutorial has been presented. This is similar to a teacher's instructional format: Practice in applying a concept follows instruction in that concept. Finally, a posttest assesses the students' mastery of each set of objectives. The best tutorial programs also include recordkeeping capabilities for student scores, which teachers may access to determine the progress of individuals. By their very nature, tutorials are complex in design, and good ones are rare. The instructional design must include a structured presentation of material that is accurate and logically sequenced. It should use relevant and stimulating graphics as well as an effective limitation of written text. Too much text on a screen display can be discouraging to poorer students and can detract from the idea being presented. If sound is important to the subject matter, as in a music lesson or a natural science segment, the programming required for the tutorial will be more complex. The sound must be accurate and logical, and it must be possible to shut it off if it seems to disrupt the instructional setting or if a student would not benefit from hearing it.

Furthermore, an effective tutorial has to allow for all possible correct responses and intelligently respond to incorrect answers. Ideally, it will be able to predict common incorrect answers and provide specific, individualized feedback according to the student's incorrect response. Finally, any tests must have validity and reliability so that student learning is evaluated with fairness and accuracy.

Bitter and Camuse (1984) discuss two of the several types of tutorial designs — *linear* and *branching* — that affect the individualization of the program. The linear design presents a series of program frames that are hierarchically arranged and proceed in a predetermined sequence, with no allowance for individual responses except in reteaching sequences that go back through the algorithm (see Chapter 2). Figure 3-3 shows two examples of the linear designs commonly found in tutorials. The linear designs are presented in a flowchart or algorithm so that students proceed from the first step to the second and so on until they reach the end of the lesson. The answers expected are prescribed and require students to think convergently.

Branching design, on the other hand, allows for more divergent thinking. Alternative answers may be accepted. It directs students to further lessons, depending upon their responses. This kind of design is desirable in most learning circumstances and can be effective in developing problem-solving abilities. Figure 3-4 is an example of the branching design, which is not so prescriptive for the users.

Tutorials are meant to be simulations of the best teaching techniques. Because their designs and programming are so complex, they must be chosen carefully and used wisely. The following are criteria that teachers may use, along with their intuition, to evaluate a tutorial that is being considered for classroom use:

1. Is the content accurate and up to date, according to the latest scholarly thinking?
2. Do the tests measure learning of the concepts presented? Do they assess thinking on levels higher than the literal level?
3. Do students learn from the tests, in addition to being assessed? Do the tests themselves have instructional value?
4. Are the graphics accurate in content, valid in design, and relevant to the subject matter? Do they complement the instruction?
5. Is the sound appropriate in its frequency, duration, and representation of nature? Can it be shut off? Is it necessary? Does it complement the instruction?
6. Can the student control the pace and frequency of the presentation? If not, does this undermine the learner's confidence?
7. Can the instructional design be clearly identified as linear, branching, or

List continues on p. 84.

Figure 3-3 Linear designs (from Gary G. Bitter and Ruth A. Camuse, *Using a Microcomputer in the Classroom,* © 1988, p. 72. Reprinted by permission of Prentice-Hall, Inc., Englewood Cliffs, New Jersey)

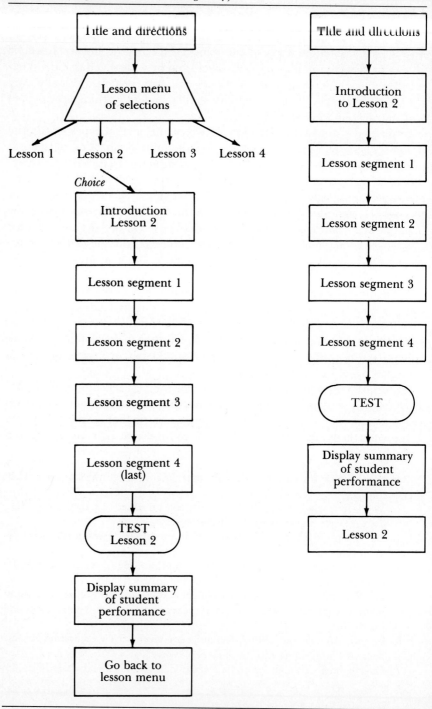

Figure 3-4 Branching design (from Gary G. Bitter and Ruth A. Camuse, *Using a Microcomputer in the Classroom,* © 1988, p. 73. Reprinted by permission of Prentice-Hall, Inc., Englewood Cliffs, New Jersey)

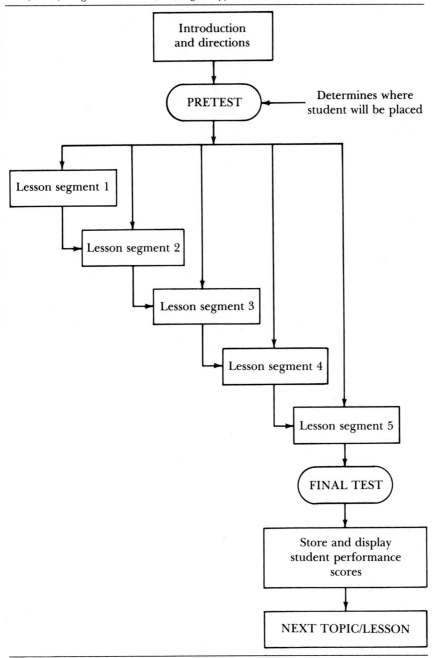

some other form of logical sequencing? Is the design appropriate for the age and needs of the student? Is the design effective and relevant to the subject matter?

8. Is the presentation of material interesting and motivating?

9. Does the program have a recordkeeping system that is efficient and makes it easy for the teacher to access records of class and individual performance?

10. Can the tutorial "stand alone" in a teaching situation? Can the student use it independently, freeing the teacher to interact individually with other students who need help?

An example of a well-designed tutorial program that meets most of these criteria is "Study Skills" (C.C. Publications, Inc., 1984), which instructs students how to research and write a paper. It consists of five sequential and progressive skill areas: Topics, Topic Development, Using Library Sources, Paraphrasing, and the Written Report. If master levels are not met in a particular skill area, students are routed through an Error Routine. Also, a workbook is provided to give students further practice with paper and pencil in specific skills — an important opportunity for transfer. There is an alternative "fast track" for faster learners, so the program does try to individualize according to different student needs. "Study Skills" is menu-driven, requiring no manual for easy student use, so the teacher is free to aid students individually. The feedback is immediate, reinforcing in a positive way when the answer is correct: "Right!" followed by an instruction to apply the concept. When a student response is inaccurate, the feedback is "No," followed by instructions to apply the concept in the correct way. Then follows remediation, depending on the number of correct responses. According to how many correct responses the student gives in the remediation section, he or she may be sent back to the original exercise. The user may leave the drills at any time by pushing two keys and returning to the main menu.

Success in the answers depends on spelling the words correctly, so the student must pay close attention to the display of the word to be typed. The criterion for advancement is about 80 percent correct answers throughout the program; the student's scores are displayed at the end of each lesson. If students meet the mastery criteria, they advance to a consecutive mastery program (P2); if they fail, they are routed to the Error Routine. Success there loops them back to the first mastery program (P1); failure there sends them to the workbook:

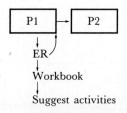

In one of the five programs, the mastery criteria are up to the teacher's discretion, and in the last one the students may be fast-tracked. These are the only allowances for teacher intervention in the programs. Another drawback is that there is no recordkeeping system to keep track of student progress. This tutorial does have some major features that are appealing for instructional purposes:

1. Remediation is offered in varying forms: in a computer subroutine and a paper workbook.
2. Transfer away from the computer is provided.
3. The programs may be independently operated by students, freeing the teacher to help others individually.
4. Teacher involvement is expected in the upper and later levels of the programs so that individual performance is monitored.
5. Feedback is positive and reinforcing when the response is accurate.
6. The concepts learned are immediately applied while prompts remain on the screen.
7. Incorrect responses are given immediate accurate application.
8. Remediation depends on mastery level.
9. Looping back to the original subroutine provides reinforcement and greater chances for success in a concept.
10. Escape from the drills is allowed at any time.

Despite the drawbacks previously noted, this branching tutorial includes most of the desirable features of an effective program.

TOOL: Word Processors

Word processing programs are so versatile in their uses, functions, and applications that they may be employed as a tool in either CMI or CAI. A word processor is transparent technology, to be used to generate teaching materials and manage teaching or else used directly in student learning of reading and writing. The computer program is the most interdisciplinary component. It crosses content areas, interrelating learning and transcending the concepts of any one field. It may be used as a database system for storing information and student writing, as a writing tool, as a material generator, and as a means to teach language use and manipulation.

The basic functions of a word processor are to create, edit, save, and print information entered onto it, as shown in Figure 3-5. This design is common to all word processors; Figure 3-5 shows the most basic functions they are able to perform. All word processors also contain the following primary features that enhance efficient manipulation of text:

1. A cursor—the flashing symbol that locates your place on the screen, within the text file.
2. Electronic characters—the numeric and alphabetic characters displayed on the monitor. Stored in the computer's RAM (random access memory), they

Figure 3-5   Word processor (adapted from Howell and Scott (1985))

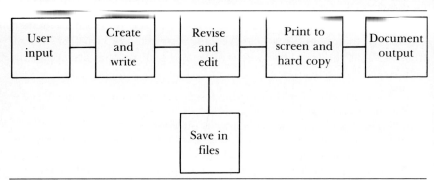

may be moved, deleted, or changed very easily, much more neatly and efficiently than with paper and pencil.

3. Word-wrap—allows each line to format itself by moving words to the next
line, depending on how many characters are permitted per line (usually between forty and eighty). The writer does not need to press the carriage return
after each line, as on a typewriter. This makes for faster, more efficient writing.

4. Capitals—using the CAPS LOCK key, the writer can make everything upper case. Both lower case and upper case are included; as on a typewriter,
individual capital letters are created with use of the SHIFT key.

5. Space bar—creates spaces between words and can be used to indent for
paragraphs (as on a typewriter). In some programs, it can also serve the function of calling other material onto the screen.

6. DELETE key—a simple way to remove characters to the left of the cursor.
The cursor is positioned to the right of the error, then the delete key is pressed
to remove characters continuously until released. This is the simplest of the
editing functions found in a word processor.

7. Scrolling function—using the cursor (controlled by arrow keys, a "mouse"
button, or other means), the entire document may be displayed on the screen,
top to bottom. As more than one screenful of text is entered, the first part
of the document moves out of sight so that the user can see the part that is
being actively worked on. The scrolling feature allows the user to bring other
parts of the document to the screen, which is handy in revising text.

8. Split screen—most word processors display the writing area and also the
writing "tools" and aids offered by the program. The aids are presented as
pictures ("icons") or by name, so the user has constant access to help in editing
or transferring text to a file to be saved or printed.

These features of a word processor have tremendous advantages over the
use of paper and pencil or a typewriter. Collette Daiute (1984) presents
situations that illustrate these advantages:

> The writer doesn't like a word or sentence: With a few commands, he or she
> can delete or alter a word or an entire sentence. Never are there erasure
> smudges or any other signs of deletion or alteration. The gaps left by dele-
> tions are closed.

The writer wishes to add a word or sentence: He or she types in the additional words, and the text on the screen is automatically reformatted.

The writer wishes to move a block of text, a paragraph or two, from point *A* to point *B*: Word processing programs include commands that make such a change more neatly than cutting and pasting, more easily than retyping.

The writer wishes to change every instance in which a certain word has been used: He or she can do that with a word processor.

The writer can go back to text stored on the disk, move to the problem sections on the screen and fix them with an ease and neatness not possible with a typewriter.

Daiute also notes some drawbacks of word processors, which teachers should take into consideration. First, because of the shimmering letters and the text's neat appearance on the screen, revision is deceiving. The teacher should determine whether hard copy is easier for students to revise. Also, many students find the screen version too abstract; only the paper version is real to them. In that case, revision may be completed on paper, then typed into the computer program for the final draft. Second, the size of the screen limits the amount of text the writer may view at any one time, so he or she may lose the sense of text as a coherent whole. With longer manuscripts, most students need a paper version to revise, especially to smooth out transitions and provide unity in the composition. Finally, it may be difficult for some students to get the time they need on school or university computers to complete a project. If demand for computer time is great, difficulty of access must be taken into consideration by the teacher when assignments are expected to be generated on school computers.

On the whole, however, the computer's positive benefits to learning and enjoying writing far outweigh the drawbacks. The emphasis in word processing is on revision and rethinking of one's ideas. A word processor makes the mechanical part of this process much simpler, so students can experience writing as a dynamic, esthetically satisfying process. Not only does a word processor allow students to record and publish what they know; it also facilitates discovery of their ideas and sharpens their thinking in ways that paper and pencil cannot.

There are many word processing programs available for CAI in writing. The earliest ones were mostly single-activity software with limited functions. More recent word processors have evolved into "idea processors." Stephen Marcus (1984) characterized this evolution in terms of generations. The first generation of word processors (as applied to writing instruction and the composing process) involved mostly drill and practice, focusing on refining students' basic skills of spelling, punctuation, and sentence combining. The second generation concentrated on "writer aids" that addressed the process of composing. The writer was aided in one of the three stages — prewriting, writing, or rewriting. This focus was based on research showing that writers spend 85 percent of their time in prewriting activities such as outlining, brainstorming, and making notes; 1 percent in writing the rough draft; and 14 percent in rewriting, editing and proofreading, and rethinking their ideas. The writer aids for prewriting in this second generation prompted students to generate preliminary ideas by means of questions similar to those a teacher might ask to elicit ideas. To facilitate writing the rough draft, word processors acted as text editors, allowing writers to add, delete, change, or move text simply and easily. Another aid focused on the revision stage, analyzing the writer's style of language use and grammar. Some of the text analyzers suggested changes and provided direct instruction in helping students revise their writing. The third generation has integrated all these capacities. Programs such as "Quill" (by DC Heath) and "The Writer's Workshop" (by Milliken) provide direct instruction in all stages of the composing process and include a word processor. Future word processing packages will no doubt extend these capabilities and refine aids to writers. It must be remembered, however, that the computer does not teach students to write; the teacher does. The computer is the technology on which students practice what they have been taught and are reinforced in the principles of the writing process — which they have learned from the teacher.

With such a vast array of word processing programs available, educators need guidelines for selecting and using one in the classroom. Thomas Boudrot (1985) offers suggestions in a five-step guide for teacher use.

Step One: Shopping for a System.   The rule, especially for beginners, is simplicity.

Software considerations. Documentation should be clear and easy to read, both for teacher and for students, and should include a chart of commands with illustrations. The manual should be helpful for review or reference. The commands themselves should be logical, clear, and easy to use.

It is important to use a word processor that allows you to print out as many characters per line as your printer will handle. You should use a program that will allow a printout of at least 50 characters per line. However, if your printer is capable of printing out 80 characters per line, but your word processor limits you to 65 characters, the equipment will not be utilized to its maximum potential. Try to match printer capability with the word processing program you are considering. Look for a package that is adaptable to a wide variety of printers.

Hardware considerations. A full-sized, typewriter-style keyboard is mandatory. The flat, touch-sensitive keys used in programming are tiring and frustrating when used in word processing. Having two disk drives will permit students to save, load, and modify files easily and efficiently, so they are well worth the investment. Color monitors are not the best for word processing, in which a very sharp, easy-to-read image is needed.

Step Two: Getting Ready.   Before introducing the word processor to students, the teacher should practice with it until he or she reaches the point of familiarity and comfort with the commands. Create activity files that include error-filled paragraphs so that students can practice inserting, deleting, changing, and moving text; beginnings of stories for students to finish; and sample tests on the word processor commands. From the manual, select and paraphrase instructions for students. For younger students, the instructions could be posted on a large board or poster. Next, select a core group of four or five students whom you can train to be helpers. Teach them the program, give them lots of computer practice, and reward them with extra credit, if appropriate.

Step Three: The First Lessons.   Use the show-and-tell approach. Pair the trained leaders with small groups of learners; have them demonstrate the program and serve as monitors of the learning sessions. In the second week, students may practice major editing commands on individual files they can save and use for practice.

Step Four: Writing Assignments.   By the third week, students should be able to begin assignments. Have them write their rough drafts on paper first, because that takes the most time. Again, pair the leaders with students for 30-minute time segments; set up a weekly schedule. One student should read the draft aloud while the other student types it in. They will hear the language as it is used, correct it, and make changes as they proceed.

Step Five: Correcting the Files.   Student writing can be viewed and reviewed in two ways: either individually (on hard copy) or as a class (on a large screen, using an erasable marker). Students critique their writing as a group, make revisions, and receive immediate feedback and guidance from the teacher. Revised files can be saved, printed out, and assembled into a booklet to be taken home at the end of the school year.

An example of a good word processor that meets most of the criteria for use by students is a system exemplifying the third generation of word processors. Minnesota Educational Computing Consortium (MECC) publishes a "composing information series" that consists of four programs: "MECC Writer," the word processor; "MECC Editor," which reviews student writing and encourages revision; "MECC Speller," which identifies misspelled and confusing words; and "MECC Write Start," a prewriting motivator. "Writer" is designed for use by middle school and secondary students. It is uncomplicated, using only one mode to write, edit, and print. Functions are accessed through the simultaneous pressing of the CONTROL key and letter keys that logically indicate their function (for example, CONTROL P for the print function). Reference or help screens are always available to a student through the CONTROL R (reference) keys. "Writer" allows students all the necessary, basic word processing capabilities:

1. Compose, edit, and print
2. Insert or delete characters, words, and blocks of text
3. Move and rearrange information
4. Arrange the information on the screen in the way it is to be printed out
5. Save files on a data disk

The manual includes a reference card and "Ten Easy Steps" to guide students through exercises that help them learn the program. This is an introductory word processing program designed specifically for student use and is intended to be embedded in other MECC products as an "implantable word processor." This flexibility permits more student interaction through writing in other courseware. Also, students need to learn only one word processing program for the entire package of related software.

The related software to be used as prewriting and postwriting support includes "Write Start," "Speller," and "Editor." "Write Start" offers ten word processing activities that encourage students "to think, to talk to one another, to share ideas, to communicate information, and, of course, to write." All of the activities contain the implantable "Writer," introduced to students by a tutorial. Also, help screens are always available during any activity by pressing the CONTROL and R keys. The user may exit any activity during the waiting time that is allowed for response.

The first five activities provide opportunities for students to generate ideas, share information with others in a journal, and create a database to build stores of ideas. The second part contains five activities that encourage students to manipulate language structures and experiment with poetic forms. The purpose is not to teach word processing, but rather to initiate student creativity and enjoyment of language in preparation for writing. The manual includes plans for implementing the activities, clear instructions for their purpose and use, and details about management options.

"Editor" analyzes student writing according to the type of writing (exposition, argument, or narration) and its specific rhetorical qualities; the style, usage, and mechanics; and a structure (both outline and pictorial) of main ideas, use of transitions, and sentence functions. "Editor" introduces outlining as a way to check for main ideas and supporting details in each paragraph *after* writing—rather than before writing, as is traditionally taught. The outline is used to verify logical structure and organization in postwriting, a practice many writers use in spite of the traditional insistence that it be used for prewriting.

"Editor" is put into operation by booting it into the computer, selecting one of the four review sections, and loading the data disk containing the text file to be analyzed. Some style analyzers are compatible with numerous word processors, which makes them very flexible for instructional use.

"MECC Editor" accommodates only "MECC Writer" and "Apple Writer II" (DOS 3.3), which may be a limitation to schools who do not have these.

One of the best features of the "Editor," in contrast to some other programs, is its capability of error correction on the spot. The writer is able to change errors immediately when they are designated and described. Not all editors offer this convenience. The program also provides the option of ignoring the highlighted error. Checking mechanical and language errors takes about ten to fifteen minutes at most but gives a writer confidence and assurance that most stylistic errors have been caught.

Deborah Kovacs (1986) discusses the reluctance of some teachers and writers to using style checkers because they believe writing is a subjective process and should be analyzed by a subjective human. They believe that the computer editors will standardize language, eliminating the creative aspect. For very advanced, professional writers of literature, such editors might well be stultifying and limiting. However, most writers and learners appreciate the non-judgmental analysis, which they can choose to accept or to reject. Students in particular can feel a real freedom in writing their initial drafts to concentrate on ideas without fear of errors if they know that an editing program will assist their revision later.

Kovacs lists criteria for selecting a "Post-writing Program" and compares several existing ones. The MECC "Editor" is the least expensive yet includes eight of the ten most desirable qualities:

1. Offers a data file editor
2. Allows on-the-spot text editing
3. Checks for grammar and style errors
4. Checks punctuation
5. Offers outline structure
6. Checks paragraph length
7. Checks sentence length
8. Reviews qualities of types of writing

It does not provide the following features, which some other editors do:

1. A readability score
2. A vocabulary analysis

She recommends evaluating the school's needs in terms of whether it should buy a totally integrated writing system or build its system one program at a time. What a school has in place and what it needs will help determine which writing programs it should buy.

"Speller" is the fourth program in MECC's composing information series. It reinforces the writing process in its emphasis on revision. "Speller" includes a dictionary on the opposite side of the diskette. First, "Speller" is booted in, and one of the four options is chosen. Then the text file on the data disk is inserted, and lastly the "Dictionary" is inserted. With all three in the computer's memory, the text is analyzed according to two categories of words: "problem words" and "confusing words." Each category may be used separately or together for the analysis. For a less mature writer, each should probably be analyzed separately to avoid confusion. The teacher may modify the basic vocabulary of 10,000 words in the "Dictionary," tailoring it to students' needs through a "Management Option." The teacher may add a maximum of one hundred words and call special attention to "flag words" that give students particular difficulty in spelling or usage.

Some teachers object to the use of a speller for student writing, saying that students don't learn to spell because they rely too much on a speller. It is important to understand that the Speller does not correct the student's words or even provide the correct spelling. All it does, in most speller programs, is point out which words are misspelled. The students must look them up or change them themselves. The writer cannot edit the word on the spot, but must write it down, go look it up, then return to the text file to find it and edit it. Surely, this procedure does not hinder students' learning to spell; indeed, it forces them to learn to spell the very words they want to use in their own writing. The motivation to solve the problem of their misspelled words is inherent in the procedure.

The "Problem Words" option identifies words not in the "Dictionary," so students have to check their own spelling. With each problem word identified, a help screen is offered as an option, informing the writer of possible reasons words are misspelled: 1) the mispelled words are not found in "Speller"; 2) they are typos; 3) they are flag words that are often misused or misspelled. The "Confusing Words" option analyzes the text for possible confusing words such as *to, too,* and *two* and explains the differences between them. Then the student may go to the text to edit such words.

The four programs constituting the Information Composing Series of MECC word processing exemplify the third generation of word processors. As a composite, they meet most of the criteria for an effective system because they reinforce the reading/writing process of preparation, implementation, and application so well.

TOOL: Planners, Story Starters, and Graphics

Planners are not actual drill and practice programs, but they help students plan their writing through cues, questions, and prompts. They also offer isolated skill practice in techniques of writing they present to students. The user is presented with questions and examples to answer and analyze. These programs usually do not include a word processor; they help writers plan their ideas, structure, and approach in prewriting activities. Then the writer uses a word processor to write what the planner has helped to generate. The planners differ from story starters in that they do not involve creative story writing or have stories built into the program. They instruct in other modes of composition, such as persuasive essays, character sketches, or expository writing. Mostly, their emphasis is on getting students to think and to overcome writer's block. This kind of program really integrates reading and writing, getting students to read examples of sample writing, then prompting them to develop their own ideas. The programs are highly interactive; they guide and prod writers to generate ideas, then develop them and structure them in the type of writing they select. They are *tools* in the sense that the writer uses them to build a base for writing that is performed later.

An example of a planner that incorporates the characteristics above is "Writing a Character Sketch" by MECC. This interactive program consists of two main sections: "Writing a Character Sketch" and "Point of View." In writing the character sketch, the student is guided first to analyze the external characteristics of characters, such as appearance, physical traits, and speech. Second, characters can be developed according to their behavior: how they act, what they say, and where they live. Then the characters are developed through others' reactions to them and through comparison and contrast. Comparisons encourage development of similes; for contrasts, students present differences using specific adjectives.

The students are led to understand character development starting from the outer characteristics and proceeding inward to the personality. In dealing with external characteristics, students may be taught the concepts of prejudice and stereotyping. The program uses "disclaimers" such as *may* and explains to students that "no piece of evidence by itself is entirely convincing." Each exercise in character development includes examples, comprehension checks for understanding, and opportunities for students to type in their own ideas (up to six lines for each exercise).

"Point of View" teaches students the first person and third person. Students may choose to write from three points of view: first-person close involvement, first-person observer, and third-person reporting. The objectives include teaching students to identify audience and purpose and to maintain a consistent point of view in writing. This section includes examples of writing from the first and third person points of view and explains the differences between their functions. Graphics of cartoon characters are also used to illustrate the characters described in the examples. The student is then quizzed on what was learned from the examples. Immediate feedback to responses is given. A correct response earns the word "Correct," with the right answer restated. An incorrect response receives a "No" plus the right answer while the text is still displayed. The next screen displays the text along with an explanation of the answer. Students' responses may be printed out at any time or stored on a data disk. Students may also leave an exercise during a response wait.

Through questions and examples, students are guided to think through the process of composing a character sketch. The "General Information Section" of the menu provides students with an overview of the learning they experience and the rationale for learning it. Thus they may develop a metacognitive awareness of what they are learning and how they are learning it, which may transfer away from the computer. As monitor of student learning, the teacher should point out this overview to the students so that they understand its value. This kind of planner software has a great deal of value for reinforcing and providing practice for students' reading and writing processes, particularly in the preparation stage.

Story starters are also useful tools for facilitating the reading/writing process in the preparation step. They differ from planners in that they have a word processor built into the program and that they focus primarily on one kind of mode of composition: creative writing. They provide experience in story mapping and plot structure. Some story starters also include graphics capabilities, particularly in programs for the early grades. The students draw pictures to illustrate what they want to write about, then use the built-in word processor to create their stories. Students may either choose from predrawn images or create their own. Some story starters even include music capabilities, by which students can compose songs to go along with the words and pictures in their stories.

Most story starters are built around branching routines that allow students to create their own story lines. A scenario is presented and multiple choices are given for episodes. As they make choices, the students plan and organize the plot and arrive at a point of climax and an eventual outcome. This kind of a program should be used by students in groups, because of the social nature of the decision-making process. Different small groups can make different decisions, then compare their story plots for episodes and turning points. The teacher can use a story starter with the entire class initially, if a large monitor or a projector is available to project the computer screen onto a large screen. Using the story starter this way serves as a catalyst for understanding plot structure and narrative text. After the class experience, student groups should map out their story episodes on paper before they enter the story into the computer program. In that way they will be prepared to use the program as a tool, and use of computer time will be more efficient.

"Story Tree" by Scholastic is an example of an interactive story starter. It fully integrates writing with reading as students learn story structure. The stories students read and help write branch out from one beginning to numerous choices of endings — much like a tree, a story tree. Students are offered opportunities to make choices about events and outcomes in the preprogrammed stories and in their own original stories. A sample story disk includes stories students can read and work on, getting ideas for writing their own. The decisions students make about the story involve three kinds of choices: 1) to *continue* the story, 2) to give the reader a *choice* (up to four choices per page), and 3) to make the story branch by *chance,* from one page part of the time and another page other times. The program includes a tutorial that gives step-by-step examples for creating a story using the three kinds of choices. Instructions are also present in every screen, so students may opt to begin an original story right away.

The built-in word processor is not sophisticated; it includes only the most elemental functions of cursor movement to enter or delete text. The main purpose of the word processor is to help in creating a story at its inception, rather than to polish or revise it, so the revision capabilities are necessarily primitive. The students may edit a story a page at a time and change its name, text, or branching connection. Each page is named initially according to the episode that occurs in the plot structure. An example of a story map or plot structure is found in the tutorial called The Checkmate Mystery. (See Figure 3-6.)

Figure 3-6   The Checkmate Mystery (reproduced from the Scholastic Story Tree™ Program with permission of the publisher, Scholastic, Inc.)

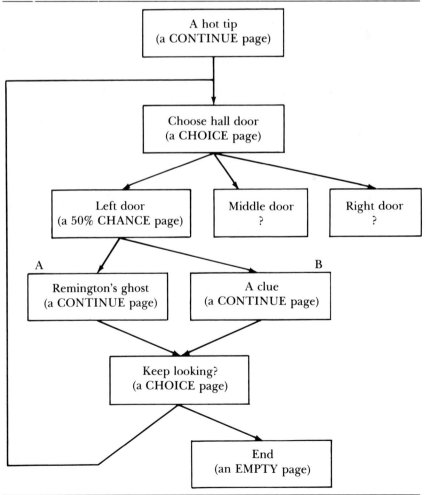

In creating their own original stories, students should be encouraged to work in groups of two or three and map out their stories on paper before they use "Story Tree." As suggested before, the entire class can be taken through the tutorial together. Then they should read from a book a story that contains episodic events, mapping them out in their groups. Each group can compare its story map to another's to assess their understanding of the story they read. Through these interrelated reading/writing activities, students will have varied opportunities to learn the narrative mode of composition, understand plot structure, and develop their own stories.

The story starter programs are highly interactive with students, probing their imaginations yet disciplining their organization and structure. These programs challenge students in the writing/reading process by providing the opportunity to plan, map out, and carry through a story adventure, from a beginning through a climax to an ending. Their writing will enhance their comprehension of narrative text; this connection should be guided and monitored by the teacher.

Graphics are also tools that may be incorporated into the reading/writing process to illustrate text and to provide visual opportunities for comprehending text. Some simple graphics packages are incorporated into word processors for prewriting and writing illustration purposes. At the other end of the spectrum are designer packages that create graphics for banners, posters, and greeting cards. Such designer packages may be used by students in instruction or by teachers in management of instruction. For the reading/writing process, graphics can be useful in the preparation stage as well as in the application step. Graphics can help students plan reading and writing, can be used to illustrate ideas as they write, and can be added in the postreading and postwriting stages to apply the ideas to another medium of communication. One graphics package, "Facemaker," has students create faces, external representations of a character they have read about or will read or write about. The students may also create very simple programming procedures to animate the faces. The faces are created by selecting prepackaged features such as hair, eyes, and nose. The features selected determine the kind of character students want to create. When they animate the face, students actually get into the personality of the character through the actions and "behavior" they program. This graphics program may be used in any step of the reading/writing process.

Another graphics package for specialized writing is "Newsroom" (by Springboard), which helps students create a newspaper. Using it, students can design, produce, and print out their own newspaper for the school, club, or class. The program includes a library of over 600 pieces of "clip art" that students can select to use to illustrate their newspaper. The software includes a word processor, onto which text is entered using any of five print styles. Even banners can be created using extra large typefaces, borders, and different tones. Finally, the program includes a wire service that can take feed from other program users through a modem.

Other graphics programs use peripherals such as a joystick, a mouse, or KoalaPad to produce pictures. A KoalaPad is a video sketch pad, 4 inches square, which permits anything drawn on it to be transferred to the monitor. The joystick, the mouse, and other graphics tools can be used to manipulate the cursor on the screen in a wide variety of graphics packages.

A different kind of a graphics program helpful to students in preparing to read and write is "Thinking Networks" by Think Network, Inc. This program includes five different organizational designs based on modes of composition: narration, theme, classification, comparison/contrast, and sequencing. Using four levels of readability for each mode, the program is useful for remedial students as well as those needing enrichment. The object of the program is to present a graphic representation or schema of story structure so that students can comprehend major and minor events. The students first read a selection from the story card at the appropriate reading level, then use the computer program to build a story network linking major and minor ideas in the story design. When the students finish their comprehension work, a completed network narrative graphic appears on the screen. Interacting with the computer "teacher/tutor," students build a network by adding a new "node" each time an event is correctly comprehended.

Figure 3-7 shows a completed network narrative design. The arrows indicate linked ideas, in order of importance. When students correctly select the main idea for a series of events, they see the arrow interconnect between idea nodes. Successful completion of the network building reveals that students understand the organization, ideas, and vocabulary of the story.

The next part of the program develops students' vocabulary. Ten to fifteen new words that were introduced in the story and reinforced in the network are taught in context, then presented briefly (as in a tachistoscope) for visual memory practice. The student then employs the words in another story that uses a cloze method.

The third part of the program presents a story model in a completed network map, which the student follows to construct a story. Because the network map is identical to the one completed in the first part, the writing involves reconstruction or retelling of a familiar story. The built-in word processor allows students to type, edit, and print out their writing. Finally, the last part of the program has the students create an original story. The graphics for learning story construction are based on schema theory (see Chapter 2) and semantic mapping techniques. Students make graphic representations of abstract text, permitting concrete visualization of story structure. Interrelating reading, writing, and graphics reinforces student learning through several sensory approaches — visual, tactile, and spatial.

TOOL: *Information Management*

In today's information age, information currently doubles about every twenty months. By the year 2000, however, it is projected to double about

Figure 3-7   Story network (reproduced with permission of Think Network, Inc., P.O. Box 6124, New York, NY 10128)

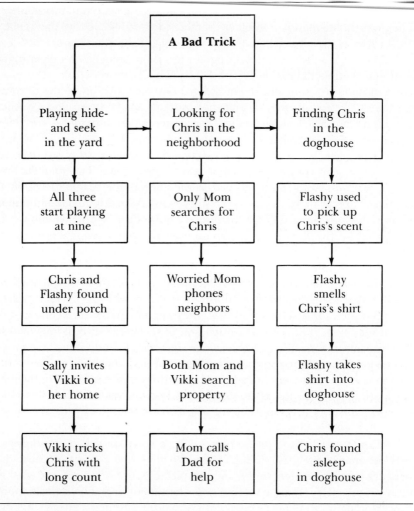

every twenty days. Our responsibility as teachers is to prepare students to handle this information, to manage, organize, store, and use it. Teaching students data management also helps them prepare for living in society as adults.

Computers can be especially helpful in creating a database for the storage and retrieval of information. The term *database* refers to an organized grouping of information on a particular topic. Familiar databases are telephone directories, class rosters, and library card catalogs. On paper, these are all static files. Using a data management computer program, however, gives us the flexibility continuously to create, design, update, and retrieve information from data files.

Besides flexibility, these all-purpose tools allow a tremendous variety of uses. Databases are primarily used for problem-solving in the classroom. For example, all students may be assigned to find information on different Indian tribes in a section of the country. When the information is gathered, students will need a method or format for classifying the data. In systematizing it, they will discover commonalities and contrasts between the tribal groups. They can analyze differences in housing, kinds of clothing, and ways of providing food. Students may also begin to perceive patterns of relationships between climate and ways of living and dressing. Students can ask the file program to find all common elements, enabling them to establish trends and test hypotheses regarding the topic. Database programs are thus useful for developing higher-level thinking abilities. When students have organized and classified information in a database, they can later retrieve it to synthesize and apply it in further reading and writing.

Creating databases should be standard preparation for writing research papers. Students could gather data on a topic, enter it into the database and share it with other students in a cooperative learning structure; all would contribute and benefit from each other's efforts.

To choose the best database program for their purposes, teachers need to know some of the major features of database design. William Hedges (1984) differentiates between the different kinds of programs and establishes criteria for choosing the right one. He describes three main database designs: the network/hierarchical database management system, the relational database management system, and the file management system. The first two are managerial systems, much more powerful than the third one, which is more suitable for classroom use and teaching purposes. For purposes of clarification, however, it is useful to describe briefly the three different systems.

The network/hierarchical database management system contains message information files that are primarily used by researchers, businesses, and stock market analysts. They access the system through a modem and telephone hookup, for which they pay a fixed fee plus a cost per hour. Examples of such systems are The Source and Dow Jones for current news and information, CompuServe for computer users and businesses, and Huttonline for stock market investors.

The second type of system is the relational database management system, which stores data in tables that show relationships. Essentially, the differences between this system and the File Management System (FMS) involve cost, power, and complexity. A relational system costs about three times as much as an FMS; it is meant for greater amounts of data and management of data; and it manipulates data on several levels and across files. A good example of a relational system is dBase II, which is usable in personal or business data processing.

For classroom and teaching purposes, the third system, the File Management System, is the most useful and easiest to teach to students. This system operates on file creation, data entry, simple sorting, and report printing — elemental functions that students should know in order to organize and use information. With this system, students can set up filing systems (much like files in a file cabinet) and print them out as needed. Some systems allow manipulation of multiple files simultaneously. Dealing with a single file in isolation could result in confusion because all related files need updating when information is changed in one of them. Maintaining several separate files may defeat the purpose of the learning objectives; this should be considered in selecting a system.

In choosing a suitable database system, Hedges cautions that the first step is to identify the tasks to be performed. The teacher or administrator needs to have in mind a clear description of what the system is to accomplish. Hedges establishes some guidelines to follow in choosing an appropriate database system:

1. *Flexibility.* The system should allow updating and changing of data entered, as well as of the format used for structuring data.
2. *Query processing.* The user should be able to enter the system with questions that get at specific information. The system should have the capability of receiving questions, searching, and retrieving specific items of information quickly.
3. *Data security.* There should be some procedure, such as a code name, for making access to confidential data difficult.
4. *Data manipulation.* Users who want to perform mathematical operations on the items should be able to obtain sums, averages, or other calculations.
5. *Efficient data storage.* Instead of making the user manipulate several files, replicating functions to get at usable information, the system should have a cross-index file that allows the user to retrieve combinations efficiently, saving storage and labor.
6. *Data integrity.* When one record is changed, all others should be automatically changed within the system as well. Discrepancies across files should be signaled, avoiding chaos and inconsistencies in data reporting.
7. *Data dictionary.* With large amounts of data, it is very helpful to have a central listing of all variables entered into the files which can be easily accessed and classified.
8. *Concurrence.* This refers to simultaneous access to the database system by multiple users — necessary for very large schools, but not necessary for classroom use.
9. *Record size and format.* The size and number of records needed will help determine the kind and the power of the system required.
10. *Main memory requirements.* A general rule is to use a system with as much memory as the computer is capable of handling. The amount of memory a computer has should be matched to a system that uses it to its capacity.

11. *Ease of learning to use.* This factor must always be considered, whether the system is used in business or in a classroom. If the tool is too difficult or time-consuming to learn, its usefulness and effectiveness are greatly diminished. When many people (such as students or new employees) have to learn it, the system must be one that is mastered easily and quickly.

Using the above criteria for selecting an appropriate database system, teachers or administrators should be able to test out the right system and plan wisely for their needs and purposes. An example of a file management system useful for both CAI and CMI by the teacher is "PFS: File" by Scholastic, Inc. It provides the means for creating files into which information is organized and easily retrieved in any order needed. "PFS: File" keeps information in forms that the user designs. After the form is designed, it can be recalled to the screen. Information is added to it, then the filled-in form is stored back in the file. Once information is stored in the file, it can be retrieved with a retrieve specification form that asks for items in the file that match a given set of characters. For example, files of all teachers in a school who teach seventh grade and are certified in reading can be retrieved, given the specifications of *grade 7* and *reading*. The characteristics in common call up the files that contain them. Figure 3-8 displays all the major functions possible with "PFS: File": Design, Add, Copy, Search/Update, and Print.

In designing a form, students learn to differentiate between major ideas and subordinate details. They learn to organize information and to standardize classifications across many related topics. They learn to compare and to contrast as well as synthesize information for further use. Above all, students learn to control vast amounts of information so that it is usable. The use of databases in a file management system is all-important for students in doing research and reports.

Another information management tool is the spreadsheet. As a practical teaching tool, it is actually a very large graph that students can use to collect and display information about many subjects. Figure 3-9 is an example of a graph that would be displayed on a computer spreadsheet. The columns are represented by letters and the rows by numbers; the spaces are the *cells*, into which information is entered. Each cell on the graph can represent a number (value) or a word (label). Each position can also store a formula that performs a mathematical function on numbers in the graph. These functions make the spreadsheet far more useful than static paper graphs. When one number is changed, the related numbers automatically change also, so the spreadsheet can be used in forecasting and predicting "what if" circumstances. For example, a baseball coach might use the spreadsheet to keep track of the times at bat, number of hits, and batting averages of a team she has scouted. By altering a few numbers, she can project what that team would be likely to do against her team. (See the chart at the bottom of p. 102.)

Figure 3-8   "PFS: File" functions (reproduced with permission of Scholastic, Inc.)

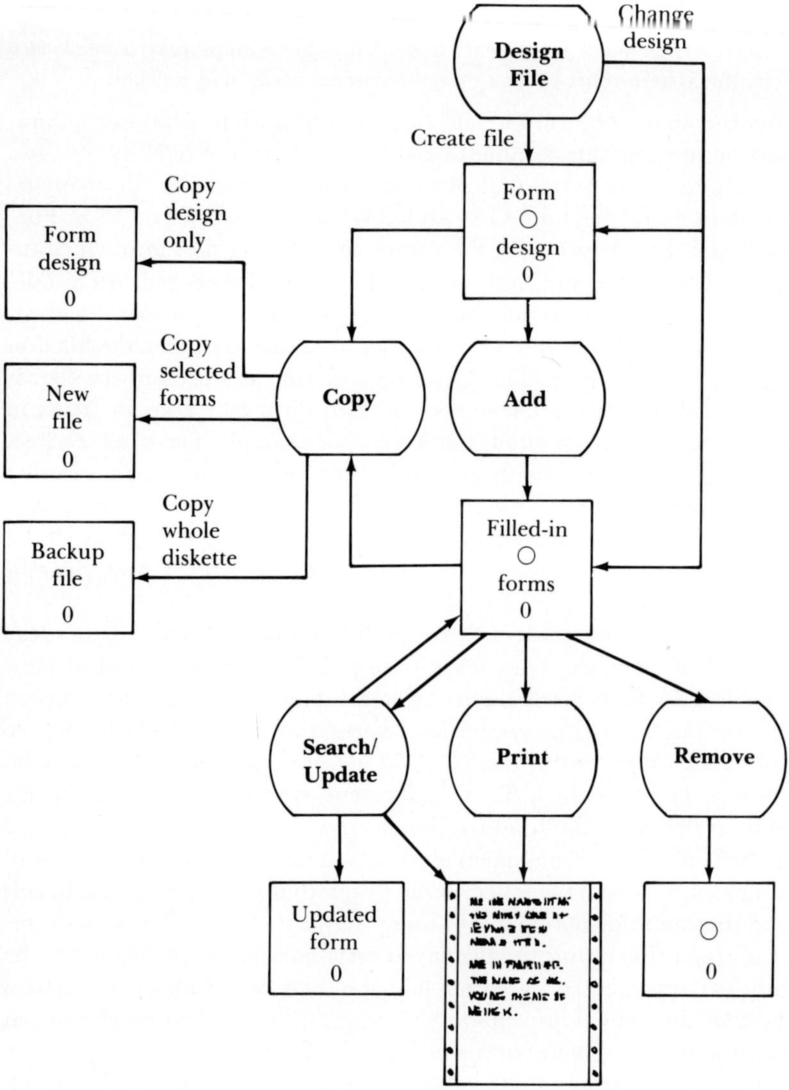

Player	At Bats	Hits	Average
Juan	20	4	.200
Chang	18	5	.277
Sam	16	6	.375
Luis	23	6	.260
Team	77	21	.278

Figure 3-9   Spreadsheet

	A	B	C	D	E	F	G	H	I	J	K	L
1												
2												
3												
4												
5												
6												
7												
8												
9												
10												
11												
12												
13												
14												
15												
16												

Another use of the spreadsheet for CMI is as a gradebook. Students' names may be entered into cells as labels and their scores on tests, quizzes, and projects as values. The scores may be weighted and averaged so that total points can indicate a grade.

Student Name	Quiz #1	Quiz #2	Test #1	Project	Total Points	Grade
Alicia	21	32	89	45	410	C
Jane	23	21	89	56	423	B
Yolanda	31	23	78	67	422	B
Lin Yu	12	26	67	45	329	D
Harry	34	29	100	34	431	A
Average	24.2	26.2	84.6	49.4	403	

Student uses of the spreadsheet in CAI are varied, depending only on the imagination of the teacher and the students. Chemistry students may use it to plot the rate of enzyme reactions; biology students to collect, graph, and analyze data of samples from the environment that they study; social studies students to collect and graph information on population statistics, then make projections regarding effects of population increase on economics and food production. The spreadsheet is valuable in both CAI and CMI for planning, forecasting, and recording information in the classroom.

In a review of spreadsheet software in the curriculum, Vaikko Allen (1985) rates six popular programs according to seven criteria:

Instructional design

Content

Appropriateness

Interest level

Ease of use

Support materials

Overall value

All of the programs are similar to "VisiCalc," the pioneering spreadsheet software, but have some other features. Some have manuals that are easier to read; others have adjustable columns, which "VisiCalc" does not have; still others have more sophisticated budgeting features, such as amortization and calculation of adjustable loan payments. The best of the programs, according to Allen, have simple text handling and extensive on-screen help. In choosing the appropriate spreadsheet, teachers will need to evaluate several programs according to such criteria.

"VisiCalc" by VisiCorp is the prototype of electronic worksheets that are suitable for teacher use for management as well as instruction. It was the first program of its type to combine a calculator capability with spreadsheet convenience. It has the power of tremendous memory and the speed of instant computation. The computer screen acts as a "window" that can be scrolled in four directions to view any part of the worksheet. Information of two kinds, names and numbers, is entered into the cells of the grid, allowing formation of charts, tables, and record sheets. Formulas may also be entered, retained in the memory, and "replicated" (repeated) elsewhere on the worksheet. If a number is changed in the worksheet, all related numbers change and are recalculated visually on the screen. Figure 3-10 is a diagram of VisiCalc features.

The program disk is not *disk-intensive* — meaning that once it has been booted, it is no longer needed in the disk drive to continue the program. A blank data disk is required to store data from one worksheet at a time. For use with a class of students, therefore, only one program disk is needed, thereby saving costs. The cost is the initial investment in the program and the blank disks needed by students. The data disks are easily initialized by a four-step procedure. The "VisiCalc" manual is fairly easy to read and includes a step-by-step tutorial that teaches the program in four lessons.

These information management tools of database programs and spreadsheets have many practical applications in the classroom. The applications include planning, organizing, recording, and storing information for further use in writing, reading, and reporting on it. These are appropriate tools for the information age and should be taught to students.

Figure 3-10   "VisiCalc" diagram

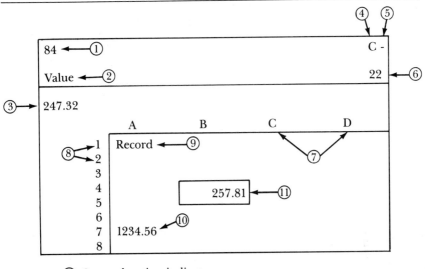

① Cursor location indicator
② Value or label indicator (also called *prompt line*)
③ Edit line
④ Order indicator (C = by column; R = by rows)
⑤ Cursor direction indicator (- = horizontal; ! = vertical)
⑥ Space left in memory indicator (0 = full)
⑦ Columns
⑧ Rows
⑨ Label
⑩ Value
⑪ Cursor

TOOL: Teacher Utilities

This category of software applications is extremely diverse, ranging from material generation to authoring systems to scheduling and management. All of the programs in this category are designed to be tools useful to the teacher in managing instruction.

Programs for material generation include vocabulary puzzles and word finds as well as tests and quiz exercises for students. Numerous popular programs for creating crossword puzzles are available to teachers. Some are great time-savers. Students should be allowed to use them, too, to create vocabulary puzzles and exercises for their classmates. Words from current reading material can be reinforced through use in the puzzles or word finds. It must be remembered that crossword puzzles do not teach word *meanings*. The puzzles should be used after students have learned the meanings of the words, to help them with spelling of the words and in simple decoding more than anything else. Some puzzles teach word relationships, such as antonyms, synonyms, and homonyms when words are paired. These puzzles are created on the computer and printed out; students then work on them on the hard copy. The teacher can also use utility programs to generate tests and quizzes. These may be multiple-choice or short-answer, using a packaged format or (with a word processor) an essay topic printed out for students to write on. Teachers should investigate the many preprogrammed utility packages to find the ones most useful to their own teaching.

Other teacher utilities involve authoring systems that can be used by non-programmers. There is a difference between authoring languages and authoring systems; the latter are programs that allow a teacher to create custom computer lessons. Such software is designed to help the teacher with the authoring process. Extensive prompts and cues tell how to provide graphics and where to add text. Preprogrammed authoring systems sacrifice a lot of sophistication and flexibility as compared with authoring languages such as BASIC and PILOT, but they do allow the novice to make custom creations. In evaluating a system to use, Linda Pattison (1985) recommends that the teacher consider two things: how easy the system is to use and how sophisticated the piece of courseware is to be. She further recommends the following selection criteria:

1. The program should provide clear screen instructions when the author disk is booted into the system, and should then show how to proceed.
2. It should have help screens that can be called up without interrupting the creation of a lesson.
3. It should provide a printed listing of the lesson once it is designed.
4. A demonstration lesson should be provided on the disk.
5. Cards or charts listing command codes and other information for easy reference should be included.

Some of the available authoring systems are very costly, running well over $1000; others are inexpensive and useful. Teachers may experiment with popular ones such as "Create Lessons," by Hartley Courseware, Inc., and "Super Sofcrates," by SIMPAC Educational Systems, to find the ones most suitable for their purposes.

The last kind of teacher utility to be considered here is the scheduling and management application. These programs include planning, curriculum scheduling, and grade management. Such programs help teachers and administrators to manage equipment inventories, report student progress to parents using standard phrases, keep track of student attendance, schedule students on computers and monitor software, plus much more. Numerous programs can assist the teacher in managing grades, performing grade calculations, and averaging scores. Some of the programs include histograms and other statistical reporting functions that may be useful to the teacher in reporting grades to parents.

An example of a utility package useful for grade management is MECC's "Grade Manager." This program allows a teacher to store and retrieve grades and offers many options. A data file can be created on a blank disk that stores approximately 1088 student records for up to 15 different classes. "Grade Manager" has five different utility programs, along with two support options for diskette and printer. The utility programs are: 1) "Classlist," 2) "Grading Method," 3) "Scores," 4) "Compute Grades," and 5) "Print Grades." Class lists are created or deleted in the first program. The list is automatically alphabetized when it is printed out, so last names have to be entered first. The second program helps the teacher to specify the grading method to be used: the score categories and either percentage or curve grading. Percentage grading uses either a five-point or twelve-point range (A – , B + , B, B – , etc.). Curve grading computes relative scores, using a score of 50 as average. The teacher can choose either option. The third program allows scores to be added or edited or printed, either individually or for the entire class. A frequency distribution can also be printed out for the scores. The fourth part computes the grades, on either a quarter or a semester basis. The final program prints out the quarter, semester and final grades for individuals or the entire class and also prints progress reports. This is quite a complete grading package, which teachers may find useful, but it is complex and requires some practice for mastery. The program is inexpensive and efficient, so it may well be worth the teacher's time to master it.

To find a program suitable for teacher use, Mary Lee Shalvoy (1985) recommends looking for the following features when considering buying an electronic gradebook:

Capacity. Depending on teacher workload, the program should be able to handle the number of students and the number of grades the teacher has.

Format. If grades are kept in a gradebook as well as on the computer disk (which is recommended), the most compatible format would probably be that of the traditional gradebook: a subject divided by assignments. The teacher should feel comfortable with the format.

Letter or number grades. Most programs print both a final letter grade and a number. Some output each assignment grade with both values. The best programs convert consistently throughout all files.

Weighted grades. Some assignments are more important and therefore count more than others. The programs should be able to handle any changes and weights easily.

Averages and statistics. Look for programs that do as much math as possible. Many calculate the mean, total average, and class rank. Some drop the lowest grades or calculate only the highest grades.

Graphs and charts. Programs with extensive graphs may be the hardest to work with. Such graphs may be unnecessary.

Comments, reports, and letters. These use standard, impersonal forms but can be a convenient avenue to communicate student progress.

Print options. Most programs have the capability of printing the different reports, rosters, and letters.

Saving process. Make sure the program allows continuous saving or has a built-in safety valve. It should also permit creation of backup disks.

Many teachers' utility programs are designed to make management and reporting easier so as to relieve some of the tedium of organization in teaching. Teachers should investigate the many different programs and select the ones that can help free them to devote more time to lesson planning, creativity, and involvement with students — the really fun parts of teaching.

TUTEE: *Programming Languages*

This is a book on teaching the reading and writing process to students. It is *not necessary* for teachers to have a knowledge of programming languages in order to teach the communication process, nor is it necessary that students learn programming languages. It is valuable, however, to understand something about programming languages and how they can benefit students in their own language growth. Instead of just responding to software created by others, students can learn to control the computer and to teach it to do what they want — using it as *tutee.* Writing their own programs, students develop thinking skills that involve problem solving. Students also learn to take risks and to accept making mistakes as part of problem solving. Furthermore, they experience procedural thinking and sequential organization of ideas.

There are currently four popular languages that are useful in education: Logo, PILOT, BASIC, and Pascal. Each one has certain characteristics that make it useful in particular learning situations. Wayne Harvey (1984) identifies four characteristics that point out a language's advantages and disadvantages. First, a language can be *interactive,* allowing the user to "talk" to the computer and get immediate feedback. Second, a language can be *modular:* Each idea is expressed as a separate piece of a program, and the pieces are later used as building blocks of large programs. Third, a language is *extensible* if a programmer can create new commands that extend the language and make it grow. Using available commands, the programmer can define other concepts and thus make the concept part of the usable commands. Lastly, a language is *recursive* if it allows parts of a concept to recur or to be called up for use elsewhere. A recursive procedure calls *itself* up somewhere in a procedure.

The Logo language has all of the above characteristics, making it very useful for beginning computer programmers to develop computer awareness and learn problem solving. Logo allows ideas to be created, tested, and

changed very easily because it is so very interactive. Because it is a procedural language, Logo allows the user to create larger concepts that are
made up of smaller ones or modules. Logo contains existing commands
(called "primitives") that the programmer can use to define new concepts,
which then become part of the language. No other language combines all
of these characteristics.

PILOT, a tool used for language processing by teachers to create lessons
and educational materials, is also very interactive, but it is not extensible
by the programmer. It is modular, too, but does not have the flexibility
of Logo when the pieces are put together. PILOT is easy to learn; it uses
ten simple English-language-related commands. It is useful more in CMI
applications than in CAI, as it is limited in its desirable characteristics.

BASIC is used primarily in solving computational problems. Of the four
characteristics previously listed, BASIC has only the characteristic of being interactive. This allows the programmer to test parts of a program on
a limited basis. The programmer does develop computer awareness in using
this language.

The fourth language, Pascal, is neither interactive nor extensible. A more
sophisticated language, it is used to solve complex problems. It is recursive and modular, but it does not get quick solutions to minor problems,
as does Logo.

Logo may be taught to students at any age level. It may be extremely
simple or very complex. Logo uses turtle graphics to solve spatial, geometric,
and graphic designs. These graphics may be used to illustrate student writing
or to inspire and motivate writing. Besides the turtle graphics, Logo also
uses naming or string variables such as words and lists that students may
create in order to generate poetry or interesting, randomly created sentences.

For our purposes in teaching language processing in reading and writing,
we should understand the list processing capabilities of Logo. Logo is based
on a language called LISP, which was designed to manipulate lists or series
of words. Having students generate lists of words, and then design a simple program that randomly selects from the lists provided, can help them
create poetry and learn that sentence parts can be manipulated for interesting
effects. William Wresch (1985) explains a simple Logo procedure for designing lists that students can play with. Using software such as "Apple Logo,"
students type in these commands:

```
MAKE "NOUNLIST [ car tree Fred Igloo snake lawn classroom ]
MAKE "VERBLIST [ walked drove wiggled calibrated opportuned ]
MAKE "ADJLIST [ sweet hairy discreet ramshackle headstrong ]
MAKE "ADVLIST [ immediately momentarily hoarsely tidily
                automatically ]
MAKE "ARTICLELIST [ a the ]
```

Students may type such lists, choosing *their own words* and having fun with
the different options of language. Once they have created the lists, they
use them to create sentences that the program randomly selects for interesting

effect. Have students type in the following commands (Wresch, 1985) to create the sentences:

```
TO PICKRANDOM :X
OUTPUT ITEM (1+RANDOM COUNT :X) :X
END

TO ARTICLE
OUTPUT PICKRANDOM :ARTICLELIST
END
TO ADJECTIVE
OUTPUT PICKRANDOM :ADJLIST
END
TO ADVERB
OUTPUT PICKRANDOM :ADVLIST
END
TO NOUN
OUTPUT PICKRANDOM :NOUNLIST
END
TO VERB
OUTPUT PICKRANDOM :VERBLIST
END

TO SENTENCE1
OUTPUT (SENTENCE ARTICLE ADJECTIVE NOUN VERB ADVERB)
END
```

The parts of speech commands above tell Logo to select at random one of the words from the appropriate list. The last command tells it the order in which the randomly selected words should be presented; in other words, it determines how the sentence order will present the words. The results can be very surprising and creative, offering new ways to look at things — which is the object of poetry. Using this program can help students to understand parts of speech and sentence structure and to build vocabulary. Students may also change the sentence order in the last command to get other results. As Wresch points out, this is just the beginning of what Logo list processing is capable of teaching students about their language. It is up to the teacher to explore these possibilities in greater depth.

TOY: Simulations

The broadest definition of a simulation is *an imitation of reality*. This type of instruction originated during World War II, as a way of training military personnel. McGuire et al. (1976) extend the broad definition to include three important criteria for a simulation as it pertains to instruction:

1. It involves a realistic setting in which students are presented with a problem.
2. It presents students with opportunities for inquiries, actions, and decisions.
3. It provides the students with information about how their actions change the way the situation evolves.

The best simulations allow students to be in control of events that are realistic, making decisions with consequences that teach them actual, probable outcomes they may face later in real life. The emphasis is on problem solving, which develops thinking skills for later use in related situations. In order to select valuable simulations, teachers should know what types are available in educational software.

Margaret Bell Gredler's characterizations of types of computer simulations are included here (see Figure 3-11) to help teachers evaluate the ones on the market. She addresses three major issues in her classifications: nature of the basic situation, use of graphics and visual displays, and kind of instructional process used. She identifies four distinct types of simulations that differ in these three issues. The first is the "structured questions and graphics" simulation. This type may be drill and practice or tutorial, offering a simulated situation about which the student then has to answer a series of questions. The second is the "variable-assignment exercises" simulation.

Figure 3-11   Criteria for classification of computer exercises (from Gredler, "A Taxonomy of Computer Simulations," *Educational Technology*, April, 1986. Reprinted with permission of the publisher)

I. Nature of the basic situation presented to the student
   1. A set of specific exercises or problems, each requiring a particular answer.
   2. Problems or situations that require experimentation to find the correct solution.
   3. A continuing situation that includes two or more variables that may take on different values.
   4. A complex, real world problem that takes new directions in response to student input.
II. Use of visuals and data
   A. Lesson presentation
      1. Graphic (or visual) demonstration of a specific item (or items).
      2. Visual presentation of a real-world problem (EX: thief holding up a store).
      3. Graphic or tabular presentation of a set of data.
   B. Feedback to student
      1. Identifies right and wrong answers.
      2. Provides clues to errors in student's selected strategy.
      3. Identifies outcomes of student's assignment of values to variables.
      4. Describes new directions that follow student input.
III. Nature of the instructional process
   1. Solve a set of discrete, specific problems.
   2. Identify new examples of concepts or rules.
   3. Discover the optimum strategy to solve a problem.
   4. Discover the random set of values identified as optimum for two or more variables.
   5. Implement the knowledge acquired in a particular subject or professional area.

This type is more flexible, allowing students more options in choosing values for the variables presented. Continuous feedback informs students of the correctness of their solutions and guides their next decisions. The third type is "diagnostic simulations," which present students with realistic problems in a particular area of expertise, such as medical diagnosis or criminal investigation. The students' decisions are compared to the optimum in real situations. The last type of simulation is the "group-interactive," which uses roles related to job functions. This type provides the greatest flexibility in decision-making, involving community or international problem situations that students must develop plans and strategies to solve.

Knowing the type of a simulation leads the teacher to ask the necessary questions regarding its instructional use. The first question concerns the nature of the basic situation presented to students. What should the teacher look for in the exercises that are of instructional value to students? Gredler presents the following criteria:

1. A set of specific exercises or problems, each requiring a particular answer.
2. Problems or situations that require experimentation to find the correct solution.
3. A continuing situation that includes two or more variables that may take on different values.
4. A complex, real-world problem that takes new directions in response to student input.

The teacher may analyze a computer simulation in order to find which criteria fit the type to be used. In the list above, the first is a drill and practice type, the second is a tutorial, the third is a variable assignment, and the fourth is a diagnostic/interactive simulation. The criteria should fit the type of simulation selected to be used in instruction.

In order to ask the second question regarding instructional value, the teacher needs to evaluate the way the lesson is presented and the kind of feedback students will experience. The lesson presentation can demonstrate reality, graphically present it, or represent it in tables or charts. The teacher needs to decide which is best for the learning to take place. Then the feedback to students should be analyzed: It may simply identify right and wrong answers, or it may provide clues to errors. Further, the feedback may identify outcomes of students' choices, or it may describe new directions that follow student input. A simulation can employ any of these four kinds of feedback, and the teacher should evaluate the simulation for the effectiveness of its feedback.

Lastly, the teacher needs to understand the nature of the instructional process the simulation employs by asking the following questions, according to the criteria suggested by Gredler:

1. Do students solve a set of discrete, specific problems?
2. Do they identify new examples of concepts or rules?

3. Are they presented with an optimum strategy to solve a problem?
4. Do they discover random sets of values identified as optimum for two or more variables?
5. Are students given the opportunity to implement the knowledge acquired in a particular subject or professional area?

Analyzing computer simulations for these three instructional issues (the basic situation presented, the use of graphics and feedback, and how students learn) helps the teacher decide how the simulation is to be used and how it will affect student learning.

A popular example of an instructional simulation is "Oregon Trail" by MECC, which will be analyzed here to illustrate use of Gredler's criteria. "Oregon Trail" is a variable-assignment simulation in which students assign values to variables that are repeated throughout the program. It presents a continuing situation that includes numerous variables, which take on different values. The feedback continuously identifies the outcomes of students' choices of values, which will help them make future decisions. Its instructional process teaches students to discover "along the trail" the set of values identified as optimum for the variables. In "Oregon Trail," students are constantly solving the life-and-death problems presented by the perilous situations.

As the manual states, "The primary intent of the simulation is to particularize events and details that will suggest the broader experience of not one, but many overland journeys." Four options on the main menu give students this simulated experience. The first is to travel the trail that is the actual adventure. The second is an overview of what lies ahead on the trail; students are asked questions that help prepare them for making decisions along the trail. These questions can stimulate student discussions and motivate them to begin pondering the problems of survival. The third option displays the names, point scores, and ratings of the "Oregon Top Ten," those students who have earned enough points to qualify as survivors. Students can reach this list by accumulating points along the way for state of health, resources left, and value of occupation in the new land. This feature makes the simulation a game with comprehensible stakes, which student groups in "wagon teams" can play to win. The final option controls the sound with the CONTROL and S function keys. An important feature is that the sound can be turned off or on throughout the program; distractions need to be controlled in classroom environments.

Students are asked to make a number of decisions when they begin to travel the trail. The first is the occupation they choose — whether a banker, a carpenter, or a farmer. Different points are awarded and varying advantages are given for each occupation, but the decision is up to the student or group of students. Next, students are to choose a leader for their "wagon team" by entering the name into the program. Up to four other people may be on the team. The next decision is the month the team decides to travel from the starting point in Independence, Missouri. Students may ask for advice by pressing Option 6; they are then told the advantages and disadvantages of leaving at a certain time. Then students must decide on the purchase of equipment and supplies with the amount of money allotted to them. At the general store, they are given a list of supplies and their costs. The team must make budgeting and supply decisions that will affect their eventual survival. The dialogue becomes highly interactive; the store owner gives advice and quotes prices, and the students respond as they make their purchases.

As they set out on the trail, students are given a report on the state of the weather, their health, and other items. They are given such options as checking supplies, looking at the map, and talking to other people. When they choose to "talk to people," they receive gossipy, hearsay reports that help to shape their decisions as they go along. As each team reaches certain destinations, they are asked to size up their situation and reflect on it. They encounter river crossings, illnesses, death, and other perils, and must think of how to solve these problems of basic survival at every turn.

The graphics are outstanding throughout the program. There are twenty-two full-color graphics (a color monitor is not required, but it should be used if available), based on paintings, lithographs, and photographs of the locations. The sound option uses actual melodies that were popular by 1848 and sung along the trail.

With this program, students improve their understanding of the hardships and problems the pioneers faced. They grow in problem-solving ability as they make decisions and adjust their thinking in order to survive the perils. Students can do supplemental research on what they experience, engage in related reading, make calculations for budgets, and write about what they encounter in a diary, letter, or journal. The program can be a dynamic catalyst for stimulating many language activities across the content areas of art, English, social studies, and math. Best of all, as a "toy" application, it can be great fun and a memorable adventure.

TOY: *Interactive Fiction and Text Adventures*

The most important feature of interactive fiction is involvement of the reader in shaping the plot and exploring new and different worlds. The reader actually becomes one of the characters, making decisions about events and outcomes, actively involved in the story development. This is in sharp contrast to the linear narrative in a book, where plot, characters, and setting are predetermined solely by the writer. Traditional stories in books are written in the first or the third person, whereas interactive fiction on the computer is presented as second person singular. The story, of course, is limited to what the author of the software has written, and the readers' responses are restricted to what has been programmed. However, different readers make different responses, so each story can be fresh and original — in effect, a collaboration between author and reader that results in a totally unique story. With interactive fiction, readers can develop a more active understanding of characterization, plot sequences, and setting as a manipulatable environment.

Just what kinds of skills this type of fiction develops in readers is not understood yet, but interactive fiction has potential for getting to the different learning modalities of students. Students who are more kinesthetic in their learning definitely would benefit by reading literature presented in this way. Also, visual skills are required as readers form visual images of clues, locations, objects, and so forth, as they predict and track events in a story. The logic used in these stories is not linear, so students develop other ways to think, mostly in patterns and synthesis of the information they must use to advance toward their goals in the story. This opportunity may revolutionize the ways students learn to process information and to understand literary forms.

Interactive fiction had its beginnings in the first adventure game, called "Adventure," created at Stanford University for a mainframe computer. In the 1970s, "Dungeons and Dragons" helped develop the field of role-playing fantasies in computer versions based on the board games. These early adventure games stressed conflict, violence, and conquest. Now the emphasis is more on cooperation among characters (the reader included) and introspection about one's plight and circumstances. Because accomplished authors such as Ray Bradbury and Arthur C. Clarke have written some of this interactive fiction, the stories have become more complex and of higher quality. The major aim is problem solving. Readers distinguish important details from irrelevant ones, look for patterns, and combine details to fit the larger framework.

The terms *interactive fiction* and *text adventure* are presented together in this section because they are related. Text adventures have the features of interactive fiction but take this educational application one step further. A text adventure is a search for information and knowledge rather than an attempt to conquer or to win something. Student experience in text adventures can be educationally valuable, particularly in teaching skills for research and use of reference materials.

An example of one of the best interactive fiction/text adventures is Broderbund's "Where in the World is Carmen Sandiego?" This program comes with a full-sized World Almanac and Facts book that students have to use as a resource and reference to solve crimes that Carmen and her band of V.I.L.E. (Villians' International Legion of Evil) fugitives commit. Furthermore, students have to consult police dossiers, maps, and the Crime Computer (all included) for facts, clues, and information pertinent to each case, thus interrelating the skills of reading, thinking, and sleuthing.

After an animated introduction, the diskette is turned over to Side B.

Students enter one of their names into the Crime Computer and are asked if they are new to the Interpol files. If so, they are given the rank of Rookie in playing the game. There are five ranks in all, increasing in difficulty up to Ace Detective. As students' problem-solving abilities improve, they go to different levels to solve increasingly complex "crimes." In each case, students must use clues provided along the way. A crime is identified, the location in the world pinpointed, and the suspect is hinted at. Then the player is given the assignment to track down and arrest the criminal. The sound is controlled through the CONTROL S function keys.

As students "arrive" at their destinations, one of thirty cities around the world, the languages spoken there are identified. For example, in Kigali the official languages are French and Kinyarwandu, but many people speak Swahili, students are told. Four options on the menu help students track down the suspect. The first, "See connections," lists all possible destinations reached by connecting flights from the scene of the crime. Students should research these in the Almanac for characteristics such as the color of the flag and the type of currency, when clues appear. The second option is "Depart by plane," which provides travel options in tracking the criminal from city to city. The third option is "Investigate," which provides three locations in the city to gather clues. The last option is "Visit Interpol," in which students narrow down their choices based on the clues they have gathered and try to solve the case. If they enter the right clues into the Crime Computer, they are issued an arrest warrant and win the game.

The factual information provided in the adventure and the wealth of information given to students in their research can be very valuable in expanding their worlds, their points of view, and their concepts of their place on this planet. Besides this richness, students can cooperate with each other and pool information as they learn. This is no mere game, but an interesting, active process for developing research skills and problem-solving abilities. Students engage in analysis of clues, synthesis of the information accumulated, and logical induction leading to the identification of the suspect. The text adventure format promotes personal involvement, with sleuthing pride at stake as the students race against the deadlines imposed on them by Acme Detective Agency. They are not stuck in a competitive goal structure for learning and playing this game; they must cooperate with each other, not compete, in order to solve the crime most efficiently. This structure is a radical departure from most other interactive fiction and role-playing formats.

This program can lead to exciting spinoffs into writing. Students may write character sketches of the seamy, degenerate V.I.L.E. suspects, using colorful adjectives and vivid verbs. They may write a police report, casting themselves as the detective in the case, or draw a "Wanted" poster and description to hang in the post office. They may combine a geography lesson and map drawing with a story or study the history of an interesting city. Students could also be led to read related literature and texts beyond the game itself, such as *The Adventures of Sherlock Holmes*. The programs can be used to cross content fields such as foreign languages, art, geography, history, literature, and economics. The educational implications and potential of this program are vast. Besides this, it is great fun for people of all ages, especially from upper elementary to adult. It can be used for individuals for enrichment, for groups to develop interpersonal skills and cooperation, and for an entire class as a springboard to transfer activities.

The "toy" applications in education have great potential for motivating students to engage in reading and writing. Beyond motivation, they have value in teaching thinking skills and problem solving. William V. Costanzo (1986) raises the question of how interactive fiction is changing the meaning of reader response. It is "redefining the relationship between the reader and the text," as he sees it, and he cautions educators to "watch closely as this relationship evolves." In a carefully planned curriculum that uses this type of literature, the teacher must be aware of its effects on student learning. It might be revealing to compare its results with use of traditional literature.

Future Trends

The educational applications of software, classified according to Taylor's four categories, have been described and exemplified by the best software available at the moment, in this author's opinion. This procedure has been followed not to promote any particular piece of courseware, but only to provide an example of the criteria developed for each type. The purpose is to help teachers make more informed choices about the software they select and to provide some direction for what is desirable in future development of the different applications. Certainly we educators have to be impressed with the great variety of educational materials available for the computer. It is up to us to make informed and wise decisions about how they are to be used with learners.

The evolution is by no means finished. Bitter and Gore (1985/86) describe the use of robots in teaching children to read and write in a second grade classroom. The children created a story and then had it retold to them by Topo, a humanoid robot created by a firm in San Jose, California. The process involved preparation, implementation, and application in our reading/writing model, and there was the potential for the robot to make concrete this abstract process. Use of robots can teach and emphasize the skills of following directions, predicting, and sequencing, among others. As Bitter and Gore point out, "Robots are an extension of computer technology and offer engaging and effective means of enriching the curriculum as well as teaching and reinforcing skills and concepts." This is one trend for the future of education.

Another trend is the sophisticated use of sound and graphics. The new

Apple IIGS is an indication of this direction. Voice synthesis systems have particularly exciting potential. Voice synthesis produces computerized imitations of the human voice, in female, male, or neuter versions. The uses of these systems range from oral feedback to reinforcement to assisting students with speech difficulties or hearing impairment. William J. Harvey (1986) sees the current limitations of this technology as a lack of memory capabilities for storing extensive vocabularies and the lack of standardization in the hardware needed to use them. Future systems, he says, will have more sophisticated automatic control of the quality of speech. Harvey concludes that video discs will help to integrate the systems and make all of them more usable for instructional purposes.

Many trends may be detected in the future, but there is one in particular that requires some comment: the technology of video discs. Because a laser beam is used to record and read data, video discs are also called laser discs. This technology is the most interactive of all. It allows the students to watch a visual program and interrupt it to get more information. Students ask questions, make decisions, enter answers, and are in control of the pace and nature of their own learning. The way this works is that a computer program is written to make use of a touch screen and a wide variety of choices from the student. The video disc adds the visual display, including photographs, video sequences, and recorded sounds. A video disc player expands the computer's functions and instructional capabilities. Judy Salpeter (1986) details its qualities: It provides excellent visual quality; it has the ability to mix still frames and video; and its random access capabilities make it an important alternative to movies, filmstrips, and slides. At the present time, video discs are not used extensively in education, despite their tremendous potential. Estimates are that fewer than 10,000 video disc players exist in K-12 schools. The biggest reason is that the prerecorded discs are still too expensive to produce, requiring almost a professional movie crew: a lighting crew, photographers, camera operators, and actors. This technology is definitely one that educators want to watch in the future. With such possibilities, it is clear that teaching in the future need never be dull.

References

Allen, Vaikko. "Software: Side by Side." *Electronic Learning,* April, 1985, pp. 52–53.

Bitter, Gary, and Camuse, Ruth. *Using a Microcomputer in the Classroom.* Reston, Va.: Reston Publishing, 1984.

Bitter, Gary G., and Gore, Kay. "Robots in the Classroom: Another of Tomorrow's Teaching Tools Today." *Computers in the Schools,* 2(4), Winter, 1985/86, pp. 15–21.

Boudrot, Thomas. "The Magical Typewriter." *Electronic Learning,* February, 1985, pp. 84–85.

Costanzo, William V. "Reading Interactive Fiction: Implications of a New Literary Genre." *Educational Technology,* June, 1986, pp. 31–35.

Daiute, Colette, "Computers and the Teaching of Writing." In *Intelligent School House* (Peterson, Dale, Ed.). Reston, Va.: Reston Publishing, 1984.

Dennis, J. Richard. "The Question Episode — Building Block of Teaching with a Computer." Illinois Series on Educational Application of Computers, No. 4. Champaign, Ill.: University of Illinois, 1979.

Grabe, Mark. "Drill and Practice's Bad Rap." *Electronic Learning,* February, 1986.

Gredler, Margaret Bell. "A Taxonomy of Computer Simulations." *Educational Technology,* April, 1986, pp. 7–12.

Harrod, N., and Ruggles, M. "Computer-Assisted Instruction: An Educational Tool." *Focus on Exceptional Children,* September, 1983.

Harvey, Wayne. "Which Programming Language Is Right for You?" *Classroom Computer Learning,* April/May, 1984, pp. 51–53.

Harvey, William J. "Voice Synthesis; A New Technology Comes to School." *Electronic Learning,* 1986, pp. 68–73.

Hedges, William D. *Computers in the Schools.* New York: Haworth Press, 1984, pp. 91–100.

Howell, Richard D., and Scott, Patrick B. *Microcomputer Applications for Teachers.* Scottsdale, Ariz.: Gorsuch Scarisbrick, 1985.

Kepner, Henry S., Jr. (Ed.). *Computers in the Classroom.* Washington, D.C.: NEA Professional Library, 1982.

Kovacs, Deborah. "Turning First Drafts into Final Drafts." *Classroom Computer Learning,* October, 1986, pp. 36–39.

Marcus, Stephen. "Computers in the Curriculum." *Electronic Learning,* October, 1984, pp. 54–58.

McGuire, C., Solomon, L., and Bashook, P. *Construction and Use of Written Simulation.* New York: Psychological Corp., 1976.

Papert, Seymour. *Mindstorms: Children, Computers and Powerful Ideas.* New York: Holt, Rinehart and Winston, 1972.

Pattison, Linda. "Software Writing Made Easy." *Electronic Learning,* March, 1985, pp. 30–36.

Salpeter, Judy. "Interactive Video: The Truth Behind the Promises." *Classroom Computer Learning,* November/December, 1986.

Shalvoy, Mary Lee. "Use an Electronic Gradebook." *Electronic Learning,* November/December, 1985, pp. 26–29.

Taylor, Robert P. (Ed.). *The Computer in the School: Tutor, Tool, Tutee.* New York: Teachers College Press, 1980.

Wresch, William. "Using Logo to Teach Writing and Literary Skills." *The Computing Teacher,* August/September, 1985, pp. 24–26.

Practical Designs for Integrating the Computer

Teachers using the computer to design instruction

This chapter gives practical suggestions for integrating the computer into all levels of a school system. Starting with an overview of national use, it looks at ways the school district can plan integration. From the district, integration has to be planned on the school level and then within the classroom itself. There follows a discussion of issues that every educator must face in planning the integration of computers into effective curricula. The suggestions made and the ideas offered are of a very practical nature. Chapter 5 continues this practical approach; it provides lesson plans that the classroom teacher may use, modify, or adapt to integrate the use of computers in the curriculum.

Instructional Uses

According to a 1985 national survey by the Center for Social Organization of Schools (Becker, 1986), 90 percent of children in U.S. schools attended schools having at least one computer. The typical school reported a ratio of approximately one computer to every forty students. A conservative estimate is that to provide thirty minutes of computer time to every student daily, a school would need to have one computer for every twelve students. As of 1985, only 7 percent of high schools and 2–3 percent of elementary and middle schools in the United States had such a favorable ratio. Use by students varied at different levels; nearly half the elementary and middle school students used computers at school, compared to one-third of all high school students. Even though the number of students using computers decreased as students got older, the length of time an individual spent with the computer increased. The typical elementary student has about thirty-five minutes per week of computer time, compared to an hour and forty-five minutes per week for the high school user. Evidently, the older the students get, the more selective and specialized is their computer use, and the more time is needed to practice the specialty.

Accordingly, the survey found that instructional use differs greatly from the elementary to high school level. More than half of computer use in elementary school is for computer-assisted instruction, particularly drill and practice and tutorials. High school students, on the other hand, spend half their computer time on programming. Across all grade levels, about one-third of the time is spent on CAI, one-third for programming, and the remaining third for other work such as word processing.

Computer use by teachers was also reported. About one-fourth of all teachers in U.S. schools use computers regularly with students. A higher proportion of elementary teachers (37 percent) use computers than high school teachers (15 percent), but the number of teachers at each school (five per school) tended to be constant at each level.

A survey of states, taken in 1986 by the journal *Electronic Learning*

(Reinhold, 1986), found that computer use in schools had gained solid state-level support and funding in all but three states. The trend was toward more spending at state and district levels, particularly for software and teacher training. Forty-three states reported having a state-level computer coordinator. The major thrust in education was in efforts to *integrate* computers throughout curriculum areas and grade levels. Accordingly, instead of mandating that students take computer courses, the prevailing policy was toward use of the computer wherever it fit. As of the 1986 survey, seven states and the District of Columbia required all teachers in the state or those in teacher training to take computer courses for certification. Fourteen states officially recommended computer courses for teacher certification, and thirty-one provided assistance to universities or students for computer training. Lastly, forty states reported that they provided in-service training to teachers who were already certified.

The 1987 survey of the states showed a "widespread interest in and commitment to technology." The overwhelming concern was for computer *integration* into the traditional curriculum. Budgets for teacher training and for software were up over the previous year's survey, and 44 percent of the nation's school districts had a computer coordinator. The number of microcomputers in the schools had increased by 18 percent in one year. The conclusion of the survey was that the benefits of computers, both for learning and for teaching, were shown "to be alive and well in America."

Such national reports are helpful as barometers against which local schools can compare their own circumstances, both within their state and nationwide.

Planning for Computer Use in the District

The first step in planning computer integration into a curriculum is an assessment of needs within the school district. Ideally, the planning should follow a top-down model that is systematic and takes into account the overview of needs and finances available. When the overall district needs are understood, planning in each school may follow an orderly process that puts into action the plans of the district. From the assessment of needs, educators may begin the planning process, which includes the resources indicated in Figure 4-1.

Each of the areas of resource should be tapped for input to planning. Key people in each area should form a planning committee to assess needs in each area, working toward developing a comprehensive district plan for computers in instruction. The information gathered through assessment of each area is used as essential background data for developing the plan.

Figure 4-1   Assessment input (courtesy of Jennifer Better House)

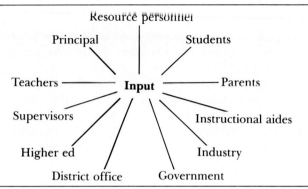

The most important data concerns the following population groups within the school settings:

1. *Student needs* for scholastic growth, diverse learning tools, and development of skills necessary for communication with society and future employment
2. *Teacher needs* for diverse instructional tools and management of instruction
3. *Administrative needs* for management, district-wide and within schools

After these prime needs are assessed by the planning committee, a course of action is established. It follows the process from developing a rationale through later modification, as indicated in Figure 4-2.

The rationale for computer use should be rooted in the overall educational philosophy of the district. A philosophy for use of computers should involve carefully considered principles, including the following:

1. Computers should be integrated as a learning tool in carefully planned curricula.
2. Computers are helpful tools in some learning circumstances, unnecessary in others. Careful concern should be given to the best tool in each circumstance.
3. Use of computers should help free teachers for more productive, quality time with students by relieving them of some management tedium.
4. An effective plan for computer use requires sufficient district resources to support the curriculum plans and faculty development.
5. There must be adequate staff development programs — both introductory courses and continuing in-service training for teachers.
6. Teachers must have computers available to practice on and to become acquainted with the diverse ways computers can be used for their instructional purposes.
7. Constant updating and awareness of changes in information technology are important, in order to gain the most from the computer's potential.
8. Computer education should be considered a basic skill requirement for all students in a district.

Figure 4-2   Developing a course of action (reprinted from *Instructional Computer Use in Education K–12,* p. 13, with permission of the Wisconsin Department of Public Instruction, 125 South Webster St., Madison, WI 53703)

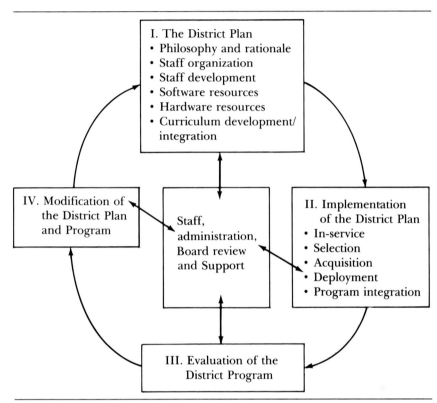

Development of the district philosophy requires an understanding of the potential computers have in education. Potential computer uses are so diverse that they should be visualized for all the services they can provide to a district. Besides being useful in instruction, computers can and should be used for administrative needs. The district's philosophy of potential use should encompass the wide range of uses detailed in Figure 4-3.

One of the most important functions of the planning committee is to devise specific plans for each section of the model for computers in instruction. The plan should be the guide that provides effective integration of technology. The Computer Education component involves making a scope and sequence progression (K–12) for introducing learning about the computer: its history, operation, and uses for problem solving. The Computer-Aided Learning section gives plans for crossing content-area instruction and for recognizing the many instructional techniques available in software.

Figure 4-3 Planning for uses of computers (reprinted from *Instructional Computer Use in Education K–12,* p. 11, with permission of the Wisconsin Department of Public Instruction, 125 South Webster St., Madison, WI 53703)

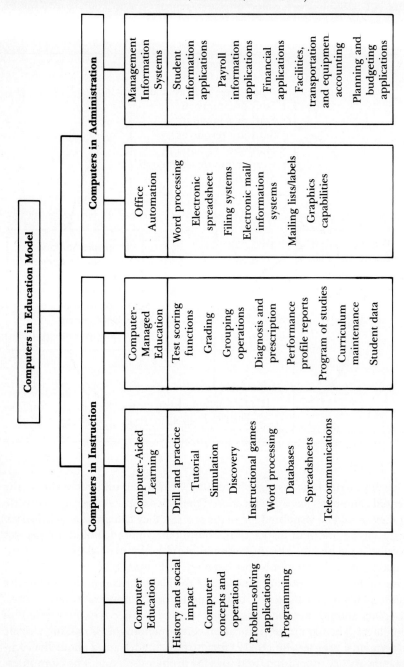

It also provides for transfer of computer skills to the "real world" in problem solving and occupations. The section on Computer-Managed Instruction requires planning for the necessary amount of staff training, as well as continuous evaluation of the plans to make sure they are meeting instructional needs. Finally, the model asks for a specified amount of time needed for district-wide implementation of the plans. A pilot-project should then be developed to implement the plan, testing it on a small scale before it goes district-wide.

Implementation of the Plan

The development of staff is crucial to putting the plan into action. Educational innovations have often failed because of lack of adequate training for teachers and staff. Training may be given individually, in small groups, or school-wide. Various opportunities should be provided for the training and incentives given or rewards offered for any person or group being trained. Such opportunities may be in the following forms:

In-service

University courses

Summer workshops

Attendance at conventions

Consultations with experts and experienced people

In order to motivate faculty to take part in such opportunities, the district needs to take two primary actions. First, make sure that enough computers are available for teachers to practice on. Ideally, teachers should be able to check out a computer and take it home, where they can comfortably practice and explore its advantages. Using the computer at home will do a great deal toward relieving the anxiety and stress associated with new technology. The summer would be an ideal time for teachers to take home computers. The machines need to be kept at a cool temperature, so home use would reduce the need for air conditioning in schoolrooms during the summer. At the very least, computers should be available on campus all day during teachers' preparation times. Secondly, teachers should be granted release time, stipends, college credit, or other incentives in order to get them started on curriculum changes brought about by computers.

Teachers and staff should be trained and involved in evaluating software for potential purchase. Each content area should have a selection staff of three or four people who review software and share their findings with other members of their department. Software can be shared across content areas and used in team-teaching plans. It is important to establish communication across departments. One suggestion for sharing software reviews within and across departments is to set up a small file system in an accessible place, perhaps the library or media center. The reviews may be filed by content areas, by functions, or by instructional techniques, such as drill and practice or games. When teachers review a new program, they should use a concise, standardized review form that has been developed by teachers specifically for the needs of the school. (See Chapter 6.)

All the software purchased by the district should be categorized and classified, just like other media resources. The district librarian should compile updated catalogs of the software and send them out to all the schools in the district for their information. Teachers in the schools should then be able to check out the software for certain time periods. Centralized cataloging is necessary to prevent duplication of purchases and to monitor the growth of the collection. This practice would tend to cut down on theft and loss and to assure easy inventory. Teachers and staff from the schools should also be able to recommend purchases to the district when they find important new software. There should be an avenue through which teachers can easily make such recommendations.

Purchases of hardware are determined through the initial needs assessments of the district. It should first be determined what already exists from school to school, what brands the computers are and whether they are compatible with each other, and what kinds of software they use. The district needs assessment should answer the following concerns:

1. What are the immediate and future needs for computers, in relation to student enrollments and projections of enrollments? What short- and long-term ratios of computers to students are being considered?
2. What specific educational applications of computers are important for schools, elementary through high school?
3. What software is available for the brands of computers already in the schools and those being considered for purchase? Is it the most appropriate software for the instructional needs of the district?
4. What are the costs of upgrading memory and adding peripherals to existing hardware in the district? Does the memory of the existing hardware match the memory requirements of the software to be purchased?
5. Which computer language should be taught to high school students? Does this language already exist in the computers available and those being considered for purchase? What is the expense of other languages?
6. What ratio of printers to computers currently exists in the district? What are the desired ratios for the short term and the long term?
7. What funding sources exist that should be tapped for purchasing additional hardware? Will the state provide funding? Are federal sources available? Will local businesses help provide funding?

Initial purchase of hardware is only the beginning of the necessary expenditure. Besides the software that must be bought for it, there are the matters of insurance and security measures for the equipment. The equipment should be carefully inventoried and visibly, indelibly labeled. Costs of security need to be figured into the continuing costs of maintenance and upkeep of the hardware, as with any other audio-visual equipment.

For the use of the computers and software on a district-wide basis, there should be a scope and sequence that fulfills the objectives of computer use. In terms of reading and writing, the focus of this book, the scope and sequence should aim to develop student skills systematically, progressing from simpler to more complex composing and information-managing tasks. The computer is used to facilitate the tasks as students mature in their language skills. The best way to educate students about technology is to integrate it into the curriculum rather than making it a separate course. Especially in teaching the processes of reading and writing, where technologies such as books, films, paper and pencils are used, the computer can be introduced as another tool for processing information. Use of the computer need not be bound to specific grade levels, although there are some preliminary skills that should be taught sequentially. For example, skills such as keyboarding are generally taught in elementary school, preliminary to or concurrent with word processing.

Teaching reading and writing is teaching students to compose and to manage information for communication purposes. Therefore, the scope and sequence for teaching the processes via computer should include the following activities that deal with composing and learning management of information, in the following approximate sequence:

Grades 4–6

Composing

Identify the main idea and supporting details in a paragraph

Begin to make outlines with composition prompters

Experiment with writing sentences and combining them using a word processor

Use interactive story adventures to learn plot structure and characterization

Practice spelling in context

Develop new vocabulary using cloze exercises and story adventures

Use drill and practice programs for grammar reinforcement

Information Management

Develop data files of new vocabulary words found in reading and print them out for the class

Collect information on a topic and organize it using a database format

Grades 7–9

Composing

Practice writing outlines

Identify main ideas and supporting details in a paragraph

Write an autobiography using a word processor and print it out

Revise poorly written examples of language using a style checker

Use interactive story adventures to learn plot and characterization and to predict story outcomes

Use text adventures and simulations to develop use of reference materials and resources

Practice spelling words in context

Use new vocabulary in cloze exercises and student-generated puzzles

Begin a class or school newspaper using newspaper computer programs and graphics packages

Use drill and practice programs to reinforce learning of grammar and language

Information Management

Organize a data file of outside reading books read by the class

Develop a data bank of new vocabulary words found in reading

Collect information on a topic found in encyclopedias and organize it using a database format

Interpret line, pie, and bar graphs and write paragraphs explaining them

Grades 10-12

Composing

Develop outlines in depth using outline programs

Identify main ideas and supporting details in longer texts, perhaps a chapter and a full-length book

Write book reviews that explain the theme using a word processor

Write a critique of a movie, providing reasons for recommending or not recommending it

Write a short story with several different endings

Predict different outcomes for a simulation

Role play and write about experiences in a simulation

Write to several different audiences on a topic, adjusting language use and vocabulary accordingly

Practice spelling in context

Correct mechanical errors in writing using a spelling checker and style analyzer

Develop new vocabulary using cloze exercises and analogy and word relationship vocabulary programs

Publish a class or school newspaper using a computer newspaper program and graphics packages

Use grammar programs for enrichment or remediation

Information Management

Survey reading preferences of class members and organize the data into a spreadsheet; calculate the results, create a graph and report the findings

Research information on a topic from several sources; organize it using a data file system; compare and contrast information found from the various sources

Such a scope and sequence for integrating computers and the variety of software for teaching language processing presents practical ideas for teachers. The school district should identify specific software programs by title for teachers' use in implementing the activities, and the district must make sure there is enough hardware and software for all schools. Every school should be equipped with at least the necessary minimum — a word processor, a database system, and a spreadsheet — to be used in instruction. The district plans should provide for hardware and software adequate to fulfill the scope and sequence they envision for integrating technology into the curriculum.

Evaluation of the District Plan

The district must consider several problematic areas in order to evaluate its plans. Questions regarding the problems each area presents will have to be raised, then the ways the plan addresses each problem must be assessed. The categories discussed below are suggested by Marilyn Gardner (1986), in describing the computer curriculum developed by Boston Public Schools. Using these categories as a guide, the school district should add to the list of problem areas during a continuing evaluation of the plan:

Curriculum

1. Does the planned curriculum account for differences in teachers' backgrounds and training?
2. How does the plan help teachers change traditional ways of teaching and presenting materials?
3. Does teacher retraining account for teachers' needs to reorganize and restructure their materials and techniques in order to use innovation?
4. Has the new curriculum clearly specified where computers fit into instruction?

Professional Development

1. Has the plan provided incentives for teachers to change their methods of instruction? Are the motivators effective?
2. How is release time provided for teachers to engage in retraining?
3. Are the leaders in technological innovation recognized and rewarded in order to avoid "burnout" and ensure continued support for the plan?
4. Are provisions made for keeping qualified staff once they are trained in using technology?

Software

1. Is there provision for teachers to be involved in helping develop software for district needs?
2. What is the vehicle or communication channel for teachers and staff to recommend software purchases to the district library? How effective is it?
3. Is there an adequate checkout system for teachers to use the district software? Is there enough software for checkout and prolonged use?
4. Is the variety sufficient for varied instructional purposes? Is the software up to date?

Economics

1. Have all possible sources of economic support been investigated for acquiring, maintaining, and expanding uses of technology, including businesses and governments?
2. Is there a procedure for acquiring public-domain software that costs nothing and that could help to build the software libraries of schools and teachers free of charge?
3. Is the district policy the most efficient it can be for providing for sharing of hardware and software among schools?
4. Does the evaluation plan provide for "proving" that technology has a positive impact on instruction and on learning in order to justify expenditures?

Administration

1. Does the district elicit cooperative input from schools, staff, and teachers, or does it only dictate policy? How involved are teachers and staff in making decisions jointly with administration?
2. Are leadership roles evenly dispersed and supported throughout the district?
3. Is there a network of support and sharing among schools guided and encouraged by the district?

Technology

1. What is the availability of equipment to schools and to teachers? Is the scheduling adequate between and within schools?
2. Is the equipment outdated so that no new software is compatible with it? Where should the older computer models be used, or should they be discarded? Can they be upgraded, and at what cost?
4. Which computers are incompatible and which compatible with different brands of software? Should certain models be used in particular schools or at different grade levels?
4. Does equipment shortage frustrate teachers? Has staff development exceeded equipment availability, and how can that be kept in balance?

Research

1. Is there a plan for systematic and controlled evaluation of effects of technology on instruction?
2. Is there provision for testing effects of technological instruction on students' learning?
3. Have teachers, staff, and administration qualified to conduct experimental

research been identified and encouraged to develop plans for conducting, reporting, and analyzing research in the district?

4. What are the questions that districts need to ask regarding the effects of technology on learning and on instruction? Do these questions include moral and ethical questions as well as academic and sociological concerns? Through what means may answers to the questions be found?

These categories provide a framework of questions that need to be raised and answered as evaluation proceeds. Modifications of the district plan for computer integration would then be based upon the answers to the questions. Thus, the planning process would come full circle.

Planning for Integration in the School Building

Long-range plans usually work for most changes in a school setting. In introducing computers, though, there is an irony connected with setting long-range plans. It is not wise to purchase a lot of software and hardware until plans have been made for what to do with them. Yet a school does not know what to do with them until faculty and staff have used them and learned what the possibilities are. As pointed out by Sheila Cory (1983), Coordinator for Staff Development Program Evaluation in North Carolina schools, implementing computers into the school curriculum is different in several ways from other changes schools have made:

Most existing faculty were not trained to use computers while they were learning to be teachers.

Money is not initially available to buy all materials needed for full computer use.

There are no precedents or models from which a school can choose to develop a "best" plan for its circumstances.

At best, implementing computer use is an unknown and an experiment. The lack of precedent is compounded within the technology industry itself, because there is no standardization of hardware. Software incompatibility is also a tremendous problem that can result in a great deal of waste for a school. Of course, such problems often arise in connection with any exciting innovation. Gene Hall, of the University of Texas at Austin, defined levels of use of an innovation in educational settings, as determined by his research on the adoption of educational innovations (1978). These levels of use pertain to personnel activities as they orient themselves to the innovation. Each school can use these levels to identify where it stands on the scale.

Levels of Use of an Innovation

Nonuse
: Users have little or no knowledge of it, no involvement, and no plans to become involved.

Orientation
: Users begin acquiring information about it and explore its values.

Preparation
: Users prepare for first use of the innovation.

Mechanical use
: Users engage in rather disjointed attempts to master the tasks needed to use it in a superficial way; they begin to set a routine pattern of use.

Routine
: Use of the innovation begins to stabilize, with little thought of improving it; users begin to evaluate its use by informal or formal methods.

Refinement
: Users vary the use of it based on their knowledge of effects on students; they initiate changes in cooperation with colleagues.

Integration
: Users collaborate with colleagues to integrate the innovation across the curriculum for maximum impact on students.

Renewal
: Users reevaluate the quality of it, seek major modifications, and search for new developments; they set new goals for themselves and the system.

A school may evaluate its level of use of the computer according to where it stands on the scale. Depending on where it ranks, the school can then plan ways for staff and teachers to grow in their use of computers in instruction. For example, at the Orientation stage, the school can begin in-service training for teachers, to help them toward preparing to use the technology. During the Preparation stage, teachers should be motivated and encouraged to take university courses and pursue higher degrees in uses of the technology. At the Mechanical Use level, the school can begin to establish committees and network support so that teachers can report on their uses and gain new ideas for more effective uses of the computer. This stage is more teacher-directed than student-directed. Because of the insecurity of dealing with the new technology, there needs to be a great deal of support and exchange of ideas among teachers within content-area departments and across departments. Once use of the innovation is stabilized and there is a degree of comfort in using it, the school should look at informal and formal methods of evaluating its use. Data may be collected through a questionnaire to teachers, through records of which software is used the most, and through evidences of student gains in learning and in attitude toward learning. When the results of the evaluations are known, the school can help its teachers grow toward refining and integrating the computer into curricula within and across content areas. "The school," of course, means the administration, which must be solidly behind growth in use of the innovation. In order to support teachers and staff in making changes to adopt computer use, administrators should update their knowledge and ideas. The whole effort for change should be directed and supported by the school administration.

Hall cautions that not every teacher will be at the same level of use of an innovation (1977). Teachers have to be assessed individually and helped to grow through the levels; they will not be able to collaborate with colleagues and contribute to school growth until they have personally mastered their own anxieties and achieved a level of comfort in classroom use of the innovation. As Hall points out, "Change is a highly personal experience." The perceptions and feelings of teachers and staff must be dealt with in helping them to adjust to change. Hall, Rutherford, and George (1977) have documented several stages of concern that teachers experience personally when dealing with the change involved in innovation. These stages should be used by a school to diagnose the effects of the activities employed in the levels of use to help teachers grow. Each teacher can be assessed through attitude inventories, questionnaires, and personal interviews regarding his or her perceptions.

Stages of Concern about Innovation

Awareness	Little concern about or involvement with innovation
Informational	General awareness and interest in general characteristics, effects, and requirements for use
Personal	Uncertainty about adequacy to meet demands of the innovation, which may include financial or status implications
Management	Concern about organization, management, scheduling, and time demands of using the innovation
Consequence	Concern about effect of the innovation on students, its relevance, positive impact, and benefits; focus on changes needed for more effective use
Collaboration	Need to coordinate and cooperate with others regarding use of the innovation
Refocusing	Individual has definite ideas about changes to the innovation that give more benefits

If the administration can recognize these stages of concern in teachers and staff, it can provide ways to address the concerns so as to help individuals grow to the next level. The progression of concern, Hall explains, appears to move "from self, to task, to impact" for people in the developmental process of adopting innovations. Teachers' in-service training on the Orientation level of use should focus on providing information about computers and how their use will affect them personally. Teachers should be led to understand their role in regard to computers, in what ways they can become knowledgeable about using them, and other personal concerns they might have. The initial concern of new users is to gain information about computers: the kinds there are, their functions, and the requirements for using them. At the beginning, staff development must address these needs for general information. As information is acquired, people's concerns become personalized. The user begins to develop feelings of inadequacy to deal with the demands of computer use. Teachers are concerned about the personal commitment they need to make, their role in making decisions about change within the school structure, and their relationship to the changes occurring. On the Mechanical Use level, teacher training should center on concerns of management — how to organize efficiently and to coordinate use of technology. Teachers' concerns are first personal, then mechanical, as accommodation to change begins. Concerns about time are utmost at the Mechanical Use level, because there is so much inefficiency and time waste until routines are established.

Not until a pattern of use or routine is established will teachers begin to be concerned about the impact of computers on their students. At this Routine level of use, personal anxieties and fears begin to subside, and social concerns appear. Teachers' concerns begin to focus on the consequences of using computers; their need is for ways to assess change. In-service development at this level should concentrate on the relevance of computer use in instruction. Teachers need help in developing methods for evaluation of the skills, performance, and attitudes of students.

Interpretation of the evaluation will lead teachers to the next level of use, Refinement of computer use to fit the diagnosed needs of students in the specific school setting. At this level, teacher training should be concerned with adaptation of hardware and software to student needs. A new needs assessment can be made and facilities changed to meet the needs. Perhaps there is a need for another computer lab or for more movable carts that can be wheeled from room to room. Whatever the physical and instructional needs are, teachers are ready to plan for refinement of computer use. They need cooperation with others to make the necessary alterations in use. Teacher training should address content-area needs for computers and how their use can cross subject areas for better integration within the whole school curriculum. This is the highest level of use of computers, a level a school should aspire to because the potential of teacher and student use will be maximized. The focus is on instructional benefits; teachers work together to achieve the desired outcomes. Teacher training thus concentrates on the development of the levels of use while meeting the stages of concern among the staff, to promote growth through the levels.

Shiela Cory (1983) documents four stages of development that school systems appear to experience. She theorizes that if a school understands what to expect as its use of computers grows, it will be able to plan accordingly. Figure 4-4 lists the stages she has witnessed in her research. They are seen to be roughly parallel to Hall's levels of use of an innovation.

Stage I, "Getting on the Bandwagon," is past for most U.S. schools, according to the 1985 survey cited previously. Most schools are undoubtedly at Stage II now, the "Stage of Confusion." Actually, the whole technology

Figure 4-4 Four stages of development for full implementation of computers for instruction (from Cory, "A 4-Stage Model of Development for Full Implementation of Computers for Instruction in a School System. Reprinted with permission from *The Computing Teacher*, November 1983)

Stage	Hardware	Software	Staff Development	Computer-Assisted Learning	Computer Literacy	Attitude
Stage I Stage of Getting on the Bandwagon	Acquisition of hardware is primary focus Emphasis on quantity vs. quality Variety of hardware within one school system Joysticks or paddles purchased	Very little software acquired Available software is teacher-written or public domain	Staff development is considered unimportant Staff develoment is almost nonexistent	Undifferentiated from computer literacy Use of arcade games Any and all software is used at all grade levels	Undifferentiated from computer-assisted learning Sometimes course taught with one computer and 30 students	Ambivalence—fear, mistrust, uncertainty, curiosity Computers are for games and fun Computers are transient in education
Stage II Stage of Confusion	Acquisition of hardware still primary focus Apples purchased to run MECC software Language cards added to Apples	Acquired software is inexpensive or free Frequently software has bugs Software often purchased by individual teacher MECC software purchased by system	Some teachers take courses from a variety of places Consultants give one-shot courses to interested faculty No overall plan for staff development exists	Somewhat differentiated from computer literacy Some teachers attempt to match software to curriculum Generally no planning for use of software	Somewhat differentiated from computer assisted-learning Courses taught at initiative of individual teacher Courses typically targeted to one segment of student population Focus is on selection of "the best language"	Some teachers excited and enthusiastic Some teachers nervous Teachers feel everyone will need to program

Figure 4-4, continued

Stage	Hardware	Software	Staff Development	Computer-Assisted Learning	Computer Literacy	Attitude
Stage III Stage of Pulling It All Together	Acquisition of hardware not the primary focus Purchases coordinated across the school system Purchase of peripherals takes place	Greater acquisition of professionally developed software Wide variety of software is purchased	A person is designated to coordinate effort Variety of courses offered through school system Participation in courses is voluntary	Totally differentiated from computer literacy Committees formed to evaluate software and recommend how to use it Software used for drill and practice, simulation, educational games and tutorials	Totally differentiated from computer-assisted learning Committee established to define computer literacy Consideration of computer literacy for all students Greater machine use in courses	Some teachers see computers as panacea for education Some teachers very resistant Many teachers gaining interest and losing fear Teachers recognize they don't need to be expert programmers
Stage IV Stage of Full Implementation	Continued acquisition of hardware Computers purchased for specific location and application Purchases characterized by simlest, least expensive machine to do given task	Purchase of software is based on plans Libraries of software exist, both at system and school level	Differentiated for different groups of teachers Tied to the system plans Offered in-house by person employed by school system Participation in courses is required	Use of software based on research findings and ongoing evaluation Primarily used with aspects of curriculum not normally served by traditional instruction Recognition that computer-assisted learning is better for some children than for others	Computer literacy is cleary defined Taught throughout all grades in sequenced fashion Taught in various classes	Prevalent attitude of respect for capabilities and limitations of the computer Understanding of computer's role in education Appreciation of computer as a tool of greater value to all

138

industry is at this stage of development, in that standardization of hardware and compatibility of software have not yet been achieved. In schools, Stage II is characterized by the lack of an overall plan. Individuals are taking the initiative to become knowledgeable, but there is no coordinated, systematic plan of action. Many teachers have misunderstandings about computer use and applications, which only compound their anxieties and mistrust of change. The software acquired is generally that which is inexpensive or free rather than that which meets needs of the school. Individuals usually acquire such software on their own initiative and at their own expense, not through system's planning.

A great many schools, however, have evolved to the third stage, "Pulling it All Together." This stage is reached sooner if the administration is committed from the beginning to plan for computer use and makes efforts to coordinate staff development and collaborative efforts school-wide. In Stage III, the focus is on staff development and curriculum design with quality software rather than on purchase of equipment. Teachers clearly differentiate between computer literacy and knowledge of computer applications and instructional uses. They focus on computer-assisted instruction and integration of the computer into the curriculum. The final stage, "Full Implementation," is where the maximum benefits to students in the school will be realized. Computers are used to meet student learning needs and styles and are but one of many varieties of technology used in a well-planned curriculum.

Cory points out some factors affecting the rate of growth for a school from one stage to the next. Chief among them is leadership from the top, within both the district and the individual schools. From the superintendent to the principals, leadership, direction, and enthusiasm must be given to staff development and acquisition of appropriate materials. Understanding of these stages can facilitate growth of computer use within a school, because they clarify points of evolution that should be considered for effective planning. Definition of the stages is an attempt to map territory that is largely uncharted because educational computer use is so new in our history.

Placement of Technology within the School Building

One of the major issues confronting a school is how and where to place computers in order to maximize student benefits. Dale Peterson (1984) discusses this issue as one of dispersion versus "critical mass." Should computers be distributed equally throughout the school, thus spreading them so thin that no student gets adequate time to use a computer? Equal dispersion will probably result in computers being used less rather than more, because planning creative ways to use a limited resource involves an extraordinary amount of work. An alternative is to cluster the computers into a "critical mass" in a particular class — a minimum number that will service a computer class. Of course, massing the computers in this way may not be fair, since it gives some students advantages over others.

Peterson terms the alternative of creating a computer lab a "middle of the road solution," It has the fairness of equal dispersion along with the advantages of critical-mass arrangements. Only a few skilled teachers are needed to operate the lab; access to it can be regulated by careful scheduling; and a lot of students can get intensive use of computers. The drawbacks are that more boys than girls will choose to use the lab, and handicapped and special-needs people will not opt to use the lab voluntarily. Another serious drawback is the separation of the lab from the classroom and from the teacher who makes assignments for its use. As noted earlier, the teacher is the monitor of learning and needs to be available to intervene and guide students. A lab apart from the classroom indicates the school's attitude toward its use — separate from the ongoing curriculum. In such a setup, uses of computers will be mostly limited to drill and practice, programming, and computer literacy (the study of the computer itself). Its capacity as a learning tool for writing, organizing research data, and building background with simulated experiences will not be utilized.

Perhaps the best solution lies in planning an eclectic placement of computers within the school. Eclectic placement considers all the alternatives and creates a variety that addresses as many needs as possible. The options are to have (1) stationary placements of multiple and single computers, (2) movable carts with multiple and single computers, and (3) a combination of stationary and portable systems. The following outline is reprinted from *Teacher Tip Book,* with permission of Follet Quality Courseware.

Organization for Maximum Use

For the sake of brevity, in this section we'll use an outline form. Factors you'll want to keep in mind include: *number of computers* available; *willingness of teachers* to use computers; *amount/type of software* available; whether there is a teacher or volunteer available to *manage the program*; and the *physical layout* of your building.

I. Stationary assignments
  A. Multiple computers
    1. Lab (Teacher or volunteer supervisor)
      • Classes are scheduled into the lab — and/or;
      • Teacher sends students, arranging previously with supervisor for assignments in blocks of time.
    2. Individual classrooms
      • Systematic purchase of computers, each dedicated to specific uses — teacher (or team) builds in maximum use of computers when building lessons.
  B. Single computer
    1. Math teacher
      • Large amount of drill/practice software.

- Advanced students may study programming: (based on tradition, programming might move into Language Arts as a study of organized patterns of expression, or secondary technical areas as a problem in machine control).

2. Library/media center
   - Carrels for various AV uses including computer.
   - Teacher sends students in to use machine as assigned.
   - Students with free reading time may use computer.
3. Special education classroom
   - Funding possibilities.
   - Teacher assigns Special Ed students into management-type programs for remediation.
   - Analysis of student progress is provided via computer-generated records.
   - Teacher monitors students sent from regular classrooms for special drill.
   - Computer is used to assist in writing IEPs.
4. Office
   - Classroom teacher, students, and administration cooperatively plan and schedule computer use.
   - Student reports to office with assigned program — essential monitoring by secretary.
5. Interested supervising teacher
   - Requires isolated part of room or adjoining area that can be monitored by teacher.
   - Large group (class) activity when hooked into larger-screen video monitor or TV.
   - Students of other teachers can come in at arranged times.

II. Movable cart
   A. Multiple computers
      1. Assignment to department or floor
         - Move between these classes by period or time block.
         - Students in computer club can help set up, (or) each group has designated student to take computer on to next assignment.
   B. Single computer
      1. Library-media center — checkout procedure similar to projector.
      2. Rotation schedule — assigned to each classroom for day of week.

III. Combination
   A. Lab
      1. Priority use of each machine is assigned to a department.
      2. Teacher may send a few students to lab or may take that computer to the classroom.
      3. Computer not in use by the designated department may be used by other students.
   B. Supervising teacher
      1. Another teacher may "borrow" system when the teacher to whom it is assigned will not be using it.

   2. System may be centrally located for specified period each week
      for use by those students with programming projects.
 C. Library media center
   1. Media specialist or aide schedules check out for the coming week.
   2. When not checked out, the system is kept as a learning center in
      the library.

Even though it might be preferable to create an eclectic selection of computer arrangements, including the classrooms, movable carts, and a lab,
a school must sometimes focus on a lab, since that is most practical and
economical at the beginning. Guidelines such as the following can help save
time and money in the initial planning stages.

The ideal lab provides for both teacher instruction and hands-on use of
computers. It also accommodates large groups, small groups, and individual
arrangements of seating. In one kind of arrangement, the student chairs
are movable desks; for large group instruction, they are placed in the middle of the room facing the teacher's computer, the large overhead monitor,
and the bulletin boards. On the sides of the room, ringing the large-group
desk seating, computers are placed in a long row, on shelves against the
walls, facing outward and attached serially to several printers spaced among
them. This arrangement allows few distractions as the teacher demonstrates
and lectures about the lesson for the day. After the group instruction,
students can move to the computers against the walls. When they are finished
with the computers, they may return to the chairs in the center of the room
to finish homework or other tasks not related to computers. This placement permits better control of wires and power outlets, providing freedom
of movement without electrical hazards. Ideally, the lab would serve a maximum of twenty students. Hardware requirements would thus be ten to
twenty computers with black and white monitors and double disk drives
and three or four printers. Several of the computers should have color
monitors, as well, for certain software that requires it.

Another configuration for placement of computers is less ideal: having
computers on tables in rows in the center of the room, facing the front.
This arrangement is less conducive to instruction because students will have
more distractions with the computers right in front of them as the teacher
is talking. Also, students will not have space to take notes or do any paper-
work at their seats. There is also greater danger from wires and power strips
that are exposed to traffic as students walk between the rows. The only
advantage to this arrangement is that students may imitate the model the
teacher demonstrates step by step on the overhead monitor without having to turn around to see it.

The school computer lab should be well planned and carefully designed,
from floor to ceiling, for the very best use. An article by Thomas Moran
(1987) discusses some of the particulars that should be considered in planning. He begins with the floors, emphasizing that they need to be static-free.

The best flooring is linoleum or tile. If that is not possible, the existing carpet will need to be sprayed with carpet guard and/or fabric softener and water a couple of times a week. This is necessary to protect the static-sensitive equipment.

Within the room, there should be no pencil sharpeners or chalk boards, Moran continues; chalk dust and pencil shavings are harmful to computers. If possible, there should be liquid boards that utilize felt tip pens. Otherwise, a teacher should use an overhead projector to write on instead of a board. Bulletin boards can be used very effectively for flowcharts, instruction, and computer information. The ceiling should be white, for better reflection, and should have fluorescent lighting. Moran recommends a dropped ceiling as a better insulator of sound and heat. For best efficiency, the computer likes a temperature range of 65 to 75 degrees Fahrenheit and a humidity range of 30 to 50 percent. The design of the room can help to maintain these ranges. Another major consideration in the design of the lab is the security it will require. The security system should be installed before the equipment is in the lab. The doors should be double-bolted, with at least one deadbolt lock. The windows must also be made secure. Moran recommends that a "portable, lockable, metal louvre system be installed on the outsides of the windows" for utmost security.

The furniture inside the lab should meet teacher needs as well as student instructional requirements. The teacher needs a lockable filing cabinet for software, grade books, and other files. There should be a teacher's desk, a computer stand, and a master monitor stand (if the monitor is not suspended from the ceiling or an overhead bar). The teacher's computer stand should be large enough to hold a computer with a double disk drive, a black-and-white monitor as well as a color monitor, and a printer. Near the teacher's desk, there should be a bookcase or shelves for technology magazines and copies of the software most used by students. The teacher should also have a closet that can securely lock up personal items.

Moran details the wiring that is required in the lab. He says there need to be the following types:

1. An independent electrical circuit for all the teacher's equipment, controlling the master computer.
2. A circuit controlling the power to all student monitors, so that the teacher may control the attention of students during instruction. The monitor control should be separate from the computer power control, so that programs or data are not lost.
3. No more than ten computers on one circuit.
4. An independent circuit for overhead lights.
5. Extra circuits for expansion of the lab or later inclusion of other technology.

To protect the circuits from overloads and power surges by circuit breakers in the main power box, each circuit of each component should be wired into a box with a master on/off switch channeled through a circuit breaker. Each component in the unit should be wired so that all are turned off as a unit. The unit consists of monitor, computer, printer, and one free circuit if necessary. Then the monitor circuits should be wired into a separate master switch for teacher control, located in the instructional part of the room. Finally, Moran recommends that the units be externally connected to power strips on all four walls, in order to protect against traffic and unnecessary handling. This is much easier with an arrangement in which the computers are against the wall.

Perhaps these guidelines can aid the design of a computer lab, so that fewer errors in initial judgment will occur. Teachers who are interested can use the guidelines to help out in the planning and most efficient use of the computer lab. Some of the guidelines are not possible for all school situations, but they can give direction to practical plans.

Selection of Quality Software for the School Curriculum

One problem in teaching the use of computers in school is that some children also have them in their homes. This may interfere with instruction, but it should also be taken as an opportunity for cooperation. One early marketing survey reported that home computers for school-age children outnumber school computers by a ratio of ten to one (Komoski, 1984). It appears that parents have a strong interest in and high expectations for school instruction in computers. Schools must plan to meet such expectations and to set up channels of communication and training for parents. Home and school should be in synchronization with each other in terms of goals, values, and concerns about computer use. Trained parents would then be able to buy hardware and software of high quality and compatible with the educational requirements and standards of the schools. Parents would cooperate and reinforce the values in the school because they helped to establish them. Komoski (1984) reports ways that some schools have initiated this kind of community and parent involvement:

1. School (or district) training of parents on how to make effective use of home computers to support school learning
2. Setting up hardware and software exchanges among parents
3. Cooperation of school and district with local libraries
4. Aid to parents in getting discounts for computer purchase — under extensions of school purchasing contracts
5. Finding federal or state funding for low-cost computers to lend to low-income families that participate in parent/child training programs
6. Holding a community computer fair to attract parent participation, involvement, and interest

Parents and computers in the home should be viewed as valuable resources for planning educational uses and software purchases. Considering that there are approximately 400 pieces of educational software published each month, by over 700 educational software companies, input from the eventual users is vital. Unfortunately, instructional information is not always provided for software packages to the same extent as for print materials, so teachers and parents are unable to evaluate the purposes for learning. Such materials as instructional objectives, teachers' guides, and scope and sequence charts are seldom included for evaluation of learning. Furthermore, the design principles and impact on the learner of software programs are usually more complicated than those of books or other print materials. Nor do the methods of evaluation for traditional materials hold for interactive video materials. New evaluation principles need to be established for new media.

Computers and software have their place in instruction; they should be used when they can address an instructional problem better than any other learning tool. Margret Hazen, Director of Courseware Development (1985), lists specific instances when computers should be used in instruction:

1. When they provide remedial or supplemental instruction—that is, when a computer acts as a tutor in a concept area that frequently presents learning difficulties
2. When a computer offers a capability (for example, simulation, calculation, graphics, automated performance recordkeeping, algorithmic data, or problem generation) that is likely to produce faster or improved learning
3. When a computer is used to aid drill, practice, and problem-solving tasks that require frequent and extensive corrective feedback to save on instructor time
4. When a computer is used to accomplish learning and instruction in remote areas otherwise not likely to receive such instruction
5. When a computer can replace costly laboratory facilities

These five conditions are unique to the computer as a learning tool. Its place in the overall curriculum to serve these conditions should be considered in the overall school plan. Its capability as motivator for learning should also be understood and planned for. For example, in prewriting and prereading, a simulation can be very useful as a springboard for ideas.

In the selection of quality software for a school curriculum, instructional criteria should be applied to types of software in order to understand their best uses. When instructional criteria are developed, the types of software will be used for their most effective purposes in student learning. The instructional criteria to be applied to drill and practice software may be the following:

Drill and Practice

It must present a variety of options for student responses.

It should give feedback that remediates rather than gives just a yes or no response.

It allows chances for success at varying levels of performance.

The teacher may easily personalize the content and the format for individual use.

For tutorials, which present new learning rather than just reinforcement and practice of old knowledge, the following instructional criteria may apply:

Tutorial

It must link old knowledge to the new concepts using semantic maps or advanced organizers.

Examples should be presented from simple to complex, concrete to abstract, and known to unknown.

It should analyze student thinking in the responses made and branch the student to appropriate remedial paths.

It should provide comparisons to other concepts.

The learning should be relevant and transfer to ongoing learning in the school curriculum.

Simulations provide a different kind of learning opportunity. Feedback is not given in the form of "correct/incorrect," but in the results of students' decisions. The primary skills taught by a simulation are analysis of a problem situation and decision-making to correct the problems. Simulations represent real-world situations by means of visual models. Students are afforded an opportunity for rehearsal of a situation before they experience it in real life. The following instructional criteria may apply to use of a simulation:

Simulation

It should present a life-like model of an actual situation, with relevant, realistic graphics, sound and text.

It should present a new and complex task that changes as students make decisions.

Proficiency in problem solving should be provided on different levels as student skills increase.

It should provide feedback that is relevant and appropriate to the decisions made. Penalties should be appropriate to mistakes made, and rewards should also be realistic.

Students should be able to learn from their mistakes and correct them in order to succeed.

Students should be able to use a wide range of decision-making skills and information that build on their prior knowledge and experience.

Student learning should be centered on thought processes — ways the problems are solved — not on the content itself.

The skills developed should transfer to actual, real-world situations presented in the total curriculum.

In use of a simulation, the teacher is a key ingredient in monitoring student learning. The teacher should ask how students have solved the problem and why they arrived at particular solutions. With constant questionning and probing, students may come to understand their own decision-making processes. Constant application should be made to other life situations as students experience the simulation. With metacognitive awareness of their decision-making, students will be able to grow in their skills and use them successfully beyond the simulated experience.

In problem-solving programs such as the Logo turtle graphics, students are given opportunities to take risks, explore, and make mistakes. Such risk-taking does not involve irremediable penalties, so students should be encouraged to experiment. The instructional criteria applied to use of this type of software should include the following:

Problem-Solving

It should provide opportunities for inductive thinking, building generalities from specific manipulations.

It should allow for student manipulation and control of creating and learning.

The problem-solving proceeds from simpler to more complex processes — for example, from manual manipulation to constructing procedures.

Students should be able to interact actively with the program, gaining immediate results from their choices and experimentation.

Opportunity should exist for cooperative learning and sharing of ideas to lessen the anxiety associated with risk-taking and to encourage language interchange.

It should provoke opportunities for transfer to skills and attitudes gained from the experience. The confidence students gain in making successful decisions should be expanded upon in life situations away from the computer.

Selection of quality software for the school curriculum must be based upon the learning students will experience. When such outcomes are clearly identified, the instructional criteria may be applied to the program. What techniques it employs in student learning will help clarify the skills, attitudes, and thinking abilities students will experience. Selection of software must be student-based yet generalizable to the overall curriculum, so that its instructional principles coincide with those of the ongoing curriculum. The guiding question will be, "How does this technology best fit into the overall plan for student learning?" Selection of quality software will provide answers to this question.

In her article on instructional theories to be used in evaluating software, Margaret E. Bell (1985) suggests that different learning theories should be used to guide the selection of educational software (see also Chapter 6). She suggests that drill and practice programs are related to B.F. Skinner's learning theory of reinforcement to promote behavioral change. Drill and practice programs, wherein the student responds to a series of options, focus on discrimation skills. Feedback on the choice is given, along with positive reinforcement for correct responses. With this method, the primary learning technique is conditioned responses.

The tutorial is based on information-processing theories that relate new information to prior knowledge stored in the learner's memories. The tutorial builds on students' experience, proceeding from known to unknown, and makes comparisons with similar and contrasting concepts. Cues are provided to aid students' associations for recall. The tutorial also utilizes Robert Gagne's learning theory of "cognitive strategies," which stresses the learner's thought processes rather than content (see Chapter 6). The tutorial presents complex problems that require students to apply information and skills in a new way, thus extending their thought processes to new situations. Simulations operate under this learning theory when they present life-like situations that require application of existing schemata to solving problems in new situations. Ways of thinking and doing are thus accommodated to new circumstances, tested out, and verified.

Problem-solving programs such as Logo are developed according to Piaget's learning theories. Students drawing complex designs with the "turtle" are allowed to experiment and explore in open-ended problem-solving. They engage in divergent thinking because the exercise has many different solutions, not just right or wrong answers. In constructing complex designs, students develop logical thinking skills and come to understand that there are many ways to solve a problem — some ways more efficient and direct than others. Students' understanding and growth has to be carefully guided, however, so that they understand what it is they are learning.

We have already examined (in Chapter 2) how Bloom's Taxonomy of cognitive development applies to different kinds of software. This learning theory can be a great aid to educators' awareness of how to select quality software that develops and extends students' cognitive growth. The software should be judged on the basis of how well it fulfills principles of the learning theory.

Software evaluation is not easy; it must follow a planned procedure. Evaluation should proceed from a needs assessment that focuses on learner outcomes identified within the overall curriculum. Each piece of software is examined for its fulfillment of the needs. Instructional criteria are applied to the piece of software to determine how well it fulfills curriculum needs. Finally, awareness of different learning theories can improve the process of selecting software by promoting the understanding that diversity is needed to meet individual learners' needs. Parents should also be included in the software evaluation and selection procedure.

Common Problems in Computer Use

In a study by Kloosterman, Ault, and Harty (1987), four secondary schools were analyzed for their progress in integrating the use of computers into their instruction. Each school had a computer lab equipped with fifteen or more computers, used for multiple purposes: computer classes for literacy and programming and subject-area or grade-level classes. Additionally, movable computer units were available for classroom use. Each school had a computer coordinator to oversee scheduling, programs, and equipment.

The four schools are considered "state-of-the-art" in their computer development. The general directions in which they are headed appear to be as follows:

Integrating Computers into Classrooms or Subjects

1. Computers viewed as tools rather than pieces of equipment to be learned about in isolation
2. Computers considered an integral part of learning rather than just a supplement to the traditional curriculum
3. Teachers using computers for their unique features, such as the capability to print a class newspaper easily

Sharing of Experiences

1. Regional meetings, workshops and training sessions set up for teachers to interact and share problems and solutions
2. Participation in conferences and workshops to support and update computer use
3. School districts sharing costs for in-service training when university courses do not meet teachers' needs

Concern about Software Quality

1. Concern about lack of instructional design, learning theories, and sound psychological principles in much educational software
2. Paucity of really relevant software
3. Some schools accessing state-funded preview centers that help in selection of quality software

Evolving Programs

1. Plans to acquire more computers
2. Plans to expand or revise their computer curricula
3. Schools finding relevant instructional applications
4. Schools struggling to keep abreast of growth in computer technology and recognition of its versatility

All four schools have experienced problems and limitations in common. The biggest problem concerns teachers' reluctance to learn about the use of computers; some teachers have poor attitudes or low interest in knowing how computer use can help them be more efficient and effective. Much more teacher participation has been found when administration is supportive and encouraging. Computer coordinators within the school could also play a big part in involving reluctant teachers. They provide assistance and demonstrate relevant applications.

Another problem is in how to use computers most effectively for learning.

The major concern is curriculum integration. Teachers need to be made aware of appropriate software and the functions it can serve. All of the schools in the study are developing computer applications of the following nature: word processors in writing labs, databases, and simulations in the social sciences, as well as reading programs in library-centered competitions.

The problem seems to be that teachers lack an overview and a methodology for classifying and organizing the great diversity of software. Perhaps they are overwhelmed by the vast amount of software that needs to be reviewed, evaluated, and organized. Traditional systems, such as the Dewey Decimal, do not work in organizing the array of software. Schools should decide on their own system, and it should be meaningful to teachers in terms of application in the curriculum. The classifications by function outlined in Chapter 3 of this book might serve as a starting point for such a system.

All of the teachers involved in the study express a need for continuing support for their efforts and growth in computer use. In order for schools to have good computer curricula, the teachers believe that the following is needed:

1. A lab for large-group work as well as movable units for small groups to use in classrooms
2. A coordinator or teacher with release time to use for coordinating computer scheduling, organizing software, and assisting teachers
3. Financial commitment from the administration for purchase and maintenance of equipment

The recommendations that come out of this study focus on preparation of new teachers in their course work. Such preparation should involve the integration of relevant software into their subject areas, word-processing experience, and exposure to different types of software. Their methods classes should emphasize problem solving and training in "thinking skills" of a more divergent nature. Perhaps such studies as these can help educators focus on ways to plan the growth of use of computers. Planning and preparation are surely needed to avoid waste and abuse of educational innovations.

Planning for Classroom Integration of Computers

The teacher, in considering use of a piece of software in the classroom, should ask the following questions:

Goals   What are my main goals? (Goals are long-term plans that may not be fully realized—unlike objectives, which are short-term learning outcomes.)

Relevance   How does each part of this program address my plans? Is each part relevant, or should some parts be deleted?

Suitability	Is this software the best material that can be used to achieve my plans?
Skills	What skills required in the computer program benefit student learning?
Transfer	Are these skills generalizable to other contexts, as principles or problem-solving heuristics? What are the best ways to promote this transfer of learning so that students recognize the relevance of the material?

Answers to such questions help teachers analyze and evaluate the benefits of using software in their curriculum. Analyzing goals and objectives and designing instruction around them assures a well-planned use of computers and other technologies. Answering the above questions almost guarantees a fresh approach to teaching that can stimulate students to greater motivation and learning. Such an exercise can be exciting to teachers, who feel challenged to address old problems of instruction in new ways — an opportunity computers surely provide.

It is easy to get excited about the use of computers, but caution is needed in integrating technology into a traditional curriculum. First of all, one finds that the "traditional curriculum" changes. The new technology alters the nature of what we have traditionally taught and the ways we have taught it. Traditional instruction tends to be limited to either an inductive (sciences) or a deductive (liberal arts) approach to problem solving. It tends to emphasize passive receptivity by students rather than active interaction. Use of computers can change traditional instruction for the better. Use of different software varies problem solving, conducts learners through a process of learning and is highly interactive.

Some possible negative effects of computer use in instruction should be taken into account in planning to use the computer (Wilson and Walsh, 1986). One possible negative consequence of using computers is that important factors affecting instruction may be neglected. For example, the computer does not address matters relating to learners' affective side: their personal values, self-worth, and personality. The danger is that this crucial area for learning may be neglected in applying computers. Another problem may be that content will be misrepresented or oversimplified in a computer program that defines concepts by prototype examples only. Concepts should be represented in all their complexity; otherwise, they may be distorted.

Wilson and Walsh point out another potential problem in using computers for learning. Too much analysis without adequate synthesis of a concept can prevent learners from seeing important patterns and effects. Analysis, although very valuable, should not be an end in itself. The instructional program can get so complex that students miss out on the final step of putting things together into a whole picture. The outcomes should be synthesis and application of the idea; teachers must evaluate the program in these terms. A further danger is that the technology itself will be valued over the instructional methodology (referred to by Wilson and Walsh as "soft technology") that underlies the educational program. Teachers must be aware of sound instructional principles in using computer programs.

Finally, there can be a problem of overly rigid instructional design, so systematized that creative approaches may not be used. Lack of creativity in a program may produce unimaginative, boring instructional designs for students. In evaluating a computer program, the teacher should insist that a balance between imaginative and technical approaches be maintained. Rigidity of design may not allow a student any flexibility and choice in making decisions, thereby limiting the development and use of the student's thinking skills.

A Prototype of Computer Integration

This author has had the pleasure of visiting a school of the future, as far as technological *integration* into instruction is concerned. It may serve as a model or prototype, in philosophy and in service, of what other schools may want to consider as they grow in the use of technology for instruction. Frost Lake Elementary School, in St. Paul, Minnesota, is designed to be a magnet school for technology and global education. As a specialized school, it draws students from across the city and aids in desegregating the system. According to district figures reported in the local newspaper, 64 percent of the 463 students live outside the boundaries of its usual attendance area, resulting in a cross-cultural and cross-neighborhood student population. The largest minority group is Southeast Asian. Racial balance must be maintained, and there is a waiting list. As a district model, the school has a fulltime technology specialist, a media specialist, and a global studies specialist, who work together to coordinate materials and curriculum and to guide the many visitors to the school.

According to the specialists, the school was given no preset guidelines from the district but has been allowed to experiment and develop in its own way. One clear philosophy that has emerged is that technology should be available when it is needed, not just when it is scheduled. Therefore, there is no computer lab to which children are sent, away from the classroom and from the teacher who planned the lesson but has no way to monitor it. Instead, there are six computers in every classroom—overall, four students to every computer in the school. Every weekend, one child in each classroom gets to take home a computer for practice and for his or her family to become involved. Parents sign an agreement to take care of the computer and not to try to repair it if it should malfunction. They agree to return it on the following Monday. The children get to choose their favorite software to take home with the computer.

The philosophy of integration is stated very clearly in the school's Media Program:

> The Media Program at Frost Lake School is designed to integrate all educational resources into the curriculum. The Media Specialists are here to help the staff to accomplish this. The Media Center attempts to provide a wide range of materials for student and teacher use. The Media Center will give the students the chance to explore, discover, locate materials, and develop a life-long interest in learning. Those materials may be books, videos, filmstrips, records, tapes, pictures, clippings, pamphlets, computer software, and people.
>
> *Grace Kurtz and Thomas Snyder, Media Specialists*

This statement of technological integration extends to all media for student learning, including people as media. Surely, this is on the highest of the levels of use suggested by Gene Hall, as discussed earlier in this chapter, a level that other schools will want to aspire to as they develop their programs.

The classroom sets of six computers are arranged differently by the different teachers. Some are arranged in semicircles, some in rows, and some on tables so that students face each other, but most are against the walls, away from the students' chairs and the main area of instruction in the room. Each subject area has identified uses of the computers for specific purposes, some of which are listed below:

A. Math
   1. Drill and practice
   2. Tutorials
   3. Test management
B. Language arts
   1. Spelling
   2. Word processing
   3. Creative writing
   4. Test management
C. Global education
   1. Simulations
   2. Databases
D. Art, music, and science
   1. Demonstrations

In addition to this classroom use, special classes are given for students and staff by the media specialists. These classes include media skills (to learn of the library and references), visual literacy (to study television programming, commercials, and stereotypes in media), word processing, database searching, and the newspaper (to study parts of it, analyze the production of it, and to produce the students' own paper). Several courses focus on books: "Story Lunch," in which students eat lunch as a book is read to them; "Reading Enrichment," in which students concentrate on the novel; and "Book Talks," which introduces students to books that they may sit and talk about with others. All of these courses are designed to maintain student attention and interest in uses of information.

The teachers in the school were hand-picked for this specialized magnet project. They were interviewed and selected for their interest in learning about technology and for specific background knowledge. The primary criterion, however, was their curiosity and interest in developing their knowledge about the uses of technology in instruction. Thus, faculty in the entire school is involved; there are no teachers reluctant to cooperate, grow, or share new ideas they gain. The specialists coordinate and conduct workshops for the faculty in the school as well as in the district as a whole. The school is thus a training ground for teachers. It conducts two-day workshops and demonstrations of teachers' own designs. The school and the faculty serve as trail blazers for the use of technology, from which other schools and districts may learn.

One classroom uses a computer system called "Discourse," manufactured by Cybernetic Communication Systems, Inc. 3M Corporation owns the marketing rights to the system in the United States and funded half of the cost for the school to pilot it. (The school district funded the other half.) A philanthropic organization in the community is planning to use the school as a test site to study the effect of the program on students whose English is limited. There will be cross-sectional and longitudinal studies of the system's effects.

On the teacher's desk is an IBM keyboard and monitor, connected to a Hewlett Packard printer and a Panasonic VHS player that allows preprogramming. Each student's desk has a keyboard, identified by seat number. In a reading lesson, the students were instructed to read their books. After a while, the teacher asked that they enter their names into the computer. Each pupil typed in a name and it appeared on the teacher's screen, identified by desk number. Then the teacher asked students to type in the name of their book, after which he printed out the information for his use. Next, students were asked to type one sentence telling what the book was about. They finished by adding two more sentences to describe the book. The teacher printed out the information.

This is just one example of how the system can be used. Using the VHS, a preprogrammed lesson allows students to set their own pace. They may generate reports for the class collectively or individually. The system records a total score and accumulates a performance record for the class and for individuals. It also calculates grades and may be geared toward criterion-referenced teaching and mastery learning, if a teacher so chooses. The system individualizes instruction, since the teacher can immediately observe each student's performance on the monitor. The teacher said that the system has changed his style of teaching because he can now "electronically look over students' shoulders, instead of physically moving around the room." It allows him to have an overview of class performance but to move to help individuals when they need him. Best of all, this teacher liked the fact that the system allowed him control and monitoring of learning, in terms of the material and the pacing of instruction. The drawback as he saw it was that student responses were limited at that time to only 274 keystrokes. (This was later to be expanded to allow paragraph-length responses by students.) The teacher uses the system about 25 percent of the time for student writing, believing that traditional writing skills must not be neglected. He admitted that students were having some difficulty in transferring from this type of system to traditional classrooms, to which they return after a year. He also said that the system is so interactive that the teacher sometimes has a problem managing so much student information. The results of the study of the system will be of great interest to all of us.

In its pioneering efforts, this school may be regarded as a prototype of a future school, integrating technology into the curriculum and using it as a learning tool to maximize instruction. Of course, any pioneer encounters problems and develops hindsight that is valuable to those who follow. When asked what they would have done differently if they had known better, the specialists gave a list of valuable insights they have gained over the two years their plans have been in operation. This list (printed with their permission) is shared as a guide for other schools that are developing their own plans for use of technology.

1. There should be more of a balanced use of funds between hardware and software, right from the beginning. Most of the initial funding was spent on hardware, leaving little for the purchase of quality software to run on it.
2. When hardware is purchased, order it *installed* by the company (which may be out of state). If it is disassembled, personnel in the school may not have the background or technological knowledge to install it, so installation should be specified by contract at time of purchase. An example is the Corvus hard-drive system.
3. A frustration (perhaps unavoidable) is that material ordered at high prices usually undergoes a drop in cost months later. This will become less of a frustration with more standardization of hardware and software, which seems inevitable in the evolution of the industry.
4. Along with the computers, it is wise to order one printer, a second disk drive, and one color monitor for each classroom.
5. One problem was that the teachers who planned the school are not the ones there now. The planning was not on-site; it was passed on to others who came in later. This results in confusion of the original objectives, in carrying out plans handed down by others.
6. As there are many hidden costs involved in repairs, upkeep, and updating of equipment, it is wise to write out maintenance and upkeep agreements while working with dealers.
7. Outdatedness of hardware and software is a major problem. Try to get guarantees from publishers and manufacturers that they will update their

products. An example is the "Academic American Encyclopedia" on CD ROM, which comes with a yearly update guarantee.

8. If possible, undertake district wide research and planning before a program for use of technology is implemented. This will minimize mistakes and inefficient uses of time, energy, and funds.

9. The biggest problem in giving workshops for teachers is that immediate implementation of the ideas is expected. Teachers are often pressured to use innovations immediately. They need a great deal of focus in using innovations, because too many scattered directions result in confusion and a drop in teacher morale.

These glimpses of the future of computers in education may help other schools, now in the planning stages, to avoid the problems these pioneers have experienced.

Chapter Four has focused on integration of computers, from the district level to the school building to the classroom. All these levels must cooperate, with clear communication, well-defined goals, and strong support and leadership. This chapter is intended to facilitate such cooperation.

References

Anderson, Elaine M., Ed. "Wisconsin Guidelines for Instructional Computer Use in Education, K-12." January, 1985.

Becker, Henry Jay. "Instructional Use of School Computers." *Center for the Social Organization of Schools, 1985 National Survey,* issue No. 1, June, 1986.

Bell, Margaret E. "The Role of Instructional Theories in the Evaluation of Microcomputer Courseware." *Educational Technology,* March, 1985, pp. 36–40.

Cory, Sheila. "A 4-Stage Model of Development for Full Implementation of Computers for Instruction in a School System." *The Computing Teacher,* November, 1983.

Gardner, Marilyn. "Developing and Implementing a Computer Curriculum: the Problems, the Contents, and the Future." *Educator's Forum,* 1986.

Gray, Robert A. "A Four-Stage Model for Integration of Microcomputers in Teacher Education." *Educational Technology,* November, 1986.

Hall, Gene E. "Concerns-Based Inservice Teacher Training: An Overview of the Concepts, Research and Practice." Paper presented at Conference on School-Focused Inservice Training, March 2–3, 1978, Bournemouth, England.

Hall, G.E., George, A.A., and Rutherford, W.L. *Measuring Stages of Concern about the Innovation: a Manual for Use of the SoC Questionnaire.* Austin: University of Texas Research and Development Center for Teacher Education, 1977.

Hazen, Margaret. "Instructional Software Design Principles." *Educational Technology,* November, 1985, pp. 18–23.

Kloosterman, Peter, Ault, Phyllis, and Harty, Harold. "School-Based Computer Education: Practices and Trends." *Educational Technology,* April, 1987, pp. 35–38.

Komoski, P. Kenneth. "Educational Computing: The Burden of Insuring Quality." *Phi Delta Kappan,* December, 1984, pp. 244–248.

Moran, Thomas. "The Ideal Computer Lab from Floor to Ceiling." *Technology Trends,* March, 1987, pp. 18–20.

Peterson, Dale. "Nine Issues: A Guide to Issues in Computer Education." *Popular Computing,* October, 1984.

Reinhold, Fran. "Computing in America: Electronic Learning's 1986 Annual Survey of the States." *Electronic Learning,* October, 1986, pp. 26–69.

Wilson, Brent G., and Walsh, Jack R. "Small Knowledge-Based Systems in Education and Training: Something New under the Sun." *Educational Technology,* November, 1986, pp. 7–13.

CHAPTER FIVE

Lesson Plans for Integration into the Classroom

A computer program that builds experience

Introduction

The purpose of this chapter is to provide actual, usable lesson plans for teachers in the classroom. The format given here — rationale, objectives, procedures, and evaluation — may be adapted by teachers as they see fit. Many of the lesson plans that follow were inspired by the work of actual teachers in graduate courses and are offered here as practical, usable ideas. The time given for each lesson is only approximate. Most of the plans are for the secondary level, grades 6–12, but the ideas may be adapted to other levels. The plans use the elemental pieces of software that every school should have: a word processor, a database, and graphics packages. Some programs are suggested specifically by name, but the ideas for using them may possibly be adapted to other, more generic software. The purpose here is not to promote particular programs or companies.

The intention of this section is to give teachers practical classroom ideas for integration of computer programs into a well-designed lesson. Each lesson has specific educational objectives related to the reading and writing process. The format is organized so that teachers may understand the rationale for the lesson, based on sound educational principles. The format is a simple one that teachers can continue to use as they begin to make up their own lesson plans to use technology creatively. Many of the lessons cross content areas and may be adapted across the curriculum. The possible uses and adaptations of the lessons are limited only by one's imagination.

Lesson 1

Grade Levels.   9–12

Time.   Three days

Rationale.   This lesson helps students distinguish main ideas from subordinate details in learning to outline information.

Objectives.
1. To preview reading and gain an overview before reading
2. To develop the skill of skimming
3. To organize ideas into main points and subordinate details

Procedures.   Working in pairs, students use the "Think Tank" outlining program. They skim a chapter in their textbook and write down the major titles, then enter them into the "Think Tank" outliner. As they read the chapter, they discuss and fill in the details under the titles, proceeding from what they think is more important to details of lesser importance. The outliner allows students to expand and contract their outlines as they gain more details. It also teaches them to develop points in great detail, which will aid them in their writing. Students print out their outlines and compare them with others'.

Evaluation.   Pairs of students compare their outlines, discuss them, and reach a consensus on a final class outline of the chapter. The class outline may be used for review and as the basis for a test.

Lesson 2

Grade Levels.   9–12

Time.   Two class periods

Rationale.   This lesson allows students to experience the creative process of composing and revising a short story.

Objectives.

1. To understand story structure and the concept of branching
2. To establish a plot line with a minimum of two options
3. To experience creative writing in story production

Procedures.   After reading and discussing a short work of fiction, students will realize that a narrative can branch into various plots and subplots. They will then apply the concepts learned in class to create their own branched narratives on the computer, using the "Story Tree" program (by Scholastic) to write and revise their narratives.

Students will work in groups of three: one typing in the responses and the other two helping to provide ideas for the story development. Each group will print out a copy of their rough draft and critique its plot line. Then they will revise it and print out the final draft.

Evaluation.   The stories will be shared with other groups, who will assess each one in peer evaluation. The grade will be based on how well the story meets the objectives.

Lesson 3

Grade Levels.   4–12

Time.   One week

Rationale.   This lesson will guide students in discovering the main theme of a story by representing it graphically.

Objectives.

1. To represent graphically the theme or moral of a story
2. To promote reading to others
3. To collaborate on communicating a theme to others

Procedures.   Students read a short story from an anthology, then discuss its meaning. Students select a character they feel can best state the message or theme. Using "Print Shop" (by Broderbund) the class creates a greeting card to be sent from one character to another, using the message or moral of the story.

Students in small groups choose a story to read — a different story for each group. The group creates a greeting card that expresses the moral of the story and prints it out. Each group presents its greeting card to the class, providing motivation for others to read that story. All greeting cards may be posted on the bulletin boards in the room as motivation for reading.

Evaluation.   Students discuss whether or not the central meaning of the story has been expressed (both graphically and verbally) in the cards.

Lesson 4

Grade Levels.   7–12

Time.   One class period

Rationale.   This lesson will help students learn to gather and organize information. It will aid them in narrowing down a topic in order to manage it for reporting.

Objectives.

1. To learn to plan research by identifying what is needed
2. To organize information into manageable formats
3. To experience writing a biography

Procedures.   Students decide whose biography they want to write. Younger students may write about someone they know personally, and older students can research their subject. The class will identify what they need to know about a person — for example, place of birth, childhood, education, occupation, and contributions to society. Two students may be assigned to use "PFS: File" (by Scholastic, Inc.) to create and print out a database format for gathering information for the biography. The database format will include whatever the class decides is necessary for the biography. When the format is duplicated, all students can use it as a guide and worksheet for organizing and using their information. Students write their biographies based on information they have researched.

Evaluation.   Collect each student's database of information. Compare it to the written biography in terms of inclusion of the information.

Lesson 5

Grade Levels.   4–9

Time.   Two weeks *(continued in next lesson)*

Rationale.   This lesson will teach students writing a character sketch to differentiate between describing outward appearance and portraying personality. Students will experience using precise language, distinguishing between close synonyms. Adjectives will be studied.

Objectives.

1. To understand stereotypes about people
2. To use precise descriptive words
3. To learn the use of reference materials

Procedures.   The class will participate in creating a face, using "Facemaker" (by Spinnaker) displayed on a large monitor. Students will select the facial features from the options given. Then each individual will write a paragraph describing the face. A list of the adjectives used for each feature will be written on the board and discussed by the class.

The students are divided into groups, each of which deals with a facial feature. Each group looks up one to three synonyms for each of the adjectives, using a thesaurus. Each group presents its options to the rest of the class, which decides which adjectives are most precise in describing the face. The class then writes a paragraph describing the face. The teacher or a student can use a word processor and a large monitor to display the class composition.

Evaluation.   The groups may be evaluated on the quality and quantity of the synonyms they find. Participation of individuals within the groups and in the class composition may be assessed.

Lesson 6

Grade Levels.   4–9

Time.   Three days *(continued in next lesson)*

Rationale.   This lesson will teach students writing a character sketch to differentiate between describing outward appearance and portraying personality. Students will experience using precise language, distinguishing between close synonyms. Adverbs will be studied.

Objectives.

1. To understand the use of adverbs in description
2. To use the thesaurus as a resource and reference
3. To create a character sketch using precise language

Procedures.   Reconstruct the face created previously using "Facemaker" and display it to the class on the large monitor. Program the face for animation, using the options given in the menu. Students will write a paragraph describing the actions of the face. List all the adverbs from students' papers on the board. Assign groups of students to look up each adverb in the dictionary or thesaurus and to find one or two synonyms for each. Each group presents its synonyms to the class, which chooses (by vote) which adverbs are most precise in describing the character's actions. The class then composes a paragraph describing the character's actions, using the adverbs agreed upon. The teacher or a student can use a word processor, displaying the composition on a large monitor.

Evaluation.   The groups may be evaluated on the quality and quantity of synonyms they find. Participation of individuals within the group and in the class composition may be assessed.

Lesson 7

Grade Levels.   4–9

Time.   Two weeks

Rationale.   This lesson will teach students writing a character sketch to differentiate between describing outward appearance and portraying personality.

Objectives.

1. To distinguish between outward appearance and personality
2. To understand the makeup of the personality of a person
3. To avoid jumping to quick conclusions in judging a person

Procedures.   The class reviews and discusses the two-paragraph composition (see Lessons 5 and 6), which has been saved on a data disk. The first paragraph describes the external characteristics of a character, and the second paragraph describes the character's actions. The class discusses what the character must be like as a person — how he or she behaves and relates to people.

Individual students write a third paragraph about the behavior of the character, carefully using both adjectives and adverbs to specify what they mean. Students volunteer to read their third paragraphs to the whole class. The adjectives and adverbs are listed on the board and their effectiveness is discussed. The class determines the differences among the three paragraphs as to what they describe about a person. Why is one of the paragraphs alone insufficient to describe a person? How does this idea relate to making quick judgments about people based solely on their external appearance, or their actions, or their behavior?

Students read and discuss a related story about stereotypes. Relate the narrowness and one-dimensionality of the characters in the story to the character sketches the students have written. Students discuss the limitations of seeing only one part of a person rather than the whole person.

Evaluation.   Collect students' three paragraphs. Holistically evaluate them, tentatively assigning a value from 1 to 4. In students' third paragraphs, especially, the specific choices of adjectives and adverbs may be evaluated. Return the sketches to students to revise and rewrite for a permanent grade. Individual participation in group work and in class contributions may also be evaluated.

Lesson 8

Grade Levels.   5–9

Time.   Two days

Rationale.   This lesson will help students to understand the use of language in poetic form. Language may be manipulated for unusual effect — especially on the computer where revision is encouraged and simplified.

Objectives.

1. To have fun with language
2. To understand creative uses of language
3. To create imaginative images

Procedures.   Students will read several free-verse poems in their anthologies and discuss how the language is used differently from prose. In pairs, students can create an original poem using the program "Compupoem" (by South Coast Writing Project). This program provides a format that students fill in with their own choice of words and syntax.

Introduce students to the thesaurus. Have them concentrate on finding words that express precisely what they want to say. They will print out their poems to share with the rest of the class, the poems may be collated as a class book of poetry.

Evaluation.   The evaluation of each poem may be based on the objectives of original use of language and creation of unusual images.

Lesson 9

Grade Levels.   9–12

Time.   Three days

Rationale.   This lesson will help students develop sensitivity to the language use and style of different authors.

Objectives.

1. To experience a writer's language by copying it
2. To emulate a writer's style by creating language that matches his or her writing
3. To evaluate language use for better writing and reading

Procedures.   Students in small groups will read a short story in the class literary anthology. Each group will read a different story, discuss it, select a representative passage, and enter it on a word processor. Each group will decide which original sentence to replace with one of its own, entering that sentence into the passage. Each group will then print out its passage and pass it on to another group. The other group must analyze the passage and decide which sentence is not the author's. The judgment must be made on style, sentence structure, language use, and content, and the group must be able to defend its judgment. Passages in which a group is not able to guess the spurious sentence are passed to another group, and so on until the student-generated sentence is uncovered.

Evaluation.   As a synthesis of this activity, students will write an analysis of the language use of the writer. Student analyses may be evaluated in terms of detail and comprehensiveness.

Lesson 10

Grade Levels.   4–12

Time.   Two weeks

Rationale.   This lesson will give students an opportunity to create an original story and to understand story elements.

Objectives.

1. To understand plot structure
2. To create an original story plot
3. To practice writing what they have gained from reading

Procedures.   Students may work in pairs or individually to continue a story that the class has originated. The class discusses a "what if" situation such as, "What if I lived in the U.S. in the nineteenth century?" Then they read a story of nineteenth-century America by a writer such as Mark Twain or Bret Harte. Students discuss the story structure in terms of events and consequences.

A student or group of students begins a story on the word processor about how people lived at that time, relating a fictional incident. The next student or group of students reads the beginning and continues the story, either relating another incident or showing the consequences of the previous one. The story continues for at least three incidents, and then a conclusion is provided to tie all the events together and resolve them.

The story is printed out for the class to critique. It is duplicated so that each individual can revise and modify it to provide better structure, more description of the setting, and more extensive development of the characters.

Evaluation.   Students' revisions may be compared to the original class-generated rough draft.

Lesson 11

Grade Levels.   11–12

Time.   Two weeks

Rationale.   This lesson will emphasize to students the practical importance of learning to write and read for lifelong uses.

Objectives.

1. To organize needed information before researching it
2. To focus on a specific career choice and investigate it
3. To understand the lifelong value of reading and writing

Procedures.   Each student makes a decision about a career he or she would like to pursue and lists all of the duties each appears to require. Then each job is discussed by the class as a whole. The class decides what information is needed about each career in order to understand it fully. A database format is constructed, including job description, qualifications, and education required. The format is created on a database program and printed out for students to use in their library research on their chosen careers. The information is entered into the database data disk, stored, and printed out for each career.

The class peruses the database of career choices and discusses each, deciding whether any writing and reading is needed for each career choice. Discuss with the class the lifelong importance of literacy on the job and off. Students collate the database of careers into a booklet for classroom reference in further writing assignments.

Evaluation.   Student gains in learning may be assessed through class discussions, information gained in research, and the final product of the career booklet.

Lesson 12

Grade Levels.   10–12

Time.   Four to five days

Rationale.   Students will learn to write a persuasive essay using logical reasons, developed from least important to most important.

Objectives.

1. To understand techniques of persuasion
2. To recognize appeals of logic, emotion, and ethics in persuasion
3. To apply understanding of persuasion in reading to writing

Procedures.   Students read a persuasive essay in their literary anthology book. Discuss why it was persuasive or, if not, what changes would make it so. On the large monitor, show students "Writing an Opinion Paper" (MECC). Summarize the major elements of persuasive writing.

As a class, the students brainstorm about what they would change in their school if they could. They should be encouraged to make positive improvements. Students then write an essay to persuade the principal, a teacher, or someone else to make the improvements they would like to see. They are to begin with least important reasons and build up to the most important; at least three reasons should be included. Students should make clear whether their appeals are to logic, emotions, or ethics. Students use a word processor and save their essays on a blank disk.

Randomly select several of the essays and, with the students' permission, display them on the large monitor. Have the class discuss the persuasive techniques used, the types of appeals made, and the effectiveness of the transition words. Review the criteria for writing a persuasive essay and identify them in each essay.

Students read another essay in their anthology and discuss it. Then they revise their rough drafts and print them out. They proofread the hard copy for mechanical errors.

Evaluation.   Students' progress can be assessed by comparing their initial drafts to the final copy. Another criterion could be how well their essays utilize the principles taught in the computer program: distinguishing between fact and opinion, supporting opinions with examples and reasons, appealing to the audience, and so on.

Lesson 13

Grade Levels.   6–12

Time.   Three days

Rationale.   This lesson helps students learn to pay attention to details and to synthesize them in order to solve a problem.

Objectives.
1. To look for clues and make predictions about an outcome
2. To use reference materials to solve a problem
3. To experience an inductive problem-solving process

Procedures.   Students form groups of three: one researcher, one analyst, and one computer operator. Using the program "Where in the World is Carmen Sandiego?" (by Broderbund), each group will research clues in the accompanying almanac, police dossiers, and "crime lab" to track down the criminal in a major city of the world.

When all groups have solved their crimes on Level 1, their times for problem solving can be compared.

Each individual will write an account of the adventure, using specific facts about the city and country the groups researched in order to "nail" the criminal.

Evaluation.   Participation in the group and fulfillment of the role assigned within the group may be assessed. The individual written accounts of the experience may be evaluated according to accuracy, details provided, and facts learned.

Lesson 14

Grade Levels.   7–10

Time.   Two to three days

Rationale.   This lesson will help students learn to write a procedural essay using specific transition words.

Objectives.

1. To reason deductively
2. To solve a problem by synthesizing information
3. To understand and use transition words effectively

Procedures.   Using a large monitor, display the MECC simulation program "Odell Lake" to the class. The students make choices to discover which is the strongest fish in the "survival of the fittest." Students react and analyze why one fish survived and another did not. Through a process of elimination, they should determine which species is the strongest.

Students write an essay explaining their conclusion. They should use specific transition words (such as "first," "then," "eventually," and "finally") to develop the procedure of survival they describe. List the transition words they use on a word processor and display them on the large monitor. Write in their definitions and functions as students explain them. Print out the list and give it to the students. Students revise their essays for a final draft.

Evaluation.   Students evaluate each other's essays using the list. Each paper should have at least five transition words or phrases, each of which should be logical in its function.

Lesson 15

Grade Levels.   6–11

Time.   Three weeks

Rationale.   This lesson will provide a simulated experience of living and survival in the westward movement of the 1850s. The experience is a springboard to writing about the experience and reading accounts of the period.

Objectives.

1. To experience personally some life-and-death decisions, without suffering their real consequences
2. To write in the journal/diary mode of literature
3. To understand the use of comparison and contrast in description

Procedures.   Display the program "The Oregon Trail" (by MECC) to the class on the large monitor. Divide the class into "wagon teams" that will make decisions together for survival as they trek westward in the simulation of the 1850s. The class as a whole will discuss the beginning and make some decisions. They will discuss the life-and-death experiences of the pioneers in westward expansion.

One group can play the simulation, making decisions and solving problems until they arrive at a destination predetermined by the teacher. Meanwhile, the other groups can read an account of the westward movement, preferably a journal or diary account. The next group can play the computer game simulation up to the predetermined point. The first group then reads the diary account. When all groups have used the simulation and read the diary, they will write their own daily diary or journal of their personal, simulated experience. Students share their experiences in class discussions.

Students collate the journal/diary entries into a resource booklet for that period of history and literature.

Evaluation.   The students take an essay test on the similarities and differences between life as a teenager today and in the 1850s. Their information will be based on the simulation experience and their readings. For grading purposes, the emphasis will be on the comparisons and contrasts they provide.

Lesson 16

Grade Levels.   6–11

Time.   One week

Rationale.   This lesson will help students understand cause-and-effect relationships in reading and writing.

Objectives.
1. To analyze the consequences of a decision
2. To recognize cause-and-effects patterns in reading
3. To write using cause-and-effect sequencing

Procedures.   Based on their journal accounts of the simulation experience with "The Oregon Trail" (see Lesson 15), students will discuss the consequences of their decisions for survival along the trail.

Students read an essay that uses cause-and-effect sequencing. Point out that "cause and effect" is a misnomer because, in the reading, the effects are presented first, then the causes are explained. The sequencing should actually be effect and cause. Students write about three of their experiences on the Oregon Trail, mentioning the effects first and then showing what caused them to come about. In class discussion, students share the experiences they have written about.

Evaluation.   Quickly skim over students' papers to check whether they include three instances of cause and effect. Return the papers to the students for revision and final drafting. Collect and assess the papers on the basis of their use of the cause-and-effect patterns.

Lesson 17

Grade Levels.   5–12

Time.   Two days

Rationale.   This lesson will allow students to "be the teacher," making up a spelling exercise for the rest of the class. It will provide incentive for students to develop in their spelling growth.

Objectives.
1. To use spelling words in a unique way to motivate learning them
2. To give students incentives to study the spelling words
3. To vary the usual routine of spelling experience

Procedures.   A small group of students enter the spelling words for the week into the "Crossword Magic" computer program to create a crossword puzzle for the class. The class completes the crossword puzzle and studies the words. Those students who get 100 percent on the spelling test get to create the next crossword puzzle on the computer.

Evaluation.   How well students complete the crossword puzzle can be evaluated. Their scores on the spelling test may also be assessed to ascertain learning.

Lesson 18

Grade Levels.   5-10

Time.   One day

Rationale.   This lesson provides practice in using words in context as well as developing skills in sentence structure.

Objectives.

1. To use words in context
2. To use sentence structure as a clue to meaning
3. To emphasize meaning through careful choice of words

Procedures.   Using a word processor, create a cloze exercise from the students' textbook. Select a passage (about 250 words) that they have not yet read. Copy the passage, but delete every seventh word beginning in the second sentence. List the missing words below the passage in random order. Either print this out to hard copy, which students can work on in pencil, or copy it onto disks for a word processing exercise. If students use a word processor to insert the words, print the words themselves to hard copy and duplicate them so that students may refer to them as they work through the text on the screen.

Evaluation.   Students who score above 60 percent understand the text at an independent reading level. Students who score between 40 and 60 percent are reading at an instructional level and need teacher help in understanding it. Below 40 percent, students are reading at a frustration level and need much practice in using context.

Lesson 19

Grade Levels.   9–12

Time.   One week

Rationale.   This lesson emphasizes to students that the purpose of reading is to understand ideas rather than to pronounce words. It also helps students break the habit of reading word by word.

Objectives.

1. To understand the idea that thought groups are to be grasped as whole ideas in reading
2. To read for meaning rather than to pronounce words
3. To understand "speed reading" in terms of speed of comprehension

Procedures.   Project the sequential lessons of the "Speed Reader II" on the large monitor. Demonstrate to students the importance of grasping ideas in thought groups during reading, rather than seeing isolated words. Emphasize that reading is for *concepts,* which are grasped in the context of grouped words. A few of the exercises can be done as a class group, to introduce proper eye movements and more efficient reading. Then have individuals practice their reading skills with the program, in segments of 15 to 20 minutes.

Evaluation.   Students bring in newspapers and practice fixating their eyes only two times per line as they speed-read a column of print. Time them for one minute, then have them write a summary of what they have read. Compare the first timed test to subsequent ones to measure progress.

Lesson 20

Grade Levels. 5-9

Time. Three days

Rationale. This lesson will help students to distinguish between fact and opinion in what they read and to apply that knowledge to current reports.

Objectives.

1. To become a critical reader
2. To distinguish fact from opinion
3. To transfer understanding from computer to other media

Procedures. Present the program "Fact or Opinion" (by Hartley Publishing Co.) to the class on the large monitor. Students can do the drill and practice exercises together and discuss the answers. Duplicate a news article and an editorial on the same subject and ask the students to compare the words, the tone, the headlines, and the treatment of the subject in each article. Which is more factual and which is more subjective?

Students write their opinion of a television program they watch. They must include at least three actual facts about it.

Evaluation. Students' papers may be assessed for differentiation between fact and opinion.

Lesson 21

Grade Levels.   6–12

Time.   Three days

Rationale.   This lesson will emphasize meanings of words in context. Even many common words have multiple meanings and need to be interpreted based on their usage in context.

Objectives.

1. To understand that words have contextual meaning
2. To learn to use words appropriately
3. To become sensitive to multiple meanings of words

Procedures.   Introduce the concept of multiple meanings of words. Ask students to say whatever occurs to them for the words *strike, point,* and *out.* Discuss the multiple meanings of each word and the necessity of context in order to understand each meaning. Project the program "Multiple Meanings" on the large monitor and have the class complete the exercises in the tutorial. Students will read a story in their anthology or textbook and pick out words with multiple meanings. How do the words affect the meaning of the story or passage?

Enter the words into the tutorial lessons, which are modifiable. Students work in small groups on the computer program.

Evaluation.   The results of students' work on the computer lesson may be assessed for indications of their progress.

Lesson 22

Grade Levels.   4–12

Time.   Two days

Rationale.   This lesson will give students practice in learning new vocabulary—not just words, but also uses in context.

Objectives.

1. To develop vocabulary found in reading
2. To analyze unfamiliar words and predict their meanings
3. To use the glossary of the textbook as a resource

Procedures.   Students skim through a chapter they have been assigned to read, looking for unfamiliar words. They list the new words as well as the page numbers on which they appear. Pair off students for work on a word processor: From the story, one student types in the sentence that uses a new word, and the other student types in what he or she guesses to be a short definition of the new word. The pairs alternate until all of the new words are presented in context and meanings guessed. Students check the meanings in the glossary of their books or in a dictionary. Students read the assigned chapter, applying the new vocabulary to their comprehension.

Evaluation.   All of the words are collected from students. A check-up quiz is given on some of the new words, and they are discussed. The quizzes are graded, but the grades can be improved if the student writes original sentences, providing further uses in context.

Lesson 23

Grade Levels.   9–12

Time.   Three days

Rationale.   This lesson will allow students the opportunity to generate ideas, seek solutions to problems, analyze situations, and share solutions with other students.

Objectives.

1. To experience reading with personal involvement
2. To write from a first-person point of view
3. To understand variations in perception, bias, and reporting of events

Procedures.   Students read a chapter, a story, or other material in the content field. They are divided into groups of three to discuss the reading selection. Using "Write Start" (MECC), each group selects the "Class Journal" option from the menu, enabling them to word-process their ideas in a journal format. Each group writes their reactions to the reading, immersing themselves in the situation as though it were their own personal experience. Students provide specific facts, but they also give their first-person feelings, thoughts, and reactions to the events and characters. They print out their journals on "Option 3." Each group shares its personal accounts with the class in an oral presentation. Discuss differences in perceptions and views.

Evaluation.   Each group member's participation and production is assessed for an individual grade. The validity of the ideas expressed in each journal is assessed for a collective group grade.

Lesson 24

Grade Levels.   7–12

Time.   Two days

Rationale.   This lesson will emphasize the importance of transition words in structuring text in time, cause and effect, and procedural sequences.

Objectives.

1. To recognize sequencing in text
2. To understand the importance of transition words and phrases
3. To manipulate text so that meaning is altered

Procedures.   Before reading a chapter, story, or other selection that is sequenced according to time, students skim the text and list all of the transition words they see. They select a passage that has five or more transition words in it, such as *first of all, therefore, finally,* and *as a result.* Discuss the functions (for example, to indicate time).

Students copy the passage onto a word processor, leaving blank spaces for the transition words. They substitute other transition words and phrases into the blanks to alter the meaning and change the sequencing. Print out the altered passage. Discuss the meaning, the logical development, and the function of the new transitions.

Evaluation.   Make lists of transitions the students have used in their passages. Have the students label the sequencing each list indicates — for example, time order, cause and effect, procedure, simple to complex or vice versa, small to large or vice versa. How well students label each sequence may be a basis for evaluating their learning.

Lesson 25

Grade Levels.   4–7

Time.   Two weeks

Rationale.   This lesson exposes students to different ways of providing information about a topic. It allows for graphic and textual variations.

Objectives.

1. To express an idea in different media
2. To gather information from a variety of sources
3. To apply "research" in different ways

Procedures.   Students work in small groups to produce a collection of information about, for example, a city they choose to study. They collect pictures or make drawings of important features of the city. They may write to the Chamber of Commerce of the city or get information about it from a museum or library. They read in an encyclopedia and other references. Students pretend they were born in the city and write an "autobiography" of their early childhood years there. They write a research report that gives facts and details about the city.

Students may dress up in costumes and act out a characteristic of the people who live in the city, or they may compose a poem about it in free verse, Haiku, or chant (including sounds and environment).

Create a cover for each collection using "Print Shop." Collate the collection and attach a cover that graphically illustrates something about the city.

Evaluation.   The participation and production of all group members are assessed. Each group's collection is given a group grade.

Lesson 26

Grade Levels.   10–12

Time.   Three to four days

Rationale.   This lesson will make concrete an abstract symbol in a story or poem.

Objectives.

1. To make concrete an abstract idea
2. To visualize an abstraction
3. To understand the meanings of symbols

Procedures.   Students read from their literature book a story or poem containing symbolism. They identify the symbol and discuss what it represents in the overall interpretation of the piece. (Examples: a flag may represent a country, a cross may represent God, or a rose may represent romance and nostalgia). In small groups, students select a symbol from the literary piece. Using the graphics tool kit "Blazing Paddles," each group "draws" or cuts and pastes a picture of the symbol and prints it out.

Using a word processor, each group describes the symbol and fully explains what it represents in the literature. They print this out and attach it to their graphic symbol. The groups share their ideas.

Evaluation.   Students' understanding may be judged by how well they explained the symbol.

Lesson 27

Grade Levels.   8–12

Time.   Three days

Rationale.   This lesson gives students an opportunity to solve a problem graphically and concretely, then write about it abstractly.

Objectives.

1. To represent an abstract idea graphically
2. To solve a problem inductively through trial and error
3. To write procedurally using a specific sequence

Procedures.   Students read a story in their anthology books, discuss it, and select some important object in it that can be drawn, such as a house, a train, or an animal. Students pair off to use the "Logo" program. Each pair will use the turtle graphics to design the object in the story. They use trial and error, mathematics, and discovery to make their designs as complex as they can. They record their commands on a sheet of paper as they develop the program, then print out their designs. Each individual writes about how the design was created, describing the procedure step by step. When procedural essays are finished, the student analyzes how the information was sequenced: part to whole, whole to part, smallest to largest, near to far or vice versa, first to last, last to first, most important to least important, most obvious to least obvious, and so on. List the sequences students suggest. The students rewrite and revise their procedural essays, making very clear with transition terms what the sequence is.

Evaluation.   Students' revised essays may be assessed according to clarity of sequence, inclusion of details, and appropriateness of transition words.

Lesson 28

Grade Levels. 4–12

Time.   One week

Rationale.   This lesson allows students to experience a free flow of ideas in the composing process, without an initial fear of making mistakes.

Objectives.

1. To defend one's opinion by arguing a point
2. To collaborate with others in taking a stand on an issue
3. To experience a free flow of ideas in the writing process

Procedures.   Students read something controversial in their textbooks or newspapers. They take sides on the issue, one group taking a stand and the other opposing them. On a word processor, students write individually every idea that occurs to them in support of their side of the issue. Turn off their monitors (but not their computers) after three minutes of writing. Tell them just to get down all their ideas and not to worry about spelling or mechanics yet. Encourage a free flow of ideas. Print out the ideas students generate. Each group discusses the ideas of its members, and someone records the major points, which are duplicated for everyone in the group. Each member writes a lengthy explanation of one of the points, which are then given to three members for use in debating three members from the other side of the issue.

Students choose a side of the issue and write a defense of their position.

Evaluation.   Students' essays may be assessed by other students — on the opposing side of the issue — as to how well they supported their opinions.

Lesson 29

Grade Levels.   4–10

Time.   Two weeks

Rationale.   This lesson will give students the opportunity to write their own play, thus learning about the dramatic literary form.

Objectives.

1. To understand the dramatic form
2. To create a dramatic play
3. To experience presentation of a play to an audience

Procedures.   Students read aloud a play in class. They discuss its form — acts, characters, scenery descriptions and directions, and dialogue. Display on the large monitor the MECC program "Show Time." The class collectively writes a short play using the program directions. "Show Time" has a built-in word processor, on which students write and edit their own script. Either the teacher or a student enters the ideas as the class produces them. Discuss the play form.

In groups of three, students write their own plays. They share their ideas and may present their plays to the class, either on the large monitor, on hard copy, or by actually acting them out.

Evaluation.   Students' plays may be assessed for their adherence to the principles of the dramatic literary form, for originality of idea, and for effective dialogue.

Lesson 30

Grade Levels.   4–12

Time.   Four days

Rationale.   This lesson allows students to make up their own study/test questions, focusing on main ideas and details.

Objectives.

1. To study for a test by asking questions about the material
2. To ask effective questions that help learning
3. To ask questions about main ideas and important details

Procedures.   Students read and discuss a chapter in their textbook. In groups of three, they make up questions about the material they have read. Each group enters the questions into the computer program "The Game Show" (by Advanced Ideas Software Co.). The groups play each other's games as a review for the test.

Evaluation.   Students' collective and individual performance may be assessed to determine the value of this study method.

Lesson 31

Grade Levels.   6–12

Time.   Two to three days

Rationale.   This lesson will provide practice in using parts of speech in meaningful ways and manipulating language to produce different effects.

Objectives.

1. To recognize usage of parts of speech
2. To "play" with language for interesting effects
3. To understand that language may be manipulated

Procedures.   Using the program "Compupoem" (by South Coast Writing Project), projected on the large monitor, the class reviews parts of speech—noun, adjective, verb, and adverb. When a noun is selected by the class, a student will look it up in a thesaurus and read aloud the synonyms given there. Students then choose a synonym and enter it into the program. This procedure is followed for each part of speech asked for in the program. The class poem is then displayed on the monitor. Select the option on the menu for variations of the poem, and discuss with the class the changes in language that are presented. Are the changes less poetic?

The class reads and discusses several Haiku poems, appreciating their structure, allusions, and creative use of language. Each student creates her or his own poem in the "Compupoem" program, using the most interesting words he or she can think of for the parts of speech asked for. Print out the poems and share them with the class.

Evaluation.   Accuracy in using the parts of speech in the poems may be the basis of evaluation, as well as originality of expression.

Lesson 32

Grade Levels.   4–12

Time.   Three days

Rationale.   This lesson will develop students' study skills by helping them to focus on main points. They identify major ideas and organize and research them for use in reviewing for a test.

Objectives.

1. To organize a unit of study into major concepts that guide student thinking about it
2. To synthesize learning and apply it
3. To reinforce learning and retention through managing it

Procedures.   When a unit of study is over and students are reviewing for a test on it, help them review with a database. Project "PFS:File" (by Scholastic) on a large class monitor. Students are to identify at least five main points they need to know for the test. Each point is discussed and reasons given why it is a major point. The class must agree on the most important ones, which are entered as the fields on the form. Print out the form and duplicate it for the students. In groups of three, students review their notes and books and fill in the information needed on the form. Each group presents its information to the class. The students take notes and discuss the findings as to accuracy, relevance, and importance.

Evaluation.   The test is based on the major points brought out by the class. The test allows students to synthesize and apply their learning. Students are evaluated on how well they use information.

Lesson 33

Grade Levels.   4–10

Time.   One week

Rationale.   This lesson will teach students to change the point of view of a text from the impersonal third person to the personal first person so that the effects of point of view can be demonstrated.

Objectives.

1. To alter text from third person to first person point of view
2. To recognize the function and effect of point of view
3. To understand the use of pronouns

Procedures.   Students copy a descriptive passage from a story onto a word processor. The passage should be at least three-quarters of a page in length and use the third person (he, she, or it). Using the "Find and Replace" function, students change the pronouns to first person (I). Change the verbs to agree with the pronouns.

Read the passage aloud. The class discusses what effect the change had on the story.

Define point of view as the perspective from which events are viewed and related to the reader.

Discuss the use of appropriate pronouns and agreement of verbs.

Students continue writing the story from the first-person point of view, maintaining personal involvement.

Evaluation.   Students' stories may be assessed for use of the first-person point of view, as well as story development based on preceding events.

Lesson 34

Grade Levels.   9–12

Time.   Two days

Rationale.   This lesson provides a means for students to assess their own language growth.

Objectives.

1. To develop sensitivity to language use
2. To understand sentence expansion of ideas
3. To judge clarity of communication

Procedures.   Present the program "Sentence Combining" (by Milliken) on a large monitor. The class follows the directions and completes the exercises. Explain that sentence combining is a technique used to enrich the information in sentences with single words, phrases, and clauses. Such enrichment can help the reader to understand more fully the point the writer wants to make. Give the students a brief sentence, such as "The cats eat." Using a word processor, the students expand the sentence using a single word (adjective or adverb). Then ask them to add a descriptive group of words (a phrase or clause). Finally, the students expand it as fully as they can. Students read aloud their sentences and discuss the clarity of their communication. If the sentence is too long or cumbersome, it will not be effective.

Students use a readability analysis program such as "Reading Level Analysis." Discuss what seems to be the desired sentence complexity for clear communication.

Students write a five-sentence paragraph on their topic, using the word processor.

Evaluation.   Students' paragraphs may be assessed for their use of modifying words, phrases, and clauses.

Lesson 35 (suggested by Ted Perry)

Grade Levels.   9–12

Time.   One week

Rationale.   This lesson presents students with "what if" decision-making hypotheses to get them to imagine and predict.

Objectives.

1. To engage in hypothesizing in thinking
2. To "change" events in history creatively
3. To recognize cause and effect

Procedures.   Project "Story Tree" (by Scholastic) on the large monitor. The class completes one of the three adventure plots, making choices and branching to alternate events. In groups of three or four, students write out alternatives for a historical event they have just read about, such as President Lincoln's stand against secession of the southern states. Students decide upon four alternatives to his position, such as (1) resign as President, (2) sell the Southern states to Mexico, (3) make the South a separate self-governing nation, and (4) establish slavery as the law of the entire United States. Students select one of the alternatives. Projecting up to the present, they describe what would have happened in history if Lincoln had acted in an alternative way. They share the scenarios they have written with the entire class.

Evaluation.   Students' writing may be evaluated according to the degree of imagination or the logic by which consequences are traced.

Lesson 36

Grade Levels.   6–12

Time.   Two days

Rationale.   This lesson gives students the opportunity to prompt each other, to monitor each other's writing, and to give immediate collaborative feedback.

Objectives.

1. To tutor other students in the writing process
2. To read and guide someone else's writing and thinking
3. To interact with a peer in the composing process

Procedures.   Pair students to work together. Position them at computers, facing each other if possible. Exchange their monitors so that each can see what the other is writing. Using a word processor, one student is to write on a topic; the other is to comment on, guide, and encourage the writing. When the writer gets stuck or distracted, he or she can type in three X's or write HELP, and the promptor can write back an idea. When the writer finishes, the students exchange roles. Both print out their essays, proofread the hard copy, and revise them on the computer.

Evaluation.   Students' essays may be evaluated to determine the success of peer prompting. Also, students' attitudes should be assessed for their enjoyment of the writing process.

Lesson 37

Grade Levels.   4–12

Time.   One week

Rationale.   This lesson will help students get involved in their reading and develop the prereading technique of predicting.

Objectives.
1. To predict the outcome of a story
2. To write the ending of a story
3. To judge story development critically

Procedures.   Introduce the story or chapter students are to read. Write the first or the last sentence on a word processor and project it on a large monitor. Ask students to decide what the text is going to be about or (if they see the last sentence) what it was about. The class adds two or three more sentences, which are typed in.

Students write the story or text, either in groups or individually. They share their ideas with the rest of the class. Students read the text. In class discussion, they compare their versions with the text and decide which they like better. They must provide substantive reasons for their opinions.

Evaluation.   Student writing may be assessed for its logical and creative development of the first or last sentence.

Lesson 38

Grade Levels.   4–12

Time.   Three days

Rationale.   This lesson will provide practice in using reference materials, extend students' vocabularies, and help students understand antonyms.

Objectives.

1. To learn to refer to the antonyms given in dictionary definitions
2. To enrich the range of vocabulary associated with a concept
3. To apply definitions for memory retention

Procedures.   Students read a chapter or a story in their textbooks. Select a passage with at least ten words that have antonyms and copy it onto a word processor (or have a student do it). Students copy down the words and look them up in an unabridged dictionary. Students find the antonym listing for each word. Project the passage on the large monitor and ask the students to agree on an appropriate antonym for each word. Change the word to the antonym form. Have the students discuss how the change alters the meanings as well as the structure of surrounding words (if this is indeed the case).

Enter the antonyms into "Wizard Memory" on the MECC program "Word Wizards," and have the class practice the antonyms in this concentration game format.

Give a short quiz on the antonyms.

Evaluation.   The participation of students in learning the vocabulary may be observed and evaluated. The results of the quiz can be used to assess learning and memory retention of the words.

Lesson 39
(suggested by Sherry Wulff, Secondary Teacher)

Grade Levels.   7–12

Time.   Several units over a four-week period *(continued in the next lesson)*

Rationale.   This lesson will allow students to create a mystery story, using cooperative learning and the full writing process.

Objectives.

1. To develop the skeleton of a mystery story
2. To use accurate information
3. To collaborate with others to develop interpersonal skills in solving a problem

Procedures.   Students read a mystery story, such as something from *The Adventures of Sherlock Holmes* or from their anthology textbook. Discuss the use of clues, foreshadowing, plot structure, and other devices that lend mystery to the story.

Students form groups of three, each with a role responsibility: one to record group ideas (the recorder), one to research ideas (the researcher), and one to lead group discussions (the initiator). On a word processor, each group creates a list of five to ten clues, two to four brief character sketches (or police dossiers), and an imaginative two-line plot summary that includes the setting (but *not* the solution to the mystery). Each group prints out this information and hands it in.

Evaluation.   The background information for the mysteries may be evaluated for its logic and plausibility as well as the accuracy of the information (which is the responsibility of the researcher in the group). The mystery background sketches should not be graded; credit should be given with a checkmark, perhaps.

Lesson 40

Grade Levels.   7–12

Time.   Four weeks *(continued in the next lesson)*

Rationale.   This lesson will give students an opportunity to develop a rough draft of a mystery story based on a background sketch provided by their peers.

Objectives.

1. To collaborate with others to solve a problem
2. To begin to construct a mystery story
3. To enjoy imaginative writing based on clues and literary devices.

Procedures.   Each group of three students selects a mystery background sketch (folded so that they do not see it), created in the previous lesson. After discussion, each group begins to write their rough drafts of the mystery story they visualize. The recorder in each group types out the story on the word processor as the group provides ideas. Students save their writing on a blank data disk. They print out their initial draft, reread it, and submit it to the teacher.

Evaluation.   Group rough drafts may be assessed for their story development, use of detail in the original sketch, and literary devices that create mystery. The rough drafts should not be graded at this time; the teacher should simply give suggestions for improvement.

Lesson 41

Grade Levels.   7–12

Time.   Four weeks *(continued in the next lesson)*

Rationale.   This lesson gives students experience in editing the writing of others, which is necessary for understanding their own writing.

Objectives.

1. To assess others' writing so that one's own may be better understood
2. To use objective criteria in judging others' writing
3. To be responsible for establishing criteria to be used in assessment

Procedures.   On a word processor projected on the large monitor, the teacher establishes a list of criteria for assessing rough drafts. Make sure students clearly understand the criteria, print them out, and duplicate them for each student. Emphasize that they are *not* to grade other students' writing, but rather assess it for its strong points and for ways it could be improved.

Pass out each group's rough draft (see Lesson 40) to another group for assessment. Each group assesses their peers' stories based on the established criteria and writes suggestions in the margins. The annotated rough drafts are returned to their owners. The groups discuss the comments and suggestions and confer with the teacher regarding improvements and changes in their stories.

Evaluation.   The comments and suggestions students make in their assessments of their peers may be evaluated through discussion and observation. Also, students' attitudes toward writing and being assessed by this method may be evaluated.

Lesson 42

Grade Levels.   7–12

Time.   Four weeks *(continued in the next lesson)*

Rationale.   This lesson builds on the previous three. The idea is that the only real writing is revised writing, and that real thinking must involve reshaped and rethought language.

Objectives.

1. To understand the process of revising and reshaping language
2. To practice revision with a word processor
3. To investigate story techniques that can lead to improved reading of stories

Procedures.   Each group writes its second draft on the word processor, using the data disk on which the rough draft was stored. Using cut and paste, search and replace, and other editing functions, they revise, reshape, and rethink their stories. They then print out their second drafts.

Each group exchanges stories with another group, which reads it and discusses it with the writers. To facilitate discussion, have each group write out two important questions they need to ask the writers of the story they read. The second drafts are returned to the teacher.

Evaluation.   The drafts may be assessed for development of plot and the use of the literary devices of mystery stories. The stories should not be graded yet, but credit should be given for revision work, perhaps with a checkmark.

Lesson 43

Grade Levels. 7–12

Time. Four weeks

Rationale. This lesson will allow students to finalize their stories and share their creations with others in the class.

Objectives.

1. To collaborate with others in the writing process.
2. To revise and rethink writing.
3. To "publish" a final version for an outside audience.

Procedures. Each group discusses the final draft of its story and decides what changes should be made in it. Using the word processor, they revise their story stored on the data disk. They may print out their revision to proofread it, or they may proofread on the screen. As a final check, they can use a spelling checker that is compatible with the word processor they are using. They print out the final version, proofread it again, and submit it to the teacher for a grade. The stories may be collated and bound in a cover created on "The Print Shop" (by Broderbund Co.). The stories may be shared with a younger class, for their reading enjoyment and writing inspiration.

Evaluation. The final versions may be assessed and graded based on plot development, mystery story literary devices, and the solution of the mystery. Initial drafts may be compared to final versions, to evaluate the effectiveness of the writing process.

Lesson 44

Grade Levels.   10–12

Time.   One week

Rationale.   This lesson will teach students to develop problem-solving strategies that they may consciously transfer to other applicable situations.

Objectives.

1. To experience using problem-solving strategies
2. To understand and verbalize the strategies used
3. To review material covered in a unit for a test or other application

Procedures.   Set up the large monitor, using "Tic Tac Show" (by Advanced Ideas), and have the class participate in creating a "game show" based on concepts learned in an ongoing unit of study. The class can play the game together. They should refer to their textbook for specific vocabulary. Lead them in using "Option 2" to build their own subject area. As a group, they can insert their own topic, questions, and answers. Discuss the kinds of problem-solving strategies they used to get the answer (for example, using a model, using clues, analyzing, or seeing patterns). Students form groups of three to write out their own version of "Tic Tac Show" based on a topic they are studying. Each group could take a different aspect of a larger topic.

Each group takes turns entering their material into the authoring system of "Tic Tac Show." The class plays the game and critiques it in terms of difficulty, quality, and learning value. Discuss the problem-solving strategies used in creating the game (brainstorming, data gathering, narrowing the topic, etc.) and in playing the game.

Evaluation.   To assess learning, the students take a test covering the topic they have reviewed in the games they created. Also evaluate their attitudes toward their learning experience.

Lesson 45

Grade Levels.   6–12

Time.   One week

Rationale.   This lesson provides a higher-level thinking exercise based on predicting the outcome of a story. Students can work cooperatively to develop their views.

Objectives.

1. To predict the outcome of a story
2. To hypothesize a character's effect upon a story
3. To integrate writing with reading to validate a prediction

Procedures.   Students will be assigned parts to read aloud in a play. They will read the first act as homework in order to prepare for the "performance" of oral reading in class the next day. Students read Act I aloud. They then pair off to use a word processor. Using two computers, they swap monitors so that they may exchange ideas on screen with each other. Students are assigned to assume the identity of a character in the play and predict what will happen to the character in the other acts. Taking turns, the pairs type in what they think will happen to the character. Each reads what the other has written, then reacts to it as though they were having a written conversation with each other. They print out their ideas.

Students pair up again to discuss their predictions. They agree upon a probable outcome for the character and together write a projected end to the play. They print out their writing and share their predictions with the class. They then finish reading the play, and assess the accuracy of their predictions.

Evaluation.   Students' understanding of the play may be assessed by having them write an argument defending their prediction for the end of the play. They may argue that their ending is better or that the play's is better, but in either case they need to provide convincing reasons based on the elements in the story.

Lesson 46

Grade Levels.   6–12

Time.   One class period

Rationale.   This lesson will aid students in understanding how to correct sentence fragments.

Objectives.

1. To learn what a complete sentence is
2. To practice manipulating language
3. To hear and see sentences modeled correctly

Procedures.   Students complete the initial drafts of an essay they have been assigned to write. A student or the teacher copies all of the sentence fragments found in their papers onto a word processor. The sentences should be projected onto the large monitor, and students can read them aloud one by one. After hearing each fragment read, the class can discuss what is wrong with the sentence.

A sentence can be defined as a group of words containing a subject and predicate and expressing a complete thought. Students should decide whether the fragment measures up to that definition. Why, or why not? How would they change the fragment to make it a complete sentence? The fragment may be changed on the screen as students watch and comment.

This procedure can be followed with each fragment. Student volunteers can change it on the word processor as the rest of the class watches.

Evaluation.   Students' rough drafts should be returned for revision. Students' final essays may be assessed in terms of their use of complete sentences.

Lesson 47

Grade Levels. 7–12

Time. One week

Rationale. This lesson teaches students to define objects carefully and accurately, using both critical and variable attributes. By doing this, students learn critical thinking skills.

Objectives.

1. To learn to distinguish critical from variable attributes
2. To define an object using attributes, rules, and discrimination
3. To solve problems using a systematic procedure

Procedures. Introduce students to the idea of critical attributes by discussing what it is that makes a table a table and distinguishes it from everything else (recommended in the manual for "Ten Clues" by Sunburst). List on the board all the attributes students name. Underline the critical attributes that a table must have in order to be a table. Boot up "Ten Clues," using a large monitor. Press "Option 1" to play the game with the class. Discuss the problem-solving skills they are using in the game (for example, analyzing, information gathering, discriminating). Point out how the exercise is intended to make them think more clearly.

Divide students into groups of five or less. Each group makes up a game of Ten Clues based on a word or concept they have been studying. Each group enters in the clues into the program, and the class plays the game as a review of ideas studied. Students write a definition essay on a word processor, choosing one of the concepts in the games played. The essay must distinguish between critical attributes of the concept and *variable* ones that are not found in every instance of the thing described. The paper should include attributes and examples of the thing in question. The definitions must be complete, accurate, and as precise as technical writing has to be. They save their essays on the data disk. Project a couple of the best essays on the large monitor and critique them as a class. Students revise and rewrite their essays and print them out.

Evaluation. Students' definition essays may be assessed for their clarity in differentiating between attributes or properties that are critical to the thing defined and those that are not present in all instances. Their essays should be judged on the basis of the critical thinking used in making the definition clear. Discuss the thinking involved and the usefulness of such discrimination in the real world, particularly in technical fields of work.

Lesson 48

Grade Levels.   6–12

Time.   Three to five days

Rationale.   This lesson helps students express an idea from any content field in different composition forms.

Objectives.

1. To express an idea in different forms of composition
2. To understand how the idea is altered by the style of communication used
3. To synthesize ideas for application

Procedures.   Students in groups compose a poem using "CompuPoem" (by South Coast Writing Project). Every key word they enter into the format should be related to the topic or an aspect of the topic they are currently studying. Each group shares its poem with the class.

Each member of the group uses a word processor to rewrite the poem into a different form: a letter, a story, an expository essay, a diary or journal, or a newspaper article. The compositions are turned in and checked (but not graded). Several are shared and discussed with the class. Discuss how the ideas were changed by the way they were expressed. The compositions are returned to the students, who revise and rewrite them, using either the same composition form or a different one. They print out their copies, exchange them with a classmate for proofreading, revise, and submit the final draft.

Evaluation.   The final drafts may be assessed on the basis of their application of the ideas expressed in different composition forms. Was the medium used the most effective one for conveying the idea? If not, have the students rewrite the idea using another mode.

Lesson 49

Grade Levels.   9–12

Time.   One week

Rationale.   This lesson helps students differentiate between fact and opinion and between subjective and "objective" reporting.

Objectives.

1. To develop as a critical reader
2. To understand the power of words to persuade
3. To recognize bias in writing

Procedures.   Students read an editorial from a newspaper. Enter it onto a word processor and display it on a large monitor. Read it through orally so that the students hear what it sounds like. Discuss the writer's views on the subject. Go through the article on the screen and underline the words students find that are suggestive, inflammatory, or connotative. Students copy down the words, then find synonyms or close substitutes that are more objective and denotative. They may use a dictionary and thesaurus, if necessary. Display the editorial again on the large screen. For each underlined word have the class agree on a substitute word, then replace each underlined word with the one they select. Reread the editorial aloud with the substituted words and discuss alterations in meaning, bias, and viewpoint. Discuss the power of words to manipulate and persuade people.

Students write their opinion of something important to them, deliberately choosing words that will persuade the audience to their way of thinking. They underline these words when they proofread their papers, then read their papers aloud (perhaps into a tape recorder) to help them determine if the writing is persuasive. Play a few of the tape-recorded essays to the class, which can critique them and make suggestions for strengthening the persuasion. Determine whether the appeal of a paper is to logic, emotions, or the ethics and morality of the reader. Overall, what is persuasive about the paper? Students revise and rewrite their opinion papers.

Evaluation.   Students' opinion papers may be evaluated based on the appeals and techniques used to persuade the reader.

Lesson 50

Grade Levels.   10–12

Time.   Four weeks

Rationale.   This lesson will help students begin to prepare for some life decisions and to be realistic about plans for their career choices.

Objectives.

1. To gather information about a career choice
2. To understand what is needed in a desired career
3. To project and predict one's attainments in the near future

Procedures.   Students read an autobiography or biography of someone they admire. Discuss the person's background and preparation for achieving what he or she did. Students decide on a possible career choice for themselves. They agree on what they need to know about a career: years of school needed, work experience, characteristics of personality, kinds of apprenticeship needed, and so on. Using "PFS File" or a similar program, construct a database format that students can use to gather information. As they research and read about their career choices, they can fill in the information in the database, either on the computer or on paper (after the form is printed out and duplicated). Students present their findings to the class, and those students who have made similar career choices can meet to share information.

Students use a word processor to create resumes for applying for the jobs they want later in life. The resumes should be projected ten years into the future, indicating what they desire to accomplish in the near future to prepare themselves for their careers. The resumes should be realistic, based on students' research into the jobs they want. The resumes should be ambitious to a degree; students should be encouraged to dream about what they would like to do in life. Yet reality must be acknowledged also — students must recognize what is necessary to prepare themselves for future opportunities. The resumes should include name and address, educational background, work experience, professional organizations, community service, awards won, and a statement of career goals. Students should decide whether they want to include any other information. Some actual resumes might be obtained from adults (for instance, students' parents or relatives) and shared with the class as examples of what can be included. Students do further reading about their chosen career fields.

Evaluation.   Students' resumes may be assessed on the basis of how accurately they perceive the life experience and preparation needed to attain their goals. The resumes may be compared to the data file assembled by each student.

SECTION THREE

Application

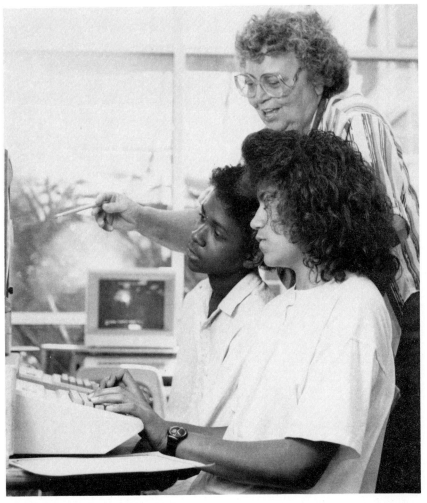

The computer as a teaching tool

Evaluating Computer Use in Teaching the Reading and Writing Processes

Determining the best software

This chapter is concerned with assessing the effectiveness of computer use in teaching reading and writing. There is a crucial need for continuous evaluation of the impact of computer use on young learners. The software industry is still in its infancy, although the quality of programs has improved greatly in the last few years. Software will continue to improve as long as educators are actively involved in telling program writers and their publishers what is needed for learning. *Teachers are the ones best qualified to dictate what education needs* for quality instruction. Therefore, teachers must keep themselves informed about current research in evaluation and the latest developments in educational technology. Teachers should also keep aware of what works and why it is working for students. Research in the area of evaluating computer use is still relatively sparse. We must keep reminding ourselves that the microcomputer has been around for little more than ten years. In such a short period of time, however, it has had an impact that has been significant and swift — though largely unguided. Evaluation and guidance by educators are essential. The next step will then be toward some kind of standardization of hardware and software, for greater efficiency and quality.

This chapter will first examine what research is telling us about the use of the computer in language arts and English. Such studies are meaningful to teachers because they give information about why we are achieving success and help us set learning objectives more realistically. We should keep in mind that these studies are preliminary and need to be validated by more research in the years ahead. These studies should encourage classroom teachers to conduct their own studies, formally and informally, and report their findings to help guide others in using computers wisely.

In the next section, we will look at software evaluation and sources of reviews that can help busy teachers sift through the mountains of new software that comes on the market each month. Lastly, this chapter will consider the evaluation of student learning by computer in our lesson plans. What are we looking for, specifically, and how can we assess our objectives for learning in the most meaningful way? We will look at how students can transfer learning away from the computer to other learning and to other life situations. What is involved in the transfer of learning? Learning to perform a skill, grasp a concept, or think in a particular way on the computer is one thing, but it must be determined whether it has value in other situations away from the computer. This chapter will pinpoint the concerns that educators must face if this new technology is to be used in the most meaningful and responsible way.

Current Research Findings

Study 1

A study by researchers at the University of Michigan used a meta-analysis to analyze findings from fifty-one studies of computer-based teaching in grades 6 through 12 (Kulik, Banger, and Williams, 1983). These studies were not solely of reading and writing instruction, but they do have meaning for us for two reasons: the quantity of the research findings and the general applications they can suggest to us in language arts and English.

The meta-analysis techniques followed procedures established by Gene Glass (Glass, McGraw, and Smith, 1981). Meta-analysis uses objective procedures to locate studies, describe their outcomes, and summarize findings and relationships between studies. The questions they asked in the search are important ones for teachers of language skills to ask: "How effective is computer-based teaching? Is it especially effective for certain types of outcomes or certain types of students? Under which conditions does it appear to be most effective?" The researchers searched three databases: ERIC, the educational materials index; dissertation abstracts; and psychological abstracts. In all, they found fifty-one studies that met their criteria for analysis: to have taken place in a classroom, used experimental groups and control groups, and measured students' final examination performance as well as attitude.

In a typical class, 63 percent of the students using computers received better scores than the average students in the control classes. Students in the classes with computer based instruction raised their scores by .32 standard deviations and performed at the 63rd percentile on the examinations. The control group, in traditional instruction, performed at the 50th percentile on the same examinations. Student attitudes were found to be more favorable in the computer-based classes than in the traditional classes — not only toward the computer, but also toward the the course itself. Lastly, the researchers found that the use of the computer substantially reduced the amount of time students needed for learning. Thus, in the three areas of performance scores, attitudes, and instructional time, the indications are that computer use is effective in the classroom. These three areas certainly concern us in teaching reading and writing by computer; we would do well to focus our own investigations there.

Study 2

A fascinating study that specifically examined the effectiveness of computer instruction in reading achievement was conducted in the Albuquerque public schools (Norton and Resta, 1986). It was particularly interesting because it pinpointed three instructional approaches to teaching reading: the skills approach, problem-solving, and simulations. Reading was defined as a problem-solving process that students use to relate existing schemata to the new schemata represented in text. The hypothesis was that software would teach problem-solving skills in reading and result in better student comprehension.

Each of the three approaches used its own software, selected to implement the thinking abilities desired for each effect. The skills approach used an integrated learning system such as "CCC" from Computer

Curriculum Corp., "WICAT" from PLATO/WICAT Corp., or "Dolphin" from Time Share Corp. The problem solving approach used such software as "Gertrude's Secrets" by Learning Co. and "The Factory," "The Pond," and "Fun House Maze" by Sunburst. The simulation approach used such programs as "Oregon Trail" and "Odell Lake" by MECC and "Jennie on the Prairie" by Addison-Wesley. All the classes in the study were made up of fourth through sixth grade students in six-week summer computer reading courses. There were 18 students in the skills group, 23 in the problem-solving class, and 20 in the simulation group. Each group was given pre- and post-tests in reading vocabulary and comprehension (Gates-MacGinitie) and in problem solving (the Purdue Elementary Problem-Solving Inventory). The instruction time for each group was $12\frac{1}{2}$ hours for the treatment and $12\frac{1}{2}$ hours with a graduate student, while the other two groups used the specified software types.

There was a significant difference in all areas tested between the skills group and the other two groups, but not between the simulation group and the problem-solving group themselves. Students profited more from instruction in simulations and problem-solving than from traditional instruction. The researchers concluded that both simulation software and and problem-solving software introduce significantly more effective cumulative strategies for teaching reading, and that teaching skills alone is not the most effective method. The simulation and problem-solving software had similar effects and may have taught general strategies that correlated to reading comprehension. Such strategies have been identified by Postman (1982): "linear, sequential, propositional, objective, hierarchical, logical and rational thinking strategies," all of which are important to the reading process. Perhaps, as the researchers suggest, the nature of reading itself needs to be redefined as "fluency with cognitive and problem-solving strategies."

Study 3

Also attempting to understand the effects of computer use on students' thinking and reading is research supported by a National Science Foundation grant (Mandinach and Linn, 1986). This study proposes that the greatest potential of computer use in education lies in its capacity to offer students a "chain of cognitive accomplishments culminating in problem-solving skills." The chain of cognitive skills was determined to have three links: language features, design skills, and generalizable problem-solving skills. This chain is sequential and cumulative; the problem is that it is underused in many learning environments. The researchers have found that learning too often remains at the initial link of the chain, so students do not acquire problem-solving skills.

The researchers discuss problem-solving software, such as "Rocky's Boots" and "Wumpus," that takes students all the way through the chain to develop problem-solving abilities. "Rocky's Boots" introduces students to logic by having them build logic machines, experimenting with the "language" of the program. It requires them to plan, test, and reformulate their designs — skills also needed in reading and writing. "Wumpus" requires problem-solving skills that develop students' procedural abilities. They must use strategic planning and logical reasoning to complete the intellectual exercise of the game. If we understand the reading/writing language process to be one of problem-solving, involving sampling, selecting, comparing, and confirming (Goodman, 1981), then such computer programs could be invaluable in developing learners' abilities for writing and reading. Mandinach observes, "The potential cognitive consequences of computers in education are just starting to emerge." As we learn more about their effects, we can become cognizant of their applications to the language arts and English.

Study 4

A positive benefit of using computers in the English curriculum appears to be their effect on students' attitudes, according to a study conducted in two secondary schools in England (Johnston, 1987). The study extended over eight weeks with 144 mixed-ability third-year students. A questionnaire survey was conducted along with an interview. Students were found to be most concerned about their learning and the quality of the programs. Their positive attitudes and expectations were based on the assumption that computers offer a better, more interesting means of learning than traditional ways. Johnston reported 74 percent responding that computers make learning more interesting than a teacher does and 83 percent that computers are more interesting than books. Just 44 percent believed that computers can help them learn better than a teacher can. In an open-ended question about what they felt they learned by using the computer, 43 percent said they believed the technical aspects of their writing (especially spelling) had improved. Just 6 percent mentioned reading. Johnston conjectured that students were not really aware of just what skills they were using while working on the computer and that teachers should be more explicit in stating the learning objectives of student's activities so as to increase awareness. In interviews, some students with reading problems reported that reading on the computer is easier because less text is presented at one time; they do not lose their place and become confused so often. Also, they felt that "colour cues" were helpful. Students also reported that typing was far easier and looked better than writing by hand, so they had more incentive to write using the computer. Students liked being able to control their own learning with the computer. They also liked having to think and make decisions for themselves; in fact, the active learning helped their concentration and prevented boredom.

The finding of this study, that students have overwhelmingly positive attitudes toward learning in the English classroom with use of the computer, has important implications for our teaching. In teaching reading and writing, we certainly need students to have positive attitudes toward their learning. Characteristics of computers that make them effective have been identified as presenting challenge, fantasy, curiosity, structure, and choice to learners (Malone, 1981). This study of attitudes tended to corroborate these desirable characteristics.

Research studies that evaluate the use of computers to teach reading and writing are not numerous at this time. Clearly, more research is needed so that we can use this new technology as wisely as possible with learners. The above studies may indicate some areas of potential research on which classroom teachers may focus in their own use of computers: student attitudes, instructional time on computer compared to traditional methods, pre- and post-test scores that compare computer instruction to other methods, and effects of various types of software. All these areas are in need of constant evaluation. Classroom teachers are in an ideal circumstance, working directly with students, to observe and study these concerns. It is important that any such findings be communicated to the rest of us in the field.

Software Evaluations and Reviews

Teachers may develop their own software review forms, which all can use and share. The form will need to be brief and concise — preferably a useful checklist that will quickly give relevant information to busy teachers. The checklist items should be related to the content field, but general data should be included as well: packaging, presentation of content, use of graphic displays, and inclusion of support materials. Consideration should also be given to human factors in the computer-human interface. These include design effects, social characteristics, and moral implications of the material presented. The more specific items will elicit information about the instructional designs and the educational value of the content of the software package.

Packages

Generally, the package should be comprehensive and should provide student materials that include a pre-instruction phase and follow-up to the actual use of the software. The student worksheets should be relevant and supportive of the learning that is ongoing in the classroom. There should be easy-to-read teacher manuals and suggestions for instructional activities. The manuals should include educationally sound rationales for use and prerequisite skills for students. The resource information should contain a bibliography of sources to which the teacher may turn for further information.

The materials themselves need to be attractively presented. The whole package of software, teaching materials, and student worksheets should be secured within a durable container. The text should be readable; not too much should appear on the screen at one time. The text should be grammatically correct and free of spelling errors. It must be logically organized to encourage students to use such good reading habits as prediction and structuring of ideas. There should be an effective combination of text and graphics, appropriate and supplemental to each other. The graphics should be set at an appropriate pace for understanding, especially if there is animation. They should not be unduly repetitive, but rather varied enough to keep students' attention throughout. The graphics should be accurate and use appropriate colors. Finally, the materials need to be durable enough to stand up to a lot of use.

Students should be able to operate the program independently so that the teacher can work with individuals while the class is using the software. The program should contain enough internal documentation to make it easy for students to follow. The directions should be clear and provide guidance through program options. The directions should be consistent and reliable, requiring a minimum of computer competency on the part of students. The cues that are given screen by screen must be appropriate in helping students learn. The software program should be well-suited to the particular model of computer and use relevant capabilities. For example, the memory requirement should match that of the computer, in order to utilize its capacity.

Teachers must be able to use the package easily without spending hours learning the program. It should require a minimum of competency so that teachers on all levels of computer use may integrate it into their lesson plans. When possible, the program should cover management of student learning by including a grading option. This option would record and store students' scores and allow the teacher to print them out. This would save the teacher a great deal of time and would also let students monitor their own progress. Lastly, the program should be reliable and perform consistently over time.

Instructional Designs

The package should be motivational to students and provide a pleasant experience for their learning. The reinforcement should be friendly and helpful, interactively involving the students by using their names, when appropriate. It should stimulate their creativity and challenge them to think and grow. Students should be allowed to make choices and decisions rather than just a programmed response. They should be challenged on several levels of thinking beyond the literal recall of factual data. The program should allow problem solving and critical thinking as well as factual recall. The progression in thinking skills should be cumulative, building upon previous material and becoming more difficult as the program continues. Learning should actively involve students and allow them control over the pace of presentation and the time allowed for solving problems. Also, students should be able to review instructions easily and continuously. They should be able to terminate a segment of instruction without having to go through the entire program.

The nature of the feedback can contribute to or inhibit student learning. If it only indicates a right or wrong response, students do not gain information that will lead them to the right answer or to changes in their thinking. The feedback should provide information that remediates and guides the student to the right answer. In the best software, students are channelled toward options depending on the kind of answer they have given so that they can discover where the errors in their thinking lay. Such options explain why the answer was wrong without giving the right answer; students are led to their own conclusions, which should be correct in the next test of their learning.

Current research on effective feedback shows that immediate feedback on the computer is *not* the most helpful to students. Instead, a slightly delayed response is preferable, because it allows students to process the information and digest it before they receive the answer. One study (Rankin and Trepper, 1978) tested college students in three groups: (1) with immediate feedback, (2) with a fifteen-second delay in feedback, and (3) with feedback after the entire presentation of material. All three groups were tested 24 hours later for their retention of the material. Groups 2 and 3 were significantly different in their success from group 1, with higher mean scores. Groups 2 and 3 were not significantly different from each other, however. The experimenters concluded that their results confirmed other research findings: that delayed feedback was most effective for retention of learning. Teachers may want to test out this hypothesis in their own use of software, to see what works best with their own students. It does seem logical that students would need processing time to absorb their new learning rather than being given a quick response that might serve to curtail their thinking.

The instruction should suit the intellectual level of the students so that it is not frustrating to them. It should be timed to fit the attention spans of the grade levels (shorter for younger grades). Most importantly, the examples used in instruction should be ones students are familiar with from their backgrounds. The examples must be integrated with the prior experience and knowledge of students, match ones used in the ongoing lesson plans in the classroom, and supplement the well-planned curriculum. If new vocabulary is introduced in the program, students should have the words pretaught before they encounter them in the software. There should be enough examples and graphic illustrations to prepare students adequately before they are tested. Effective integration of software depends on sound teaching practices, just like any other educational technology.

The supplements to the text should be used for appropriate instructional reasons. The graphics, sound, and color should supplement the text rather than detract from it and should provide motivation and interest. It must be possible to regulate the sound; the user should be able to turn it off when it bothers other students. Also, the sound must be appropriate to the instruction and supplement it. On the other hand, when the sound is turned off, the lesson should still be workable unless it specifically deals with sounds.

Presentation of the lesson should be clear and logically organized. Students should be able to follow the sequencing very easily and begin to predict the format, which must be consistent in organization and structure. The purpose of the lesson should be very clear to students; they should be able to recognize it and assess whether it has been achieved in the package. Teachers should ask students about the purpose of the lesson so as to give them a verbalized awareness of it. Teachers must constantly foster this important part of students' metacognitive development.

Content Value

The subject matter content must have educational value. It can be a game, a simulation, or a drill and practice program, but it must have value in teaching students to think, solve problems, and understand concepts. Generally, the software program will be used to supplement instruction in a well-designed lesson — to provide practice, review, or an experience with concepts or skills. The concepts are inherent in the curriculum of the course and specified with clear objectives. The computer reinforces the curriculum if it is well integrated into the learning objectives that the teacher sets.

Naturally, the content must be accurate. It should be the most current information available, with no factual errors. The examples given should not be oversimplified or exaggerated. The graphs, charts, maps, and other supplemental graphics should be accurate. Of course, no gender, racial, or ethnic stereotypes should be presented.

Human Factors

Educational software must consider the human being with whom the machine interacts. The science called ergonomics studies this interaction of humans and machines, and teachers should be aware of the effects of design, the social characteristics, and their moral implications in CAI software. These factors affect attitude and behavior of the whole human being — as important a concern for teachers as subject matter learning.

An important consideration in presentation of CAI material is the design of the screen display. Rambally and Rambally (1987) recommend four criteria in judging screen design: (1) simplicity, (2) spaciousness and relevance, (3) standardization, and (4) screen change capabilities. Students should be presented with material that is "organized and structured in such a manner as to avoid non-essential complexity," the Ramballys contend. Factors that influence simplicity include the dialogue, the location of pertinent information the student can access, and the reading speed expected. The student-computer dialogue, generally offered in the menu options, is the communication mode for the interaction. It should be presented so that inexperienced students can easily understand it. Therefore, the current screen menu should pertain to the options for the current step only, not the one preceding or following. Furthermore, the options on any one menu should number no more than nine; otherwise, hierarchical menus should be used. Students should be able to access the main menu at all times in order to control their own progress or review other selections. Also, the options presented on any one menu should be arranged in order of probability of selection, from high to low. Students should be able to locate important information readily, so it must be given in a prominent and consistent manner. If important facts are highlighted or given in a blinking display, these techniques should be limited and used sparingly, since they tend to induce eye fatigue. In split-screen presentations, the screen separation should be made evident with lines or contrasts so as to avoid confusion. Finally, the reading speed must be adjustable and under student control, so that it can be slowed down for careful study and review of missed information.

Information must be well-spaced, organized, and uncluttered if it is to be real on a computer screen. The verbal information presented in any one frame should be limited, highly relevant, and spaciously displayed. Otherwise, reading errors will occur more frequently and students will become stressed and frustrated. It is important that verbal information be carefully selected and strategically presented for student interaction. The terminology used, as well as the input/output format, should be standardized throughout the entire software package so that it is predictable and becomes reassuring with repeated use. The mode of operation should also be standardized. The basic scrolling, windowing, and paging operations must be easy to perform and consistent in design. Whether scrolling up and down through the program, changing pages all at once, or pulling down windows, the operations that display data must be simple to control. In evaluating CAI software, teachers must understand design for human interaction.

The social characteristics to consider involve how many students at a time may interact with a program. Drill and practice programs that emphasize speed and automaticity of basic skills are probably best utilized by individual students (Cosden and Lieber, 1986). However, in problem-solving programs, the best results are achieved when students are grouped together in cooperative learning groups of two, three, or four. Groups larger than that tend to develop friction and social problems, mainly because there is not enough access to the keyboard and computer screen for all (Cox and Berger, 1985). Not only do students in cooperative learning groups perform better in problem solving than individual users do, but they also develop better attitudes toward using computers (Johnson et al., 1986). With grouping, there is more social interchange and attitudes are more positive; students ask each other questions, give answers and explanations, and provide feedback on the correctness of responses. An interesting finding has been that grouping students of different abilities produces better results than grouping students of similar ability, even though this can result in frustration when the ability gap is large. The conclusion in the research literature is that using the computer in problem solving offers rich opportunities for social interactions among groups of students. Choices of software should be varied, to allow students this opportunity for sharing ideas.

The moral issues pertain to the content of the programs themselves, particularly in certain games that promote war, aggression, and competition. Some early computer games emphasized monsters and mazes, with violent consequences for the characters involved.

Some recent computer games do not use violence at all (for example, "Where in the World is Carmen Sandiego"), even though so-called criminal characters are involved. Also, competition that necessitates a winner and a loser may be immoral to use in the classroom, especially if it damages some child's self-esteem. Some games end in capital punishment or death and are therefore inappropriate for use with young people. Teachers must consider such moral implications of software before using it for learning in the classroom.

The General Review Form

Because of all the considerations discussed so far, any software package must be carefully reviewed by the teacher before it is used with students. This can take a great deal of time. It is recommended that a whole department of teachers take part in reviewing and reporting on the use of a new piece of software. The reviews could be reported on a brief form to be shared with all content-area faculty or across disciplines school-wide. The reviews could be housed within a department or the school library where all faculty interested in new software could have access to them. Figure 6-1 is an example of a software evaluation form that is easy to fill out and requires little time to read. By skimming the two-page form, teachers could make a quick decision as to whether or not they would like to use the program it covers. This form can be customized for a particular subject, department, or faculty concern. Above all, the review form used should answer teachers' pertinent and specific questions about the role of the software in the curriculum

Figure 6-1 is adapted from forms created by teachers in graduate courses. It is a model that teachers can use in creating forms for their own content area and particular situation.

Figure 6-1   Software evaluation form

Program name: _____ Publisher: _____ Cost: _____
Subject area: _____ Reviewer: _____ Date: _____
Hardware: _____
Age level intended: _____ Time length: _____

Instructional Use

__demonstration __drill or practice __instructional games __problem solving
__simulation __tutorial __word processing __graphics
__database __interactive fiction __text editing _____other

Instructional Grouping

__individual   __small group   __large group   __class demonstration

Checklist. Check the appropriate category for each item (yes, no, or not applicable).

Packaging

Yes   No   N/A

1. Is container attractive and durable in design?
2. Are instructional manuals for teacher included?
3. Are worksheets and directions for use by students provided?
4. Are other resources and bibliographies included?
5. Are directions clear and logically presented?
6. Is minimal competency required to understand and use the program?
7. Is there sufficient internal documentation on how to use the program?
8. Are grading options and records management included?
9. Are external and internal documentation grammatical and free of errors?
10. Are graphics included to illustrate external and internal text?

Instructional Design

Yes   No   N/A

1. Are directions shown on the screen and easy to follow?
2. Is the level of difficulty appropriate for the user?
3. Does program clearly state its purpose and achieve it?
4. Can user adjust rate and speed of presentation?
5. Can user enter and exit the program easily and readily?
6. Is program interactive with the user?
7. Does feedback guide the user to the correct response?
8. Do graphics, sound, and color enhance the content?
9. Is content logically presented?
10. Can the instruction be easily integrated with the user's prior experience?

Figure 6-1, continued

Content Value

Yes   No   N/A

____ ____ ____   1. Does the content have clear educational value?
____ ____ ____   2. Is the content accurate and reliable?
____ ____ ____   3. Is the content logically organized, from simple to complex?
____ ____ ____   4. Does the content present current information with no factual errors?
____ ____ ____   5. Are the examples appropriate and representative of reality?
____ ____ ____   6. Are maps, graphs, charts, and other visuals accurate and realistic?
____ ____ ____   7. Does the content avoid exaggeration and misrepresentation of facts?
____ ____ ____   8. Is the content appropriate to the grade level suggested?
____ ____ ____   9. Is presentation of the content interesting and stimulating?
____ ____ ____   10. Is the content free of sexual, racial, and ethnic stereotypes?

Human Factors

Yes   No   N/A

____ ____ ____   1. Are the screen displays uncluttered and simple to read?
____ ____ ____   2. Are menu options easily accessible and simple to read?
____ ____ ____   3. Are menu options ordered logically?
____ ____ ____   4. Are eye-fatiguing techniques limited?
____ ____ ____   5. Is the data display simply presented and controlled?
____ ____ ____   6. Are there opportunities for cooperation in the program?
____ ____ ____   7. If there is competition, is it positive and motivational?
____ ____ ____   8. If there are moral issues or value judgments, are they positive?
____ ____ ____   9. If there are moral issues or value judgments, are they necessary and appropriate to the age level and experience of the students?
____ ____ ____   10. Can the user control the speed and pace of learning?

Overall Evaluation

____Excellent   ____Good   ____Fair   ____Poor

Major Weaknesses: _____

_____

General Comments and Recommendations: _____

_____

Specific Reading and Writing Considerations in Software

There are two well-known approaches to teaching reading. They are based on theories of the reading process and how students learn to read. The selection of software to teach reading and language use should be determined by which theory a teacher subscribes to (Miller and Burnett, 1986). One theory is that isolation of subskills is the most effective method for teaching reading (Otto and Askov, 1974). However, the author of this book subscribes to the theory that is based on holistic, psycholinguistic processing (see also Moffett and Wagner, 1976). To become mature readers, students must learn to read for meaning. The holistic approach activates and utilizes their life experience and prior knowledge, in terms of both content and text form (see Chapter 1). Since teachers will select software according to the theory they favor, the program review must include this consideration.

The first question for the teacher to ask is, "How do I think reading should be taught?" If the answer is "skill by skill," one would choose from the array of drill and practice programs that afford practice, review, and reinforcement of skill. If the answer is through active hypothesis testing, holistic text, and interactive involvement with text, then one may more freely choose from simulations, interactive fiction, and educational games. These programs would allow the student to use reading and writing in a problem-solving context with holistic interaction.

Other questions follow. If a teacher focuses on subskills, which subskills should be taught, in what order? Should they be linear and sequential? Also, how many skills should be taught in one program, and how should they be tested? If teacher does not agree with the software's packaged presentation of the subskills, the program should be modifiable. Teachers using the holistic approach use reading and writing situations interrelatedly, as reinforcements of each other, and on an individual need basis. This is radically different from teaching prescribed, hierarchically arranged skills to an entire class. In the holistic approach, the emphasis in the software is on active cognitive involvement by the learner in discovery and hypothesis-testing situations, so drill and practice software that presents skills in isolation would have to be eliminated from consideration.

Most teachers no doubt find themselves somewhere along the continuum between these two extremes. It is nonetheless important for them to be aware of where the software stands on the continuum and how it affects learners. Criteria to consider in choosing software to teach reading and writing include the following:

1. The program supports my theory of how reading and writing should be taught.
2. The skills students will use are consistent with my theory.
3. The program allows the teacher to modify subskill sequencing, frequency of presentation, and levels of difficulty so as to meet individual skill levels.
4. The program is interactive with students, having them make decisions rather than just react with prescribed answers.
5. The concepts and text format presented build on students' experience and prior knowledge.
6. The program facilitates the transfer of skills to the traditional technologies of books, paper, and pen.

Adding these criteria to the general software evaluation forms will help teachers of reading and writing make wiser decisions in selecting software.

Software Evaluation Resources

Busy teachers should be aware of resources that can provide time-saving shortcuts. The first place to go for information on a potentially interesting new software program is to one of the published indexes of reviews. If the review is favorable for a teacher's or a department's needs, the software package itself can then be reviewed first-hand. One or more of these review sources should be ordered for the school library for teachers' information and for guidance in updating the school's software. The following is a list of sources of software reviews:

The Yellow Book of Computer Products for Education has been published annually by the National Educational Association since 1984. This catalog of software considered "worthy of consideration for purchase" includes programs in most grade levels and subject areas. Three important criteria for teachers are (1) ease of use, (2) instructional value, and (3) technical reliability. The programs most highly rated by the NEA are updated annually in this catalog.

Only the Best: The Discriminating Software Guide for Preschool–Grade 12 is published by Education News Service in Sacramento, California and costs $21.95 yearly. Approximately one hundred of the most highly rated programs are gleaned from sixteen evaluation services. The programs are described and accompanied by excerpts from reviews. Software for special education is also provided. The outstanding programs are chosen by the editors of *School/TechNews,* who put this guide together annually.

MicroSift is a directory published by Northwest Regional Educational Laboratory at 300 SW Sixth Avenue, Portland, Oregon 97204. Besides the paper version, it is available through the RICE and ERIC online databases. The directory includes software for Apple, Atari, Commodore, IBM, and Radio Shack computers. Approximately 500 reviews are written by a network of educators throughout the United States, covering most subject areas. The areas evaluated in each program are objectives, major strengths and weaknesses, content, and structure. An evaluation summary table is provided for each program. The publisher allows copying of the reviews without copyright restrictions.

Micro-Courseware PRO/FILE and Evaluation is produced by EPIE (Educational Products Information Exchange) in conjunction with Consumer's Union and is available at EPIE Institute, P.O. Box 839, Watermill, New York 11976. This is an ongoing series of courseware evaluations covering all curriculum areas and grade levels. Including approximately 720 evaluations so far, the series rates technical quality, cost effectiveness, ease of use, and instructional quality. Software for Atari, Apple, IBM PC, Radio Shack, Commodore, and Texas Instruments computers is evaluated on 8½ " × 11 " cards, easily filed in a plastic carrying case.

TESS: The Educational Software Selector is an annual catalog published by EPIE Institute, P.O. Box 839, Watermill, New York 11976 and costs $59.95. The catalog reviews software for all major computers. Also included are approximately 2,000 references to published reviews of titles in all subject areas and grade levels. The catalog is organized by subject matter and includes a section on English/Language Arts software. Each software program reviewed is categorized by type (game, tutorial, etc.), uses (home, school), and scope (multiple subjects, multiple years); a description of the program and its hardware requirements is also included, and the publisher and program components are given. The *TESS* database contains more than 6,700 product descriptions from about 560 suppliers. It covers instructional software for over 100 subjects, at levels from nursery school through graduate school.

Software Reports: The Guide to Evaluated Educational Software is a biweekly looseleaf publication that reviews software in twenty subject areas, across all grade levels. A summary of the program, a description of it, and an annotated graded evaluation are included in each review.

Educational Software Directory, compiled by Marilyn Chartrand and Constance Williams, is published by Libraries Unlimited, Inc., located at P.O. Box 263, Littleton, Colorado 80160. This subject guide to software presents a whole section on Language Arts software. The entries are alphabetized by title. Information includes grade levels, hardware requirements, price, and description. The directory contains five sections: software, publishers and distributors, bibliography, subject index, and title index.

The software review services listed above should be considered for purchase for a school or district library, where teachers will have easy access to them. The problem of finding time to review a new software piece would be lessened with such information. Teachers hearing about new software would be able to read about it and obtain professional ratings, then decide whether it is worth spending time reviewing it themselves. These up-to-date services would keep teachers well informed about software developments.

The following online sources provide further resources for evaluation information:

Online Sources

The Computer Database is available on "DIALOG." It is updated every two weeks and contains 30,000 references to 500 computer-related journals. Its purpose is to give information about hardware, software, peripherals, and services for computers, electronics, and telecommunications.

Microcomputer Index is also available on "DIALOG." This index contains about 10,000 references to articles on uses of computers in business, education, and the home. Thirty microcomputer journals are culled for general book reviews, software reviews, applications, new product descriptions, and other information.

Education Resources Information Center (ERIC) is available on "BAS" and "DIALOG." Updated monthly, it indexes more than 700 journals on education and related subjects. Included in the documents portion are the *Microsift* evaluations of software.

Resources in Computer Education (RICE) is available on "BAS" and is updated monthly. It provides information on producers of educational software and educational computer applications. A *Microsift* evaluation is included with some of the software descriptions.

Besides the indexes and online sources of software reviews, some professional journals regularly carry software reviews, and others occasionally do. Teachers will want to consider the following journals for their libraries, as they contain the most up-to-date information.

Classroom Computer Learning, 19 Davis Drive, Belmont, California 94002. Telephone: 415-592-7810.

Computers, Reading and Language Arts, CRLA, P.O. Box 13247, Oakland, California 94661-0247. Telephone: 415-530-9587.

Curriculum Review, 517 South Jefferson, Chicago, Illinois 60607. Telephone: 312-939-3010.

Educational Computer, 3199 DeLaCruz, Santa Clara, California 95050. Telephone: 408-988-0135.

Educational Technology, 140 Sylvan Ave., Englewood Cliffs, New Jersey 07632. Telephone: 201-871-4007.

Electronic Learning, 730 Broadway, New York, New York 10003. Telephone: 212-505-3000.

Journal of Learning Disabilities, 11 East Adams St., Chicago, Illinois 60603.

Journal of Special Education Technology, Association of Special Education, Utah State University, Logan, Utah 84322. Telephone: 801-750-3243.

Media Review, Box 425, Ridgefield, Connecticut 06877.

Software Review, 520 Riverside Ave., Westport, Connecticut 06880.

The Computing Teacher, International Council for Computers in Education (ICCE), University of Oregon, 1787 Agate Street, Eugene, Oregon 97403. Telephone: 503-686-4414.

Schools should consider including such professional publications in their libraries, just to keep teachers current on what is happening in their fields. Subscriptions to the journals are less expensive than indexes of reviews, and they will add to the professionalism of teaching resources. Teachers may want to request an issue to peruse before buying a subscription, in order to assure themselves that they will find the publication useful.

Evaluation of Student Learning by Computer

To assess student learning, teachers must examine the objectives of a lesson. The objectives identify the type of performance expected or the learning outcomes for a student. Robert Gagne (Walker and Hess, 1984) has described the specific categories of learning outcomes that CAI software

most often aims to achieve. Understanding the learning outcomes educational software is designed for, teachers can evaluate the students' success
in learning them. The writers of the better software programs are aware
of learning principles and try to utilize them to design the program for the
most effective learning. The particular learning outcomes that teachers
should be aware of include the following (adapted from Gagne):

1. *Verbal information.* Students will be able to exhibit knowledge of meaningful terms and ideas, recalling the words and labels appropriate to the
body of knowledge. Teachers can evaluate the learning outcomes of verbal
information by having students recall and *state* their understanding of what
they have learned. The performance expected of this learning outcome is
the ability to remember and talk about what was gained verbally in a program. In the teaching of reading and writing, teachers emphasize the learning outcome of verbal information necessary for communicating.

2. *Concrete concept.* Students acquire understanding of a concrete concept
when they are able to point out a property of an object, an event that occurs, or a spatial direction. Teachers can evaluate the learning outcome
of concrete concepts by having students *identify* physical representations of
the concept learned in the program. The performance expected of this learning outcome is the student's ability to recognize and mark in some manner
the concrete representation of the concept. In teaching reading and writing,
teachers require students to identify symbols, both alphabetic
and multisymbolic (such as in art or graphics), that are necessary for
communicating.

3. *Defined concept.* Students must be able to demonstrate a concept by
identifying the components of the concept and indicating how they are
related. For example, the concept of story has within itself numerous components: characters, plot, action, and setting. Students will be expected
to recognize the component parts and to relate them into the integrated
whole of a story. This learning outcome of a defined concept can be evaluated
by having students *apply* it to other examples of it. (For example, other
stories would be recognized and maybe even written by students.) This
learning outcome is crucial in the teaching of reading and writing, which
involve understanding relationships and synthesis. Students must recognize
the component parts of a text, relate them, and synthesize them into a whole.

4. *Rule.* Students understand rules when they see the relationships between two or more concepts and are able to extend the principles of the
rule to new instances of it. For example, metaphor is a concept that is related
to personifications, similes, and other kinds of comparison. If students
understand the relationships between the different figures of speech, they
will be able to explain them, find other examples of them, and use them
in their own writing. Teachers evaluate students' learning of a rule through
student *demonstration* of its application. In their reading and writing, students

are constantly making relationships between concepts, so this learning out-come is directly related to the teaching of these processes.

5. *Problem solving.* Students learn to solve problems by applying known (previously learned) rules to unfamiliar situations. They must decide which rules will generalize to a solution of the new problem. Skills in problem solving are developed only when there are opportunities to practice them. Evaluation of students' ability to solve problems is made by observing the rules or principles they select in solving a problem. If the rules apply, then the solution will be reached successfully. To help students generalize their skills, they should be guided to an awareness of how they solved the prob-lem. They can then use the skills in other situations. The learning outcome of problem solving is therefore dependent on *judgment,* involving the selec-tion of rules, principles, and procedures for making right decisions. In reading and writing instruction, the teacher should present many oppor-tunities for students to make decisions, interpret writing, and decide how to arrive at conclusions in their reading and in writing, both on computer and in print.

To achieve the learning outcomes identified above as important to teaching reading and writing, a computer program must display "instructional events" (Gagne et al., 1981). Not all nine of these events occur in all types of educa-tional software, as they may not all be necessary. However, teachers should be aware whether or not they occur, in order to assess their effects on stu-dent learning. These external events displayed on the monitor are designed to create internal learning reactions in students, reflected in student per-formance. The performance, of course, can be observed and assessed.

Instructional "Events"

1. Gaining student attention to elicit internal alertness
2. Informing students of lesson objective to create expectancy
3. Stimulating recall of prior learning to provide student retrieval of memory
4. Presenting stimuli with distinctive features to help students' selective perception
5. Guiding learning to develop students' knowledge
6. Eliciting performance to encourage students' responses
7. Providing valuable feedback to give students reinforcement
8. Assessing performance test and aid students' retention
9. Providing learning transfer to help students generalize learning

Not all software programs use these "events" of instruction. Drill and prac-tice programs employ only two of the events: they elicit response by asking questions (#6) and provide feedback (#7), usually as knowledge of results only. The purpose of this type of CAI software is to provide practice for previously learned knowledge, not new knowledge, so it is not necessary to include all the events. Simulations, on the other hand, use a number of the instructional events, because their purpose is to teach students to solve problems presented by a situation. In a simulation, the student has to make relationships between elements of the situation, apply learned rules from previous knowledge, and manipulate the variables in order to arrive at a solution to the problems. Simulations usually contain the following instructional events: motivation, presentation of objectives, presenting stimuli, eliciting performance, and providing feedback. In varying the types of software, teachers provide different opportunities and ways for students to learn.

All of these nine instructional events are important to learning, especially in a good tutorial program. A tutorial is considered to be primary instruction rather than supplementary. In other words, a tutorial teaches *new* information instead of reinforcing or providing practice for previously learned material. As indicated in Chapter 3, tutorials present instructional sequences that are either linear or branching. These sequences can use all nine of the events for instruction, but typically the linear tutorials present text, ask questions, and provide feedback. (See Figure 6-2.)

Figure 6-3 diagrams Gagne's proposal for incorporating the nine instructional events in a good tutorial. This sequence is the "ideal" for most effective learning.

Recognizing the instructional sequences of presentation of content helps teachers understand the effects on learning. Such an awareness leads teachers to demand the best software, because they understand the process of instruction as well as the process of learning.

Transfer of Learning by Computer

Does what students learn on the computer transfer to other learning? Determining this involves the same problems as the transfer of education in general. How do we teachers know that what we do really relates to

Figure 6-2   Typical instructional sequence (from *Instructional Software: Principles and Perspectives for Design and Use,* by Decker F. Walker and Robert D. Hess. © 1984 by Wadsworth, Inc. Reprinted by permission of the publisher.)

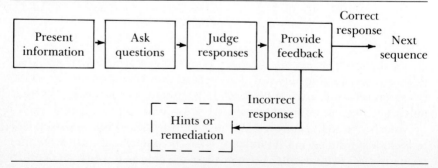

Figure 6-3   Gagne's events of instruction (from *Instructional Software: Principles and Perspectives For Design and Use,* by Decker F. Walker and Robert D. Hess. © 1984 by Wadsworth, Inc. Reprinted by permission of the publisher.)

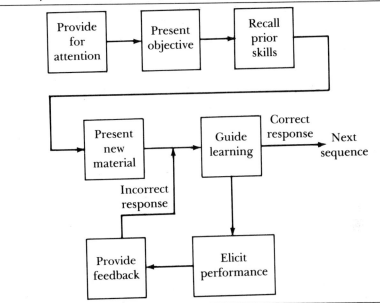

students' lives and gives them skills useful beyond our classrooms? We want school learning to generalize to the outside world, but how do we orchestrate or even evaluate such transfer of learning?

First of all, instruction in the classroom must be carefully designed so that objectives and goals can be understood and achieved before they can be evaluated. According to Gagne and Briggs (1974), "The best way to design instruction is to work backwards from the outcomes it is expected to have." In teaching reading and writing, the outcomes must be clearly understood before evaluation can begin. Outcomes should be stated broadly enough that they can be seen to generalize to other situations outside the classroom. The outcomes of student learning on the computer should be realized in a broad context of skills and abilities that have application to technologies such as paper and pencil and books. Obviously, students cannot carry computers around constantly; they will need to use more commonly available means of communicating. Therefore, the learning they acquire on the computer must be seen to have transfer value to other situations. The learning outcomes should be stated so as to reflect the need for transfer.

Learning on the computer is affected by the medium itself, and different learning experiences are created by different software programs. For example, simulations provide practice in problem solving, and tutorials give skills practice. The learning outcomes are in part determined by what type of program is used. In general, however, the major learning outcomes on computer that can be generalized are the ones described by Gagne (see the list at the beginning of the previous section). Those outcomes can be analyzed for their relevance to the teaching of reading and writing and their transfer to other technologies.

1. The learning outcome of verbal information, in which students have to *state* their understanding of knowledge gained, can be measured, evaluated, and transferred to other situations. Students must have a literal understanding of what they read and experience before they can achieve comprehension on the interpretive and creative levels. The ability to verbalize this understanding by recalling specific names, dates, and labels is a broad learning outcome that can be generalized to all situations. Whether they use paper and pen, a typewriter, or a word processor in writing, students must be able to use specific verbal data to communicate their knowledge and understanding to a reader. In reading, as well, students must be able to gain information and then restate it in order to show their understanding of what they have read. This general learning outcome is one major goal teachers may set for students in designing the curriculum. It is measurable; teachers can evaluate its success and its transfer to other classroom learning and life experience. Teachers should tell students why this outcome is valuable, so that they will have a conscious understanding of the skill and its use elsewhere.

2. The learning outcome of concrete concepts is a broad goal that can be generalized to other learning. In reading and writing, students have to *identify* concrete representations of abstract symbols they have used in print. If they read or write about geometric shapes, for example, they must be able to identify those shapes in objects they encounter in real life. The value of reading is to extend and widen experience, so the outcome of being able to identify what one has read about is clearly a generalizable goal in learning. It is a measurable outcome, as well. Computer programs, such as simulations, would incorporate this learning outcome as a goal, generalizable to the real world and to other technologies.

3. The learning outcome of defined concepts is less measurable because it is more abstract. However, it is crucial in the teaching of reading and writing. It involves higher-level thinking skills and the ability to synthesize parts into a whole. In language use, this is necessary for composing meaning in reading and in writing to an audience. Transfer of this learning would be seen in student's *application* of the rules and principles involved in synthesizing language. Rules of grammatical usage and punctuation are examples of defined concepts that students should apply to their own reading and writing. Their understanding of these rules can be evaluated indirectly, in the way they apply them. These concepts can be generalized to other

technologies and experiences throughout life. When the concepts are applied in word processing, for example, the teacher should make the students aware of the transfer of this learning to other situations.

4. The learning outcome of rules is evaluated through students' *demonstration* that they are able to see relationships between concepts. They demonstrate them in their own reading and writing. Students' understanding of literary devices, for example, can be evaluated on the basis of the similes, metaphors, and personifications they use in their writing. The writing is an opportunity for them to demonstrate that they recognize the rules that govern the use of these literary techniques and that they know when it is appropriate to use them. This learning outcome is broad enough that it may be generalized to other situations. When students can demonstrate their understanding of a rule such as the use of commas and by applying it, the teacher can evaluate their learning. They can generalize their learning of a rule to other encounters with it, if the teacher guides them to conscious awareness of where it applies.

5. The learning outcome of problem solving is the most complex to evaluate, since it depends on *judgment*. Students can solve a particular problem in an educational game on the computer, but if they do not gain a conscious awareness of how they did it, the skills may not be generalized to other situations. To generalize the problem-solving skills, students must be given another opportunity to practice them in a new situation. The teacher must first recognize what skills the students are learning in a computer program. Then students should be presented with an opportunity in reading and writing to provide for transfer and practice of problem-solving skills. For example, students may solve the "crime" in the computer program "Where in the World is Carmen Sandiego?" by using the problem-solving skills of research and application of clues to the situation. To transfer those skills to other classroom learning, students would need another opportunity to do research and to apply information to solve a problem — one they found in reading a book, for instance. The teacher should point out the value of these skills and their usefulness in other situations, so that students become aware of the connection and can make the transfer.

Computers cannot be used in isolation from other learning or from life. Teachers construct a well-designed curriculum that has short-term objectives and long-term goals, and they integrate computer use in ways that help to achieve those objectives and goals. Learning outcomes are the expected results of the objectives and goals set. The learning outcomes can be conceptualized broadly enough that they are understood as human performances needed in coping with other situations in the classroom and in life. If students are given conscious awareness of their learning and opportunities to practice in other situations, the learning outcomes can be transferred. Learning on the computer is like learning with any other technology:

Its benefits and values need to be evaluated and transferred beyond the technology itself

Evaluating Lessons Using the Computer

Learning outcomes can be recognized, objectives set, long-term goals established, and the lesson designed well. But when it is implemented, what makes a lesson effective — in particular, one that uses the computer? Figure 6-4 is a model form for evaluating a lesson, based on Gagne's nine events of instruction (described earlier in this chapter). The events are a guide to designing a good lesson as well as to diagnosing just where one went wrong. Realizing that one or more of the events is weak can help the teacher

Figure 6-4   Lesson evaluation form (adapted from Sales, Carrier, and Allen, 1986)

Circle the number on the scale that indicates your rating of its success. (1 is low; 5 is high.)

Part I. Overall Lesson

Lesson title: _____

Lesson objectives: _____

Instructional Events	Event Rating	Changes Needed
Gaining attention	1 2 3 4 5	Provided focus on task.
Student knowledge of objectives	1 2 3 4 5	Built expectations of task.
Building schemata	1 2 3 4 5	Brought in students' prior knowledge.
Presenting content	1 2 3 4 5	Clearly sequenced the content.
Providing guidance	1 2 3 4 5	Gave examples, clear directions.
Eliciting performance	1 2 3 4 5	Provided practice for concepts.
Providing feedback	1 2 3 4 5	Guided student learning.
Assessing performance	1 2 3 4 5	Accurately evaluated learning.
Enhancing retention and transfer	1 2 3 4 5	Gave further practice in new situations

Part II. Computer-Related Activities

1 2 3 4 5   The computer program aided in achieving objectives.
1 2 3 4 5   The program was relevant to overall learning objectives.
1 2 3 4 5   The software was a valuable component of the lesson.
1 2 3 4 5   Student motivation to learn on the computer was high.
1 2 3 4 5   Skills learned can be transferred to other classroom learning.
1 2 3 4 5   Reading and writing skills were effectively practiced.

understand why a lesson failed to achieve its objectives. Gagne's nine events apply to both the computer and the non-computer parts of a lesson. The events are for general instruction, so they must be adapted to our focus on lessons that teach reading and writing with the computer. The rating scale in Figure 6-4 is designed to be quick and easy, using a scale of 1 to 5.

Evaluation of student learning on the computer means different things to different educators. To some, evaluation must be based on assessment of retention of learning: Students are evaluated on what they remember from the lesson. To others, evaluation should reflect the amount of learning students gain initially. Still others focus their evaluation on student attitudes — affective changes that occur in learning. In teaching reading and writing, evaluation of learning can include all three perspectives, but *application* of what has been learned must be the ultimate criterion. This is because the product is what is judged. The product of reading is comprehension; it is demonstrated in understanding the material on several levels of meaning. The product of writing is the composition; it is demonstrated in expression of ideas to an audience. We are concerned with the process by which the products are derived, but our evaluation is of the products. The computer as a language processor helps in the process of reading and writing, and it can also aid us in attaining superior products. The use of some quality programs enhances comprehension with problem-solving and decision-making; a composition can be "professionally" published with the editing and printing features of a word processor. Evaluation of learning in reading and writing instruction that makes use of the computer must include an understanding of the effects of the medium itself. It is hoped that this book has contributed to the understanding of the educational implications of the computer as a medium of instruction.

References

Cosden, Merith A., and Lieber, Joan. "Grouping Students on the Microcomputer." *Academic Therapy* 22(2), November, 1986, pp. 165–172.

Cox, Dorothy A., and Berger, Carl F. "The Importance of Group Size in the Use of Problem-Solving Skills on a Microcomputer." *Journal of Educational Computing Research* 1(4), 1985, pp. 459–468.

Gagne, Robert M., and Briggs, Leslie J. *Principles of Instructional Design.* New York: Holt, Rinehart and Winston, 1974.

Gagne, Robert M., Wager, Walter, and Rojas, Alicia. "Planning and Authoring Computer-Assisted Instruction Lessons." *Educational Technology* 21, September, 1981, pp. 17–26.

Glass, G.V., McGraw, B., and Smith, M.L. *Meta-Analysis in Social Research.* Beverly Hills, Calif.: Sage Publications, 1981.

Goodman, Kenneth. Reading in *A Dictionary of Reading and Related Terms* (Harris and Hodges, Eds.). Newark, Del.: International Reading Assn., 1981.

Johnson, Roger T., Johnson, David W., and Stanne, Mary Beth. "Comparison of Computer-Assisted Cooperative, Competitive, and Individualistic Learning." *American Educational Research Journal* 23(3), Fall, 1986, pp. 382–392.

Johnston, Vivien M. "Attitudes towards Microcomputers in Learning: 1. Pupils and Software for Language Development." *Educational Research* 29(1), February, 1987, pp. 47–55.

Kulik, James A., Bangert, Robert L., and Williams, George W. "Effects of Computer-Based Teaching on Secondary School Students." *Journal of Educational Psychology* 75, 1983, pp. 19–26.

Malone, T.W. "Toward a Theory of Intrinsically Motivating Instruction." *Cognitive Science* 4, 1981, pp. 333–369.

Mandinach, Ellen B., and Linn, Marcia. "The Cognitive Effects of Computer Learning Environments." *Journal of Educational Computing Research* 2(4), 1986, pp. 411–427.

Miller, Larry, and Burnett, J.D. "Theoretical Considerations in Selecting Language Arts Software." *Computing Education* 10(1), 1986, pp. 159–165.

Moffett, J., and Wagner, B.J. *Student-Centered Language Arts and Reading,* 2nd ed. Boston, Mass.: Houghton Mifflin, 1976.

Norton, Priscilla, and Resta, Virginia. "Investigating the Impact of Computer Instruction on Elementary Students' Reading Achievement." *Educational Technology,* March, 1986, pp. 35–41.

Otto, W., and Askov, E. *Rationale and Guidelines: The Wisconsin Design for Reading Skills Development.* Minneapolis, Minn.: National Computer Systems, 1974.

Postman, Neil. *The Disappearance of Childhood.* New York: Delacorte Press, 1982.

Rambally, Gerard, and Rambally, Rodney. "Human Factors in CAI Design." *Computing Education* 11(2), 1987, pp. 149–153.

Rankin, R.J., and Trepper, Terry. "Retention and Delay of Feedback in a Computer-assisted Instructional Task." *Journal of Experimental Education* 64(4), 1978, pp. 67–70.

Sales, Gregory C., Carrier, Carol A., and Allen, Glenn D. "Evaluating Lessons That Use Computers." *The Computing Teacher,* May, 1986, pp. 46–48.

Walker, Decker F., and Hess, Robert D. *Instructional Software: Principles and Perspectives for Design and Use.* Belmont, Calif.: Wadsworth, 1984.

A P P E N D I X

Publishers of Reading and Writing Software

Student writing with a word processor

Active Learning Systems
P.O. Box 1984
Midland, MI 48640

Addison-Wesley Publishing
    Company
2725 Sand Hill Rd.
Menlo Park, CA 94025

Advanced Ideas, Inc.
2902 San Pablo Avenue
Berkeley, CA 94702

Advanced Technology Applications
3019 Governor Dr.
San Diego, CA 92122

American Educational Computer
2450 Embarcadero Way
Palo Alto, CA 94303

American Software Design Co.
7450 Ivyston Ave.
Cottage Grove, MN 55016

Apple Computer, Inc.
10260 Bandley Dr.
Cupertino, CA 95014

Ashton-Tate
3600 Wilshire Blvd.
Los Angeles, CA 90010

Atari, Inc.
1265 Barregas Ave.
Sunnyvale, CA 94086

A.V. Systems
P.O. Box 49210
Los Angeles, CA 90049

Bantam Software
666 Fifth Avenue
New York, NY 10103

Basics & Beyond, Inc.
P.O. Box 10
Amawalk, NY 10501

Behavioral Engineering
230 Mount Hermon, Suite 207
Scotts Valley, CA 95066

Bolt, Beranek and Newman, Inc.
10 Moulton Street
Cambridge, MA 02238

Borg-Warner Educational
    Systems
600 W. University Drive
Arlington Heights, IL 60004

Broderbund Software
17 Paul Drive
San Rafael, CA 94903

Byte by Byte
1183 West 1380
North Provo, UT 84604

Educational Activities
P.O. Box 392
Freeport, NY 11520

Educational Computing Systems
106 Fairbanks Road
Oakridge, TN 37830

Educational Teaching Aids
199 Carpenter Ave.
Wheeling, IL 60090

Edupro
445 E. Charleston Road
Palo Alto, CA 94306

EduSoft
P.O. Box 2560
Berkeley, CA 94702

EduTech, Inc.
303 Lamartine Street
Jamaica Plain, MA 02130

EduWare Services
185 Berry Street
San Francisco, CA 94107

Electronic Arts
2755 Campus Drive
San Mateo, CA 94403

Encyclopedia Brittanica Educational
   Corp.
425 N. Michigan Ave.
Chicago, IL 60611

Ginn and Company
191 Spring Street
Lexington, MA 02173

Grolier Educational Software
Sherman Turnpike
Danbury, CT 06816

Grolier Electronic Publishing
95 Madison Ave.
New York, NY 10016

Harcourt Brace Jovanovich
1250 Sixth Ave.
San Diego, CA 92101

Hartley Courseware
P.O. Box 431
Diamondale, MI 48821

D.C. Heath
125 Spring Street
Lexington, MA 02173

Holt, Rinehart and Winston
383 Madison Ave.
New York, NY 10017

Houghton Mifflin Co.
One Beacon Street
Boston, MA 02108

IBM (Systems Products Division)
P.O. Box 1328
Boca Raton, FL 33432

Ideatech Co.
P.O. Box 62451
Sunnyvale, CA 94088

Intellectual Software
798 North Ave.
Bridgeport, CT 06606

Jamestown Publishers
P.O. Box 6743
Providence, RI 02940

Jostens Learning Systems, Inc.
600 W. University Drive
Arlington Heights, IL 60004

Kendall Hunt Publishing Co.
P.O. Box 539
2460 Kerper Blvd.
Dubuque, IA 52004

Koala Technologies Corp.
2065 Junction Ave.
San Jose, CA 95131

Krell Software Corp.
1320 Stony Brook Rd.
Stony Brook, NY 11790

The Learning Company
545 Middlefield Rd., Suite 170
Menlo Park, CA 94025

Living Videotext
2432 Charleston Road
Mountain View, CA 94043

Logo Computer Systems
555 W. 57 St., Suite 1236
New York, NY 10019

McGraw-Hill
1221 Avenue of the Americas
New York, NY 10020

Milliken Publishing Co.
1100 Research Blvd.
St. Louis, MO 63132

Milton Bradley Co.
443 Shaker Rd.
E. Longmeadow, MA 01028

Mindscape, Inc.
3444 Dundee Rd.
Northbrook, IL 60062

Minnesota Education Computing
  Consortium
3490 Lexington Ave., N.
St. Paul, MN 55112

Peachtree Software
3445 Peachtree Road, NE
Atlanta, GA 30326

PLATO/WICAT Systems, Inc.
8800 Queen Ave., S.
Minneapolis, MN 55431

Precision Software
3452 North Ride Circle
Jacksonville, FL 32217

The Psychological Corp.
7500 Old Oak Blvd.
Cleveland, OH 44130

Radio Shack Educational Division
1400 One Tandy Center
Ft. Worth, TX 76102

Random House School Division
201 E. 50 Street
New York, NY 10022

Reader's Digest Microcomputer
  Division
Pleasantville, NY 10570

Reston Publishing
11480 Sunset Hills Rd.
Reston, VA 22090

Scarborough Systems
25 N. Broadway
Tarrytown, NY 10003

Scholastic, Inc.
Warehouse
1290 Wall Street
West Syndhurst, NJ 07071

Schoolhouse Software
290 Brighton
Elk Grove, IL 60007

Science Research Associates
155 N. Wacker Drive
Chicago, IL 60606

Scott, Foresman & Company
1900 E. Lake Ave.
Glenview, IL 60025

Sensible Software
210 S. Woodward, Suite 229
Birmingham, MI 48011

Sierra
Sierra On-Line Building
Coarsegold, CA 93914

Simon & Schuster
Sylvan Ave.
Englewood Cliffs, NJ 07632

Skillcorp Software, Inc.
1711 McGraw Ave.
Irvine, CA 92714

SOFTSWAP
San Mateo County Office of
  Education
233 Main Street
Redwood City, CA 94063

Software Research Corp.
3939 Quadra Street
Victoria, British Columbia
Canada U8X 1J5

South Coast Writing Project
University of California
Santa Barbara, CA 93106

Spinnaker Software Corp.
1 Kendall Square
Cambridge, MA 02139

Springboard Software, Inc.
7807 Creekridge Circle
Minneapolis, MN 55435

Sunburst Communications, Inc.
39 Washington Street
Pleasantville, NY 10570

Telephone Software Connection
P.O. Box 6548
Torrance, CA 90504

Think Network, Inc.
P.O. Box 6124
New York, NY 10128

T.I.E.S.
1925 County Road B2
Roseville, MN 55113

Tyson Educational Systems
P.O. Box 2478
Miami, FL 33055

Unicom
297 Elmwood Ave.
Providence, RI 02907

University of California
Mathematics/Computer Education
   Project
Lawrence Hall of Science
Berkeley, CA 94720

Walt Disney Personal Computer
   Software
6153 Fairmount Ave.
San Diego, CA 92120

World Book Discovery, Inc.
5700 Lombardo Centre, Suite 120
Seven Hills, OH 44131

Xerox Education Publications
245 Long Hill Road
Middletown, CT 06457

Zweig Associates
1711 McGaw Avenue
Irvine, CA 92714

INDEX